A Handbook *for* Classroom Instruction *that* Works

Association for Supervision and Curriculum Development
Alexandria, VA USA

Association for Supervision and Curriculum Development
1703 N. Beauregard St. • Alexandria, VA 22311-1714 USA
Telephone: 1-800-933-2723 or 703-578-9600 • Fax: 703-575-5400
Web site: www.ascd.org • E-mail: member@ascd.org

Printed in the United States of America.

ASCD Product No. 101041
ASCD member price: $26.95   nonmember price: $31.95

sll/2001
        Library of Congress Cataloging-in-Publication Data

A handbook for classroom instruction that works / Robert J. Marzano ...
[et al.].
      p. cm.
Includes bibliographical references (p.) and index.
  ISBN 0-87120-522-X (alk. paper)
  1. Effective teaching--United States--Handbooks, manuals, etc. 2.
Learning--Handbooks, manuals, etc. I. Marzano, Robert J.
  LB1025.3 .H364 2001
  371.3--dc21
                                        2001004896

07 06 05 04 03 02   10 9 8 7 6 5 4 3

A Handbook for Classroom Instruction that Works

INTRODUCTION

We stand at a unique point in the history of U.S. education—a point at which the potential for truly meaningful school reform is greater than it ever has been. This is not just because we are at the beginning of a new century and a new millenium, although these are certainly noteworthy milestones. Rather, it is because we now have more than 30 years of accumulated research that provides some highly consistent answers to the question of what types of instructional strategies work best to improve student achievement. Much of that research has been synthesized and described in the book *Classroom Instruction That Works: Research-Based Strategies for Increasing Student Achievement* by Marzano, Pickering, and Pollock (ASCD, 2001). Briefly, based on a survey of thousands of comparisons between experimental and control groups, using a wide variety of instructional strategies in K–12 classrooms, across a variety of subject areas, we were able to identify nine categories of instructional strategies proven to improve student achievement:

1. Identifying similarities and differences
2. Summarizing and note taking
3. Reinforcing effort and providing recognition
4. Homework and practice
5. Representing knowledge
6. Learning groups
7. Setting objectives and providing feedback
8. Generating and testing hypotheses
9. Cues, questions, and advance organizers

This handbook is intended as a self-study guide to the effective use of specific strategies in each of these nine categories. Although you can use this handbook without having read *Classroom Instruction That Works*, we recommend that you do so, particularly if you are interested in the research that underlies the recommendations in this handbook.

How to Use the Handbook

This handbook is organized into 11 sections. Sections 1 through 9 address the nine categories of instructional strategies listed. These strategies can be applied to all types of content, at all grade levels, with all types of students. Section 10 addresses instructional strategies that are most appropriate with specific types of knowledge, such as vocabulary terms, generalizations, and processes. Finally, Section 11 presents a framework for using the instructional strategies to improve your effectiveness in unit planning.

Except for Section 11, all sections follow the same format. Each section begins with a brief introduction describing the nature and purpose of the strategies discussed in the section. Generalizations that can be drawn from the research about the strategies also are presented. These discussions are brief with no detailed citations to the research literature. Again, if you are interested in a thorough discussion of the research on these strategies with full academic citations, we recommend *Classroom Instruction That Works*.

The introduction in each section is followed by one or more "modules" that specifically address the strategies within the section. Each module contains eight components:

1. Introduction
Each module begins with a brief introduction to the strategies presented in the module. It explains why the specific strategies in the module have been grouped together.

2. Reflecting on My Current Beliefs and Practices
This component asks you to reflect on how and why you currently use strategies that you will be studying in the module. The intent is to stimulate your thinking about your use of the strategies so that you will have a basis of comparison as you read about the strategies in the module.

3. Recommendations for Classroom Practice
The heart of each module is a set of recommendations for classroom practice. These recommendations may deal with specific strategies and

techniques or they may be generalizations about classroom practice. Each strategy or recommendation is discussed and exemplified.

4. Checking My Understanding

After the discussion of recommended classroom practices, a hypothetical situation or problem is presented. The intent is to give you an opportunity to apply what you have learned in the previous discussion. If you find it difficult to complete this hypothetical situation or problem, we recommend that you reread the content in "Recommendations for Classroom Practice."

5. Assessing the Impact on Students

Each module contains rubrics that can be used to assess how the strategies affect students' learning.

6. Planning My Classroom Activities

A series of questions is presented that, when answered, help you determine how you might use the strategies presented in the module in the context of your current practice.

7. Assessing Myself

A series of questions helps you assess how effectively you use the strategies presented in the module.

8. Module Reflection

A series of questions asks you to reflect on what you have learned about the strategies presented in the module and what you have learned about yourself as a teacher and a learner.

As we mentioned before, the handbook is as a tool for self-study. You can work through the various sections and their related modules at your own pace and identify your own sequence in terms of which sections you consider. You need not address all sections of the manual. In fact, you can derive benefit from the handbook by selecting only those sections of interest to you.

Another useful approach to using this handbook is to form study teams. The study team format is one of the best ways to build skill and confidence in the strategies presented in this handbook because it brings to bear collegial support structures that encourage analysis, discussion, problem solving, and solution sharing in ways consistent with best practices in staff development. Study teams fulfill the following two salient functions relative to the use of this handbook:

- They provide a context for teachers to assess the extent to which the strategies in the handbook are effectively used.
- They provide an opportunity for teachers to use the strategies with structured peer support.

Some educators might question how study teams are possible within the structure of K–12 schooling. They wonder how study teams can function in the context of how the school day is arranged. To help you envision how you might use study teams with this handbook, consider the following scenario.

A Study Team Scenario

A majority of the faculty at Haystead Middle School agreed to use the *Handbook for Classroom Instruction That Works* as the focus of study during the upcoming school year. Those members of the faculty who volunteered to work on the project organized themselves into study teams of four to six individuals. Teams agreed to meet for two hours once every other week during both semesters of the year. Some teams met during the school day on released time; others met after contract hours. Because of her interest in the project and to show support for it, the principal joined one of the teams. She also arranged the school schedule to allow teachers to meet during common planning periods. Finally, the principal helped arrange for team members to receive recertification credit upon completion and acceptance of a paper describing their learning at the end of the semester.

Meeting dates, times, and location were agreed upon at the first meeting, during which time a team leader was selected. The team leader's job included making sure the meeting began and ended on time; arranging for meeting rooms, materials, and refreshments; and completing a summary sheet at the end of each session outlining what had been discussed, who had attended, and the goals for the next meeting. These summary sheets were forwarded to the principal, who met with the team leaders monthly so the team members could exchange ideas, coordinate efforts, and share resources.

Although the team leaders were volunteers, they were given a stipend of $300 per semester in partial recognition of the responsibilities they had assumed.

Each team began by selecting one section of the handbook that was of most interest to team members. Prior to a scheduled meeting, each team member was required to read each module in the section and complete all the activities. The first order of business at a meeting was to share responses to the following parts of the modules that were the subject of study:

- "Reflecting on My Current Beliefs and Practices"
- "Checking My Understanding"
- "Assessing Myself"
- "Module Reflection"

For some sections, this interchange was enough to give team members ideas about various ways to use the information presented in the modules. For some sections, however, team members agreed to engage in some action research. One or more members of the team would try out a technique described in a module and hypothesize the effect of using this technique on students. After the technique was implemented, data were collected using the rubrics in the "Assessing Student Learning" section of the module. The data were then brought back to the next group meeting, which was spent analyzing and interpreting the data and discussing the implications for classroom practice.

Periodically and at the end of each semester, each study team evaluated its progress in terms of the learning of individual team members and the effect of the project on student learning.

Designing an Approach That Works for You

Ultimately, professional development is personal. No two teachers are alike. Therefore, no two teachers need exactly the same information to enhance their performance. The same is true for individual schools. The scenario was presented to stimulate your thinking regarding the use of this handbook. Given that the content does not have to be addressed in any particular order, individual schools and teachers can design study programs that meet their individual needs and styles.

IDENTIFYING SIMILARITIES AND DIFFERENCES

Study Group Tip

If you are using this handbook in a study group, your group might want to read and discuss the research summary about identifying similarities and differences in the companion book, *Classroom Instruction That Works.*

This section concerns four related activities: comparing, classifying, creating metaphors, and creating analogies. Each of these processes involves identifying how items, events, processes, or concepts are similar and different. When we compare, we examine how things are alike and different based on characteristics: Heather's car is silver, front-wheel drive, with a bike rack on top; Bob's car is red, four-wheel drive, with ski racks on top. When we classify, we consider how items are similar and different and then group them using similarities to define categories: hibiscus and black-eyed susans are perennials; pansies and marigolds are annuals. Metaphors link two things that appear to be quite different on the surface but have some likeness, such as "My Life had stood—A Loaded Gun" (Emily Dickinson). Analogies involve relationships between pairs of elements. With analogies we look for similarities between two pairs, as in ruler is to length as measuring cup is to volume.

Research tells us that students need explicit structure when they first begin identifying similarities and differences. As they progress, however, students can use the process on their own to stimulate a wide-ranging exchange of ideas. Research also shows that graphic and symbolic representations can help students to understand and effectively use processes for identifying similarities and differences. In this section, we offer strategies and suggestions for using what the research tells us works in the classroom. We encourage you to use these and other approaches for using the process of identifying similarities and differences to enhance students' learning.

List of Figures

COMPARING

To compare is to identify similarities and differences between or among things or ideas. We each frequently engage in the process of comparing. We compare movies we have seen; we compare restaurants where we have eaten; we compare ski runs on our favorite mountains.

In the classroom, we can use this process deliberately and rigorously to deepen students' understanding of the knowledge they are learning. We can compare Heathcliff in *Wuthering Heights* to Mr. Rochester in *Jane Eyre*; we can compare the shape of the graph of $y = 2x + 3$ to the shape of $y = 2x - 3$; we can compare strategies used in the battles of Gettysburg and Antietam during the Civil War.

Before reading "Recommendations for Classroom Practice," take some time to reflect on your current practices and beliefs about comparing by completing the Reflecting on My Current Beliefs and Practices—Comparing worksheet in Figure 1.1 (p. 10).

Recommendations for Classroom Practice

Comparing is a complex process that students will need to learn about and practice. In this module, we discuss several approaches to use in the classroom:

- give students a model for the process,
- use familiar content to teach students the steps for comparing,

- give students graphic organizers for comparing, and
- guide students as needed.

Give Students a Model

Students understand the process of comparing on some level because they compare things every day: "Friday's lunch in the cafeteria was better than today's"; "Fat Boy Slim's new music video is way cooler than the new 311 video"; "Ms. Bloomer's calculus class is a lot harder than Mr. Stacy's." To push students beyond the kind of comparing that they do automatically every day, we need to teach a systematic process and hold students accountable for rigorously using it. A model for comparing might include a set of steps for students to follow like those in Figure 1.2 (p. 11).

Comparing activities have broad applications. The key to an effective comparison is to identify important characteristics (those that will enhance students' understanding of the similarities and differences between the items). If students are comparing Malcolm X and Martin Luther King Jr. during a history class, describing similarities and differences between the two men in terms of "where they were born" might be interesting but does not add much to students' learning. A more useful characteristic might be "religious views" or "role in the Civil Rights movement."

FIGURE 1.1

Reflecting on My Current Beliefs and Practices—Comparing

What is the purpose of asking students to compare?

What kinds of activities do I use to help students compare?

I can think of a time that I asked students to compare, and I was pleased with the results. Why did it go well?

I can think of a time that I asked students to compare, and I was not pleased with the results. Why did it not go well?

What questions do I have about using comparing in my classroom?

FIGURE 1.2

Model for Comparing

Steps for Comparing

1. Select the items you want to compare.
2. Select the characteristics of the items on which you want to base your comparison.
3. Explain how the items are similar and different with respect to the characteristics.

Steps for Comparing for Younger Students

1. What do I want to compare?
2. What things about them do I want to compare?
3. How are they the same? How are they different?

(Adapted from *Dimension of Learning*, Marzano et al., 1997.)

We can make many comparisons at a surface level that do not contribute much to our learning. For example, we could compare the Lewis and Clark expedition to Pike's 1806 Arkansas River expedition on the basis of who went on the expeditions, how long each trip lasted, what kind of clothes the members of the expedition wore, and which expedition was written about the most. We might learn that Lewis and Clark became more famous than Pike, even though the Pike expedition was better dressed. Does this information add to our understanding of the importance of these expeditions? Probably not. Students will have a much better understanding of the Lewis and Clark expedition and Pike's 1806 expedition if they base their comparison on meaningful characteristics, such as each expedition's purpose, areas explored, and outcomes.

Use Familiar Content

Everyday comparisons can help students understand the steps in the comparing process. For example, if students are comparing Friday's cafeteria lunch to Tuesday's lunch, they can compare them based on a set of characteristics, such as nutritional content, variety of foods, and type of cuisine. Explaining how the items are similar and different in terms of these characteristics uncovers for students the information that lies behind the claim that Friday's cafeteria lunch was "better" than Tuesday's. Understanding and following steps in a process for comparing helps students when they use the process with content knowledge.

Give Students Graphic Organizers

Students can use graphic organizers as a visual tool to help them make comparisons. A Venn diagram uses two intersecting circles to show how items are similar and different. Similarities are shown in the intersection of the circles, and differences are indicated in the parts of each circle that do not overlap. Teachers can demonstrate the use of Venn diagrams in a couple of different ways. A Venn diagram might be used to compare two things.

In the example in Figure 1.3 (p. 12), one Venn diagram is used to compare the characteristics of rain forests and deserts. The characteristics include plant life, animal life, and climate. You can also use Venn diagrams to compare one characteristic at a time.

In the comparison shown in Figures 1.4 (p. 13) and 1.5 (p. 13), two Venn diagrams show similarities and differences between two specific places—the Amazon Rain Forest in South America and the Mojave Desert in the southwestern United States. Each Venn diagram contains similarities and differences for only one characteristic each: one for climate and one for animals.

Students can also use a comparison matrix to graphically represent similarities and differences among items (see Figure 1.6, p. 14). The comparison matrix helps students systematically organize information about the items or events they are comparing.

You may need to provide more detailed instructions when students use a comparison matrix. Including a space for students to write their conclusions helps them bring together the pieces of the comparison and reflect on what they have learned.

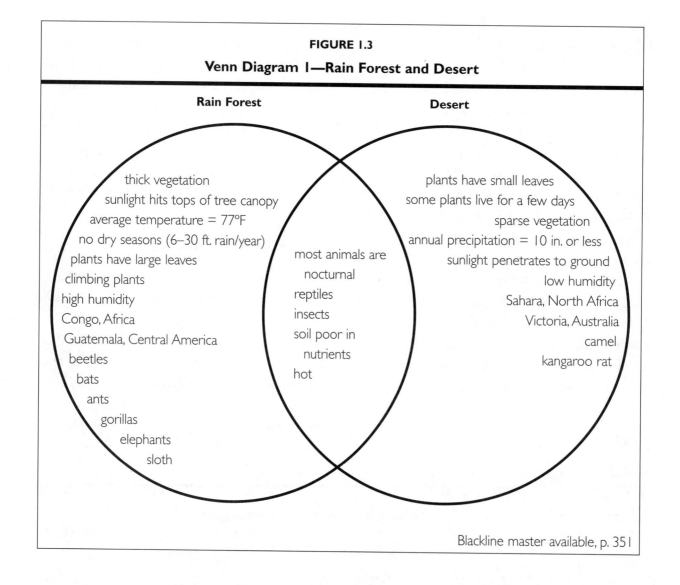

FIGURE 1.3

Venn Diagram 1—Rain Forest and Desert

Rain Forest

Desert

thick vegetation
sunlight hits tops of tree canopy
average temperature = 77°F
no dry seasons (6–30 ft. rain/year)
plants have large leaves
climbing plants
high humidity
Congo, Africa
Guatemala, Central America
beetles
bats
ants
gorillas
elephants
sloth

most animals are
nocturnal
reptiles
insects
soil poor in
nutrients
hot

plants have small leaves
some plants live for a few days
sparse vegetation
annual precipitation = 10 in. or less
sunlight penetrates to ground
low humidity
Sahara, North Africa
Victoria, Australia
camel
kangaroo rat

Blackline master available, p. 351

FIGURE 1.4

Venn Diagram 2—Rain Forest and Desert Climate

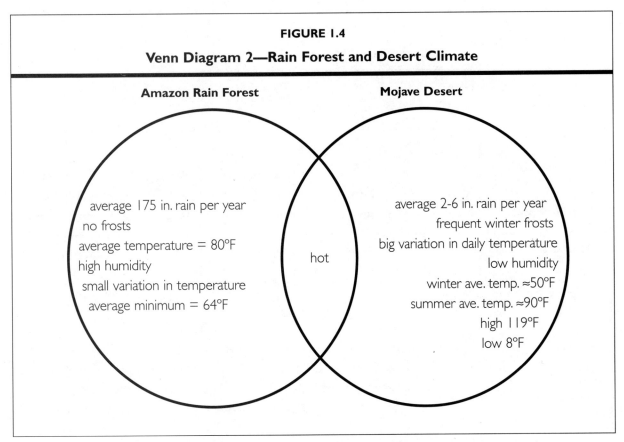

Amazon Rain Forest

Mojave Desert

average 175 in. rain per year
no frosts
average temperature = 80°F
high humidity
small variation in temperature
average minimum = 64°F

hot

average 2-6 in. rain per year
frequent winter frosts
big variation in daily temperature
low humidity
winter ave. temp. ≈50°F
summer ave. temp. ≈90°F
high 119°F
low 8°F

FIGURE 1.5

Venn Diagram 3—Rain Forest and Desert Animals

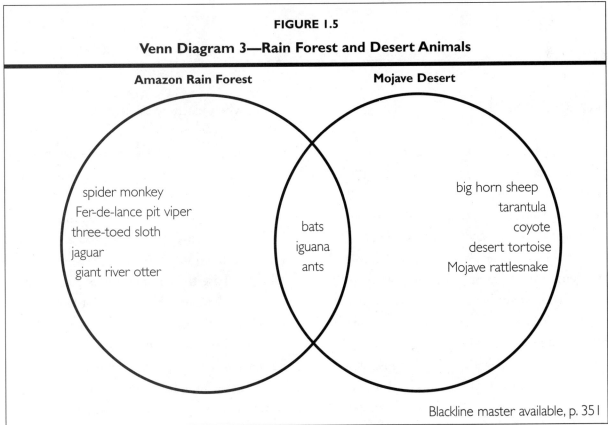

Amazon Rain Forest

Mojave Desert

spider monkey
Fer-de-lance pit viper
three-toed sloth
jaguar
giant river otter

bats
iguana
ants

big horn sheep
tarantula
coyote
desert tortoise
Mojave rattlesnake

Blackline master available, p. 351

FIGURE 1.6
Comparison Matrix—Basic Measures

Characteristics	Items to be compared				
	1-cm square	2-cm square	Rectangle: width 4 cm length 6 cm	Rectangle: width 3 cm length 7 cm	Rectangle: width 3 cm length 8 cm
Perimeter	4 cm	8 cm	20 cm	20 cm	22 cm
Area	1 sq. cm	4 sq. cm	24 sq. cm	21 sq. cm	24 sq. cm
Conclusions	Two rectangles can have the same perimeter, but different areas. That also means that a square and a rectangle could have the same perimeter, but different areas. Also, two rectangles can have the same area, but different perimeters. If you double the size of a square, the perimeter doubles, but the area increases 4 times.				

Blackline master available, p. 352

Guide Students As Needed

When students are first learning to use the process of comparing, you can give them more of the information they need to complete the task. For example, you might identify the items to compare and the characteristics to use in the comparison. In this case, students describe how the items are similar and different based on the characteristics you have identified. You also might ask students to summarize what they have learned. Although these structured comparisons are somewhat limiting because students are working with a defined set of items and characteristics, this structure can be very useful when teaching students the process of comparison.

After students have had some practice completing more structured comparison activities, you can give less structure and less guidance. For this type of activity, you might identify the items for students to compare and ask them to choose the characteristics upon which to base the comparison. Students have more freedom and they also must think and work more independently. As they become more comfortable with the process of comparing, students must grapple with the issue of choosing meaningful characteristics to use to compare items you have identified.

Tools to Facilitate Comparing in the Classroom

To guide your students effectively you need to be confident of your own understanding of how to use comparing. Figure 1.7, Checking My Understanding—Comparing (p. 16), gives you an opportunity to apply what you have learned in the previous discussion. If you find it difficult to complete the comparison matrix, we suggest you reread "Recommendations for Classroom Practice." The other assessment and planning tools that follow will help you guide your students when using comparing processes in the classroom.

Assessing the Impact on Students

Rubrics are one tool you can use to gauge students' progress. Sample rubrics are provided in Figure 1.8 (p. 17) for evaluating students' progress in using the comparing process. These rubrics can be revised, when appropriate, for students to use as part of the self-assessment process to help them reflect on their work.

FIGURE 1.7

Checking My Understanding—Comparing

Complete this matrix by adding one more living thing and one more characteristic. Focus on similarities and differences.

Characteristics	Items to be compared				
	Pine Tree	**Tulip**	**Elephant**	**Shark**	
External body features					
Habitat					
Sources of energy					

What knowledge did you need to complete this task?

What insights did you gain about the process of identifying similarities and differences while using the comparison matrix?

Blackline master available, p. 352

FIGURE 1.8

Rubrics for Comparing

Comparing Rubric

4   The student uses important, as well as some less obvious, characteristics to compare the items. The student accurately identifies the similarities and differences and explains his conclusions in a way that shows a complete and detailed understanding of the items.

3   The student uses important characteristics to compare the items. The student accurately identifies the similarities and differences and explains his conclusions.

2   The student uses characteristics to compare the items, but not the most important characteristics. The student's comparison and conclusions show some misconceptions about the items.

1   The student uses insignificant characteristics to compare the items. The student's comparison and conclusions show many misconceptions that indicate the student does not understand the items.

0   Not enough information to make a judgment.

Comparing Rubric for Younger Students

4   The student uses important features to compare the items. The student also uses some features that are not easily seen. The student identifies similarities and differences without making mistakes. The student tells what she learned in a way that shows a complete understanding of the items.

3   The student uses important features to compare the items. The student identifies similarities and differences without making mistakes. The student tells what she learned.

2   The student uses features to compare the items, but the student does not use the most important features. The student makes some mistakes in the comparison.

1   The student uses features that are not important to compare the items. The student makes some big mistakes in the comparison.

0   The student does not try to do the task.

Planning Classroom Activities and Assessing Myself

Answering a series of questions will help you discover how you might use the strategies for using comparing presented in this module. You can use the Planning for Comparing Worksheet, Figure 1.9 (p. 19), to guide your thinking when planning comparing activities for students.

Rubrics help assess student learning. You can also use a tool to assess yourself—how effectively you are using comparing strategies. Use Figure 1.10 (p. 20) to evaluate your effectiveness in teaching comparing strategies.

Module Reflection

Review your responses to the questions in Figure 1.1, Reflecting on My Current Beliefs and Practices—Comparing (p. 10). How has this module affected your thinking about teaching and learning? What have you learned about yourself as a teacher and learner? Use the space provided to record your thoughts.

- Reading this information affirms some of what I already knew about comparing

- Now, I better understand some things about comparing

- I think I will change how I use comparing in my classroom

FIGURE 1.9

Planning for Comparing Worksheet

What knowledge will students be learning?

Do I need to set aside time to teach students comparing? How will I teach them the process?

Will I ask students to use a graphic organizer?

How much guidance will I provide students?

How will students explain their work and communicate their conclusions?

How will I monitor how well students are doing with comparing?

What will I do to help students who are not comparing effectively?

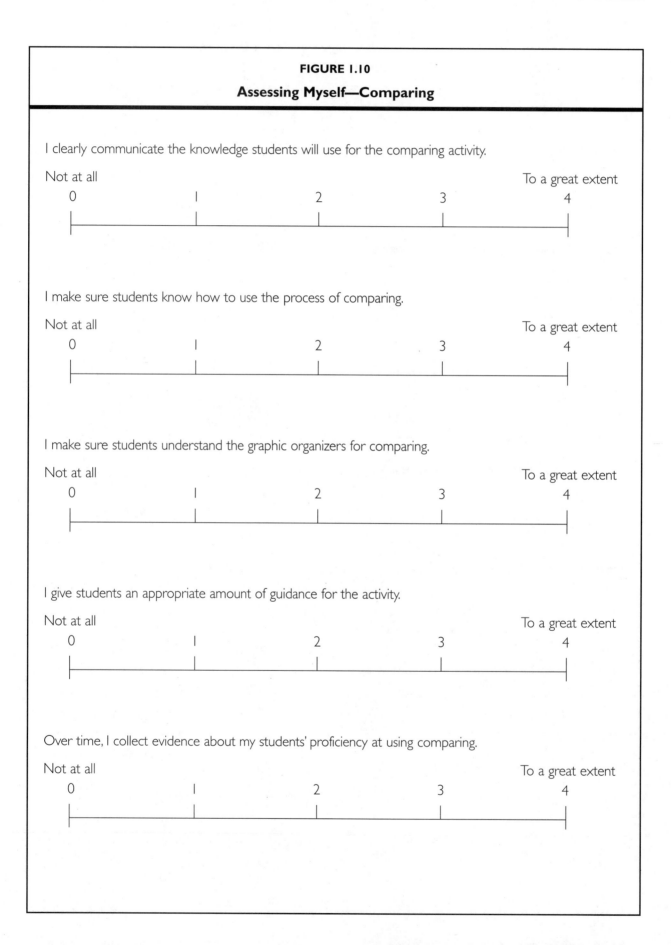

FIGURE 1.10

Assessing Myself—Comparing

I clearly communicate the knowledge students will use for the comparing activity.

Not at all   To a great extent
  0   1   2   3   4

I make sure students know how to use the process of comparing.

Not at all   To a great extent
  0   1   2   3   4

I make sure students understand the graphic organizers for comparing.

Not at all   To a great extent
  0   1   2   3   4

I give students an appropriate amount of guidance for the activity.

Not at all   To a great extent
  0   1   2   3   4

Over time, I collect evidence about my students' proficiency at using comparing.

Not at all   To a great extent
  0   1   2   3   4

CLASSIFYING

Classifying involves grouping things into definable categories based on like characteristics. Like comparing, it is something we do in our day-to-day lives. We classify the clothes we put into our closet. We classify the food we put on our kitchen shelves. Some of us classify the music CDs in our collection. Snowboarders provide a glimpse of the way they classify things when they talk about bad, rad, lame, sick, wack, and phat riding.

Certain rules govern these classifications: classical music CDs go together, Bob Dylan CDs have their own category, country goes with country. Even though we use rules to classify our CDs, snowboard riding, our clothes, and foods, most of us aren't expending much effort to decide if the canned tomatoes should go with the canned fruit or the canned vegetables. In the classroom, students can use a systematic process to classify important pieces of content knowledge. Students might classify organisms according to kingdom, phylum, class, order, family, genus, and species, or mathematical functions as linear, quadratic, trigonometric, exponential, or logarithmic.

Before reading "Recommendations for Classroom Practice," take some time to reflect on your current practices and beliefs about classifying by completing the Reflecting on My Current Beliefs and Practices—Classifying worksheet in Figure 2.1 (p. 22).

Recommendations for Classroom Practice

Classifying is a complex process that students will need to learn about and practice. In this module, we discuss several approaches to use in the classroom:

- give students a model for the process,
- use familiar content to teach students the steps in classifying,
- give students graphic organizers for classifying, and
- guide students as needed.

Give Students a Model

If we want students to move beyond classification schemes that are defined for them, such as the food groups or the animal kingdom, we need to give them opportunities to classify items using their own rules for category membership. We might ask them to classify historical battles, works of literature, or types of exercises. When we ask students to complete these types of assignments, we need to teach them explicit steps for classifying, as shown in Figure 2.2 (p. 23), and help them to understand the process as a systematic strategy with rules and expectations. This process involves the critical step of determining the rules that govern category membership.

FIGURE 2.1

Reflecting on My Current Beliefs and Practices—Classifying

What is the purpose of asking students to classify?

What kinds of activities do I use to help students classify?

I can think of a time that I asked students to classify, and I was pleased with the results. Why did it go well?

I can think of a time that I asked students to classify, and I was not pleased with the results. Why did it not go well?

What questions do I have about using classifying in my classroom?

How things are classified influences our perceptions and behavior. When rules for category membership change, we change the way we think about items. Imagine if we classified food items in a grocery store according to color. Purposefully grouping items into different categories can give us a different perspective on those items. When a green, square object is grouped with other square objects, we tend to notice it is square. When the green, square object is grouped with other green objects, we tend to notice it is green. In the classroom, using classifying can influence what students see and think about what they are learning.

Use Familiar Content

You can use everyday examples to help students understand the process of grouping items and describing the rules for membership in a category. When asked, any snowboarder can explain the difference between "wack" and "phat" moves on the slopes—moves that fit into each category share a certain set of

---

FIGURE 2.2
Model for Classifying

Steps for Classifying

1. Identify the items you want to classify.
2. Select what seems to be an important item, describe its key attributes, and identify other items that have the same attributes.
3. Create the category by specifying the attributes that the items must have for membership in the category.
4. Select another item, describe its key attributes, and identify other items that have the same attributes.
5. Create the second category by specifying the attributes that the items must have for membership in the category.
6. Repeat the previous two steps until all items are classified and the specific attributes have been identified for membership in each category.
7. If necessary, combine categories or split them into smaller categories and specify the attributes that determine membership in the category.

(Adapted from *Dimensions of Learning*, Marzano et al., 1997.)

Steps for Classifying for Younger Students

1. What do I want to classify?
2. What things are alike that I can put into a group?
3. How are these things alike?
4. What other groups can I make? How are the things in each group alike?
5. Does everything fit into a group now?
6. Would it be better to split up any of the groups or put any groups together?

characteristics. Students can begin to understand that classifying influences our thinking and behavior by considering some classification systems that we take for granted. How would our behavior change if books in a library were grouped by size? How does our thinking change if we group an elephant first with people and things in a circus, and then with other wild animals that live in Kenya? Thinking about what defines a particular group and why an item fits into the group helps students to learn more about the content they are studying.

Give Students Graphic Organizers

Graphic organizers are tools students can use as a visual guide to the classifying process. Two popular graphic organizers for classification are shown in Figures 2.3 (p. 25) and 2.4 (p. 26).

Guide Students As Needed

When students are first learning to classify, you can provide the items and the categories for the classification so that the activity is structured and students' attention can be focused on why items belong in certain categories. A structured classification activity can be appropriate for students in many situations. For example, if you want students to learn the specific characteristics of each of the four major food groups, you might provide a list of foods and ask students to explain where each belongs and why. Students' performance on this type of activity is based on how accurately they place the items into the categories.

After students have had some practice completing structured classification activities, you can give them items to classify, but ask them to form the categories themselves. This type of activity often extends students' understanding of the content they are studying. For example, asking students to group foods into one of four food groups can tell you how well they know the given rules for membership in each category. However, asking students to disregard these four food groups and form their own helps them to delve into what they understand about the characteristics of various foods. This activity requires students to think in a different way and forces them to answer the question: How would *I* group these items and why?

Tools to Facilitate Classifying in the Classroom

To guide your students effectively, you need to be confident of your own understanding of how to use classifying. Figure 2.5, Checking My Understanding—Classifying (p. 27), gives you an opportunity to apply what you have learned in the previous discussion. If you find it difficult to reclassify the items and answer the accompanying questions, we suggest you reread "Recommendations for Classroom Practice." The other planning and assessment tools that follow will help you guide your students in classifying activities in the classroom.

Assessing the Impact on Students

Rubrics are one tool you can use to gauge students' progress. Sample rubrics for evaluating students' progress in using the classifying process are provided in Figure 2.6 (p. 28). These rubrics can be revised, when appropriate, for students to use as part of the self-assessment process to help them reflect on their work.

FIGURE 2.3

Classification Organizer

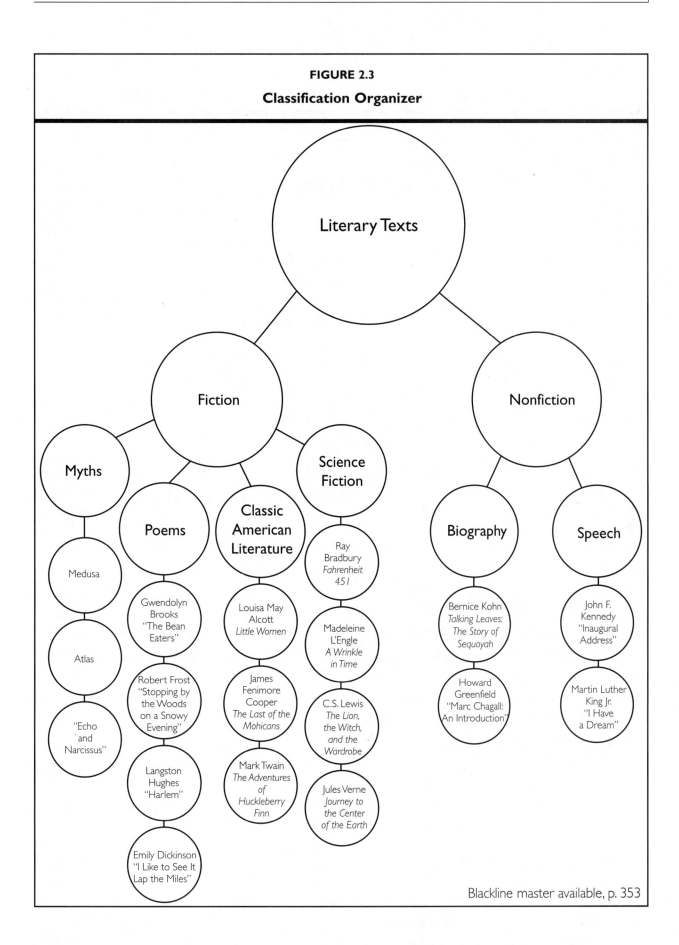

Blackline master available, p. 353

FIGURE 2.4
Classification Organizer—Art Materials, Techniques, and Processes

Categories		
Art Materials	**Art Techniques**	**Art Processes**
Paint	Overlapping	Adding in sculpture
Clay	Shading	Subtracting in sculpture
Charcoal	Varying Size	Casting jewelry
Pencil	Varying Color	Constructing jewelry
Wood	Collage	Mixing color
	Perspective	
	Stippling	
	Glaze	Blackline master available, p. 354

Planning Classroom Activities and Assessing Myself

Answering a series of questions will help you discover how you might use the strategies for using classifying presented in this module. You can use the Planning for Classifying Worksheet, Figure 2.7 (p. 29), to guide your thinking when planning classifying activities for students.

Rubrics help assess student learning. You can also use a tool to assess yourself—how effectively you are using classifying strategies. Use Figure 2.8 (p. 30) to evaluate your effectiveness in using classifying.

FIGURE 2.5

Checking My Understanding—Classifying

The table below lists items grouped into three categories of resources. Take a moment to study these categories and the items in each.

Categories

Natural Resources	Human Resources	Capital Resources
Land	Police officer	Bricks
Forests	Mail carrier	Hammer
Rivers	Teacher	Bus
Oceans	Engineer	2" x 4" lumber
Sunlight	Taxi driver	Table saw
Coal	Construction worker	Dump truck
Pastures	Accountant	Dishwashing machine
Mineral deposits	Telephone operator	Jackhammer
	Salesperson	Computer

Now it's your turn. Reclassify these items using categories that you determine. Take a moment to examine the new categories. Then answer the following questions:

What steps did you follow to reclassify the items?

What do you see differently about the items now that you have reclassified them?

What are the benefits are of reclassifying items? Why might a teacher ask students to reclassify items?

FIGURE 2.6

Rubrics for Classifying

Classifying Rubric

4   The student organizes the items into meaningful categories and thoroughly describes the defining characteristics of each category. The student provides insightful conclusions about the classification.

3   The student organizes the items into meaningful categories and describes the defining characteristics of each category.

2   The student organizes the items into categories that are not very meaningful, but addresses some of the important characteristics of the items.

1   The student organizes the items into categories that do not make sense or are unimportant.

0   Not enough information to make a judgment.

Classifying Rubric for Younger Students

4   The student puts the items into meaningful groups. The student tells the important characteristics for each group. The student makes conclusions.

3   The student put the items into meaningful groups. The student tells the important characteristics for each group.

2   The student puts the items into groups that do not have a lot of meaning.

1   The student puts the items into groups that do not make sense.

0   The student does not try to do the task.

FIGURE 2.7

Planning for Classifying Worksheet

What knowledge will students be learning?

Do I need to set aside time to teach students the process of classifying? How will I teach students the process?

Will I ask students to use a graphic organizer?

How much guidance will I provide students?

How will students explain their work and communicate their conclusions?

How will I monitor how well students are doing with classifying?

What will I do to help students who are not classifying effectively?

FIGURE 2.8

Assessing Myself—Classifying

I clearly communicate the knowledge students will use for the classifying activity.

Not at all   To a great extent

0   1   2   3   4

I make sure students know how to use the process of classifying.

Not at all   To a great extent

0   1   2   3   4

I make sure students understand the graphic organizers for classifying.

Not at all   To a great extent

0   1   2   3   4

I give students an appropriate amount of guidance for the activity.

Not at all   To a great extent

0   1   2   3   4

Over time, I collect evidence about my students' proficiency at using the process of classifying.

Not at all   To a great extent

0   1   2   3   4

Module Reflection

Review your responses to the questions in Figure 2.1, Reflecting on My Current Beliefs and Practices—Classifying worksheet (p. 22). How has this module affected your thinking about teaching and learning? Use the space provided to record your thoughts.

- Reading this information affirms some of what I already knew about classifying

- Now, I better understand some things about classifying

- I think I will change how I use classifying in my classroom

CREATING METAPHORS

When we create metaphors, we identify a general or basic pattern in a specific topic and then find another topic that seems quite different at the literal level but has the same general pattern. Authors frequently use metaphors to give readers strong images. Shakespeare's Macbeth describes life with a metaphor:

> *Life's but a walking shadow, a poor player*
> *That struts and frets his hour upon the stage*
> *And then is heard no more: it is a tale*
> *Told by an idiot, full of sound and fury,*
> *Signifying nothing.*
>   (Shakespeare, W. *Macbeth*, Act V Scene V)

Macbeth likens life to a theatrical performance that exists for an "hour upon the stage" and then disappears, implying that life lacks substance and is merely a brief drama that does not leave a lasting mark. This passage further compares life to a tale full of noise and excitement and commotion, but meaningless in the end. The abstract relationship—a brief moment full of commotion that dissolves into nothingness—connects life to the images in Macbeth's description. Creating metaphors isn't just for Shakespeare. We can use metaphors and help students create metaphors to better understand academic content from history (the United States is freedom and promise) to mathematics (the graph of the sine function is a rollercoaster).

Before reading "Recommendations for Classroom Practice," take some time to reflect on your current practices and beliefs about using metaphors with your students by completing the Reflecting on My Current Beliefs and Practices—Metaphors worksheet (Figure 3.1, p. 33).

Recommendations for Classroom Practice

Creating metaphors is a complex process that students will need to learn about and practice. In this module, we discuss several approaches to use in the classroom:

- giving students a model for the process,
- using familiar content to teach students the steps in creating metaphors,
- giving students graphic organizers for creating metaphors, and
- giving students guidance as needed.

Give Students a Model

Students encounter metaphors in many different contexts. Authors use metaphors to give readers strong mental images, such as "he was walking on thin ice," "she was a grizzly bear in the mornings," or "her eyes were pools of blue." Metaphors are also common in specific content areas. In science, teachers might use the following comparisons: "a cell is a factory" or

FIGURE 3.1

Reflecting on My Current Beliefs and Practices—Metaphors

What is the purpose of asking students to create metaphors?

What kinds of activities do I use to help students create metaphors?

What metaphors apply to the content areas that I teach?

What questions do I have about using metaphors in my classroom?

"a DNA molecule is a ladder." In health or biology class, students might connect the heart to a force pump, the kidney to a water filter, or the eye to a camera. Teaching students to develop metaphors provides them with a tool to explore ideas and information at deeper levels. You can present students with steps as a process for creating metaphors, as shown in Figure 3.2.

Use Familiar Content to Create Metaphors

Common metaphors can help students understand the steps in the process of creating metaphors. Students have probably heard sayings like "You're walking on thin ice," or "Her eyes were pools of blue." They themselves make metaphorical comparisons every day—

"my brother is a tyrant," "chemistry is a monster," "cafeteria lunches are dog food." You can use these kinds of examples to help students learn a deliberate process for making these connections. What does it mean if I say, "My brother is a tyrant." As students identify the important information for both elements, they will begin to see the similarities between the two. Students can make a list that might look like the one that follows.

My brother	Tyrant
makes me do his chores	*absolute ruler*
calls me names	*makes rules that are not fair*
I lock myself in the bathroom to escape	*citizens flee*
sometimes he locks me in the bathroom	*arrests people*

FIGURE 3.2
Model for Metaphors

Steps for Creating Metaphors	**Steps for Creating Metaphors for Younger Students**
1. Identify the important or basic elements of the information or situation with which you are working.	1. What is important here?
2. Write that basic information as a general pattern by • replacing words for specific things with words for more general things, and • summarizing information whenever possible.	2. How can I say the same thing in a more general way?
3. Find new information or a situation to which the general pattern applies.	3. What else has the same general pattern?

Stating the relationship between "my brother" and "tyrant" in more general terms—*cruel ruler who treats innocent and weaker people unfairly*—helps students understand the reasoning behind the connection they are making in the metaphor.

Use Graphic Organizers for Creating Metaphors

You can give students a graphic organizer to help them understand and use metaphors. The metaphor organizer in Figure 3.3 (p. 36), showing the human heart as a heat pump, is a good example.

Guide Students As Needed

Modeling the process of creating metaphors helps students understand how to identify the literal parts of a metaphor and describe the abstract relationship. Once students are familiar with the process, you might identify one element of the metaphor and the abstract pattern, giving students a kind of scaffold to build on as they complete the metaphor. You can vary how structured the metaphor tasks are, according to students' level of understanding and skill.

After students have had some practice completing metaphors, you can gradually remove the scaffolding by presenting one element of the metaphor and asking students to provide the second element *and* a description of the abstract relationship:

Disease is _____ .

The brain is _____ .

The Great Wall of China is _____ .

Sedimentary rock is _____ .

To complete metaphors like these, students must use what they know about the given element and make connections to similar things, events, or processes. Explaining their metaphors will help students analyze their reasoning and refine their metaphors. It is important to give students some guidance until they are comfortable with the rigor of more complex metaphor activities. For example, you might allow students to work in pairs or monitor their individual progress and offer assistance when they need it.

Tools to Facilitate Creating Metaphors in the Classroom

To guide your students effectively, you need to be confident of your own understanding of how to create metaphors. Figure 3.4, Checking My Understanding (p. 37), suggests metaphors that describe the Internet and gives you an opportunity to apply what you have learned in the previous discussion. If you find it difficult to reclassify the items and answer the accompanying questions, we suggest you reread "Recommendations for Classroom Practice." The other assessment and planning tools that follow will help you guide your students to create metaphors in the classroom.

Assessing the Impact on Students

Rubrics are one tool you can use to gauge students' progress. Sample rubrics are provided in Figure 3.5 (p. 38) for evaluating students' progress in using metaphors. These rubrics can be revised, when appropriate, for students to

FIGURE 3.3

Metaphor Organizer—Human Heart Is a Heat Pump

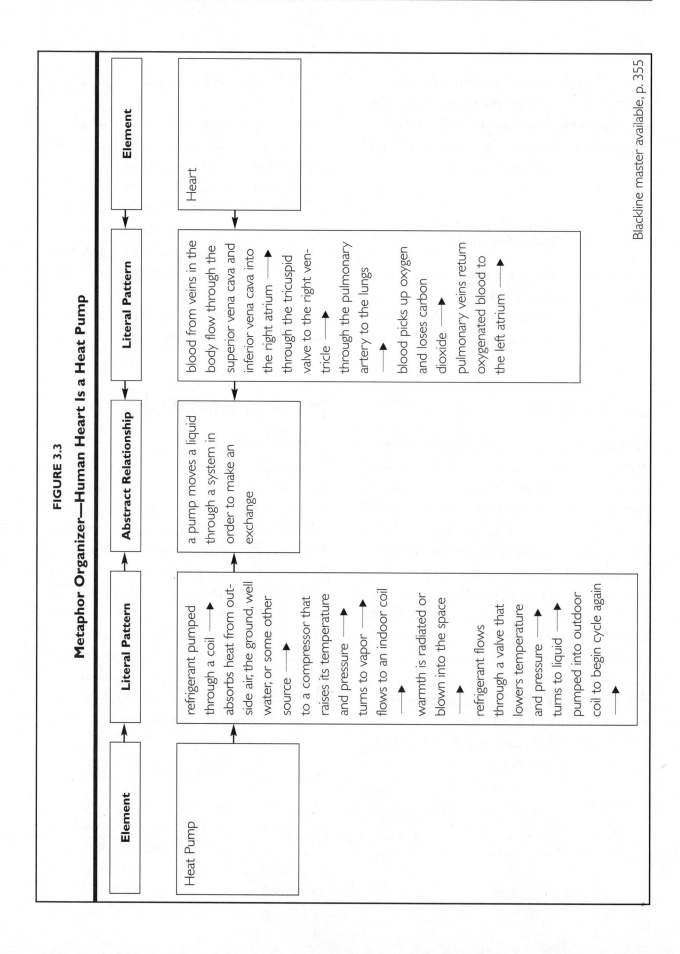

Element	Literal Pattern	Abstract Relationship	Literal Pattern	Element
Heat Pump	refrigerant pumped through a coil ➞ absorbs heat from outside air, the ground, well water, or some other source ➞ to a compressor that raises its temperature and pressure ➞ turns to vapor ➞ flows to an indoor coil ➞ warmth is radiated or blown into the space ➞ refrigerant flows through a valve that lowers temperature and pressure ➞ turns to liquid ➞ pumped into outdoor coil to begin cycle again ➞	a pump moves a liquid through a system in order to make an exchange	blood from veins in the body flow through the superior vena cava and inferior vena cava into the right atrium ➞ through the tricuspid valve to the right ventricle ➞ through the pulmonary artery to the lungs ➞ blood picks up oxygen and loses carbon dioxide ➞ pulmonary veins return oxygenated blood to the left atrium ➞	Heart

Blackline master available, p. 355

FIGURE 3.4

Checking My Understanding—Metaphors

The following metaphors describe the Internet. Imagine you are a student and the teacher asks you to explain each metaphor. Select the one that you believe best describes the Internet and explain that metaphor. Then create a new metaphor of your own. As you complete this assignment, notice what the task asks you to do with the knowledge. How does it take you beyond simply recalling information?

• The Internet is an information superhighway.

• The Internet is a giant flea market.

• The Internet is a coffee shop.

Which metaphor do you think best describes the Internet and why?

Write your own metaphor to describe the Internet:

• What knowledge did you need to complete this task?

• What would you need to do in the classroom to prepare students for a task like this?

FIGURE 3.5

Rubrics for Metaphors

Creating Metaphors Rubric

4   The student identifies the important information of the situation in detail and concisely and accurately states the abstract relationship that explains the general pattern. The student identifies another situation that has the same general pattern and accurately explains their relationship in detail.

3   The student identifies the important information of the situation and states the abstract relationship that explains the general pattern. The student identifies another situation that has the same general pattern and accurately explains their relationship.

2   The student identifies some information about the situation, but the statement of the abstract relationship shows some misconceptions.

1   The student identifies trivial information about the situation. The statement of the abstract relationship shows that the student does not understand the general pattern.

0   Not enough information to make a judgment.

Creating Metaphors Rubric for Younger Students

4   The student identifies the important information of the situation in detail. The student tells what the general pattern is. The student finds another situation that has the same pattern. The student explains how the two situations are related.

3   The student identifies the important information of the situation. The student tells what the general pattern is. The student finds another situation that has the same pattern.

2   The student identifies some information about the situation. What the student says about the general pattern has some mistakes.

1   The student identifies information that does not explain the situation. What the student says about the general pattern has some big mistakes.

0   The student does not try to do the task.

---

use as part of the self-assessment process to help them reflect on their work.

Planning Classroom Activities and Assessing Myself

Answering a series of questions will help you discover how you might use the strategies presented in this module in the context of your current practice. You can use the Planning for Metaphors Worksheet in Figure 3.6 (p. 39) to guide your thinking when planning metaphor activities for students.

Rubrics help in assessing student learning. You can also use a tool to assess yourself—how effectively you are using the strategies for creating metaphors presented in the module. Use Figure 3.7 (p. 40) to evaluate your use of metaphors in the classroom.

FIGURE 3.6

Planning for Metaphors Worksheet

What knowledge will students be learning?

Do I need to set aside time to teach students the process of creating metaphors? How will I teach them the process?

Will I ask students to use a graphic organizer?

How much guidance will I provide students?

How will students explain their work and communicate their conclusions?

How will I monitor how well students are creating and using metaphors?

What will I do to help students who are not creating and using metaphors effectively?

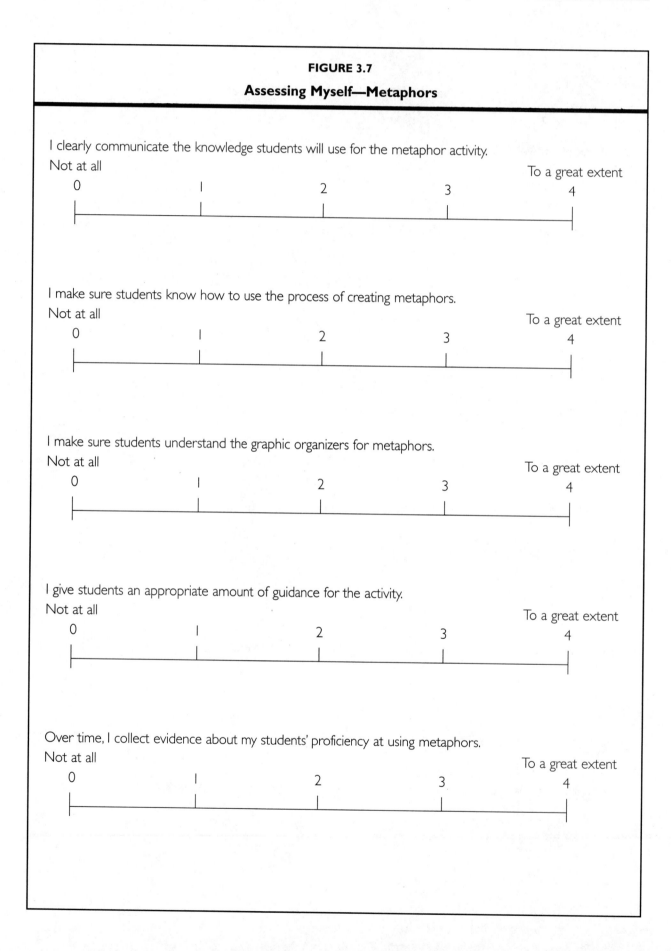

FIGURE 3.7

Assessing Myself—Metaphors

I clearly communicate the knowledge students will use for the metaphor activity.

I make sure students know how to use the process of creating metaphors.

I make sure students understand the graphic organizers for metaphors.

I give students an appropriate amount of guidance for the activity.

Over time, I collect evidence about my students' proficiency at using metaphors.

Module Reflection

Review your responses to the questions in Figure 3.1, Reflecting on My Current Beliefs and Practices—Metaphors worksheet (p. 33). How has this module affected your thinking about teaching and learning? Use the space provided to record your thoughts.

● Reading this information affirms some of what I already knew about metaphors

● Now, I better understand some things about metaphors

● I think I will change how I use metaphors in my classroom

CREATING ANALOGIES

Creating analogies is the process of identifying relationships between pairs of concepts (e.g., identifying relationships between relationships). Like metaphors, analogies help us make connections between things that seem very different. Typically, an analogy follows the form A:B::C:D (read "A is to B as C is to D") (Sternberg, 1977):

> happy:sad::big:small ("happy is to sad as big is to small").
> Happy and big are opposites of sad and small, respectively.

Analogies can help explain an unfamiliar concept by making a comparison to something that we understand. For example, concentrations of particulates in water are commonly stated in measures that are difficult to comprehend: one part per million, one part per billion, one part per trillion, one part per quadrillion. What does one part per trillion mean? An analogy to familiar items and relationships that we can imagine helps us to make sense of one part per trillion:

> one:trillion::one square inch:the area of the city of Chicago
> one is to a trillion as one square inch is to the area of the city of Chicago
> OR

> One:trillion::one square foot tile:a kitchen floor the size of Indiana
> One is to a trillion as one square foot tile is to a kitchen floor the size of Indiana
> OR

> One:trillion::one drop of milk:the milk in a row of milk tanker trucks 10 miles long
> One is to a trillion as one drop of milk is to the amount of milk in a row of milk tanker trucks 10 miles long

In each of these analogies, the relationship is a simple mathematical proportion that relates a quantity of one to a large number. One part of lead per trillion parts of water is an abstract statement, but one drop of milk in a 10-mile line of milk tanker trucks is more concrete. The relationships are easier to imagine because we have concrete representations for things like one square inch, a square foot tile, or a drop of milk. We can use analogies for similar purposes in the classroom. Before reading the recommendations for classroom practice, take some time to reflect on your current practices and beliefs related to using analogies with your students by completing the Reflecting on My Current Beliefs and Practices—Analogies worksheet in Figure 4.1 (p. 43).

FIGURE 4.1

Reflecting on My Current Beliefs and Practices—Analogies

What is the purpose of asking students to create analogies?

What kind of activities do I use to help students create analogies?

What analogies can I think of that apply to the content areas that I teach?

What questions do I have about using analogies in my classroom?

Recommendations for Classroom Practice

Creating analogies is a complex process that students will need to learn about and practice. In this module, we discuss several approaches to use in the classroom:

- giving students a model for the process,
- using familiar content to teach students the steps in creating analogies,
- giving students graphic organizers for creating analogies, and
- giving students guidance as needed.

Give Students a Model for the Process

An analogy pushes us to think about how items and concepts are related: how do these two things interact, and how is this relationship similar to the relationship between the second pair of items? At first, content-area analogies might seem very complicated to students because they involve several elements and relationships among and between the elements, such as in the examples that follow.

heart:human::compressor:heat pump ("heart is to human as compressor is to heat pump")
The heart circulates and oxygenates blood in a human as a compressor vaporizes refrigerant and circulates air in a heat pump.
one:multiplication::zero:addition ("one is to multiplication as zero is to addition")
When a number is multiplied by one, the result is the number; when a number is added to zero, the result is the number.

Providing students with steps in a process for creating analogies, as given in Figure 4.2, can help them work with academic content.

Use Familiar Content to Teach How to Create Analogies

Analogy problems are common in testing situations. Students will encounter analogy problems on many state standards tests, on the PSAT, the SAT, or the ACT. The types of relationships that are common to these analogy problems appear on page 45.

FIGURE 4.2
Model for Analogies

Steps for Creating Analogies	**Steps for Creating Analogies for Younger Students**
1. Identify how the two elements in the first pair are related.	1. What is the connection between the first two things?
2. State their relationship in a general way.	2. How can I describe this connection?
3. Identify another pair of elements that share a similar relationship.	3. Do the second two things have a connection like the first two?

Similar Concepts
Adjacent concepts are synonyms or similar in meaning.

> *hungry:ravenous::tired:exhausted*

Dissimilar Concepts
Adjacent concepts are opposites or dissimilar in meaning.

> *grim:cheerful::hilly:flat*

Class Membership
Adjacent concepts belong to the same class or category.

> *carrot:potato::brown:purple*

Class Name or Class Member
One element in a pair is a class name, the other is a member of the class.

> *3:natural number::2:irrational number*

Part to Whole
One element in a pair is a part of the other element in the pair.

> *spark plug:engine::variable:function*

Change
One element in a pair turns into the other element in the pair.

> *caterpillar:butterfly::tadpole:frog*

Function
One element in a pair performs a function on or for another.

> *pilot:airplane::lawn mower:grass*

Quantity/Size
The two elements in the pair are comparable in terms of quantity or size.

> *one minute:two years::one penny:ten thousand dollars*

(Adapted from Lewis & Greene, 1982.)

Providing students with examples of these relationships can help them to recognize patterns in the analogies they come across and guide them as they learn the steps for creating analogies. You might start with some of the common analogy relationships described above to introduce the structure of an analogy to students. To illustrate, you might introduce the "class name/class member" relationship with a few examples, such as

> *whale:mammal::snake:reptile*
> *newt:amphibian::salmon:fish*
> The Adventures of Huckleberry
>   Finn:*classic American literature::*
>   Great Expectations:*classic British*
>   *literature*

Once students understand the structure of analogies, they can begin to discover the complexities of the relationships implied by the form *a is to b as c is to d*, and create new analogies that explain different relationships.

Use Graphic Organizers to Create Analogies

Students can use a graphic organizer as an aid for creating analogies. The graphic organizer describing the Great Depression (Figure 4.3, p. 46) shows the relationship
Stock Market Crash of 1929: United States economy::exposure to germs:human body.

Guide Students As Needed

Analogies emphasize similarities, but they also show differences. The more students examine

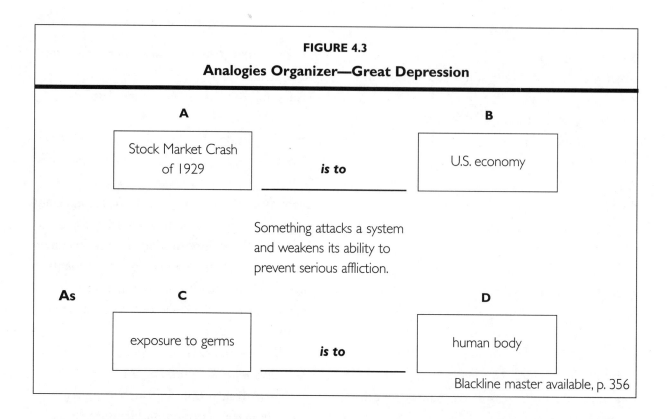

FIGURE 4.3

Analogies Organizer—Great Depression

A

Stock Market Crash of 1929

is to

B

U.S. economy

Something attacks a system and weakens its ability to prevent serious affliction.

As

C

exposure to germs

is to

D

human body

Blackline master available, p. 356

the details of the relationships between the elements in each pair of an analogy, and the connection between the pairs, the better they will understand that analogies can reveal differences as well as similarities. For example, consider the following analogy:

brain:human::central processing unit: computer

In a human, the brain controls activities vital for survival, such as movement, sleep, thirst. Other parts of the body and the external environment send signals to the brain, which interprets these signals. The brain makes things happen and communicates with other parts of the body by sending electrical signals through neurons. Similarly, the central processing unit (CPU) in a computer processes information. The CPU interprets signals or instructions and executes programs, makes decisions, stores

information, and communicates with the other parts of the computer. However, if students push this analogy and consider the differences, they will begin to see how an analogy eventually breaks down. For example, the brain is an electrical and chemical "machine." That is, neurons in the human body send electrical and chemical signals. A computer does not use chemical signals. Uncovering the differences beneath the surface of this analogy helps students to refine their understanding of how the human brain and a computer work.

To introduce students to analogical thinking, you can give them complete content-area analogies like the previous example discussed, or the following:

down:up::under:over

In this case, students must explain the relationship between the items in each pair of the analogy, as well as the relationship between the two pairs.

You can also give students incomplete analogies and ask them to fill in the missing elements and explain the relationships. For example:

evaporation:steam::_____:liquid

This type of activity requires more work, but still gives students a predetermined relationship that they must uncover. After some practice with analogies, you can give students the first pair of elements and ask them to provide the second pair. Students may struggle with open-ended analogy tasks, but this struggle pushes their understanding to another level.

Tools to Facilitate Creating Analogies in the Classroom

To effectively guide your students, you need to be confident of your own understanding of how to create analogies. Figure 4.4, Checking My Understanding—Analogies (pp. 48–49), gives several analogies from different content areas that you are to explain and provides you with an opportunity to apply what you have learned in the previous discussion. If you find it difficult to complete the assignment on analogies, we suggest you reread "Recommendations for Classroom Practice." The other assessment and planning tools that follow will help you guide students in creating analogies in the classroom.

Assessing the Impact on Students

Rubrics are one tool you can use to gauge students' progress. Sample rubrics are given below for evaluating students' progress in using analogies (Figure 4.5, p. 50). These rubrics can be revised, when appropriate, for students to use as part of the self-assessment process to help them reflect on their work.

Planning Classroom Activities and Assessing Myself

Answering a series of questions will help you decide how you might use the strategies presented in this module in the context of your current practice. You can use the Planning for Analogies Worksheet, Figure 4.6 (p. 51), to guide your thinking when planning analogy activities for students.

Rubrics are a tool to help assess students' learning. You can also use a tool to assess yourself—how effectively you use the strategies presented in the module for creating analogies. Use Figure 4.7 (p. 52) to evaluate your effectiveness in using analogies.

FIGURE 4.4

Checking My Understanding—Analogies

Below are several analogies from different content areas. Before each analogy is a statement of the content knowledge that is the focus of the analogy. Imagine that your teacher asks you to explain each analogy in Set 1 and complete each analogy in Set 2. As you complete this assignment, notice what the task asks you to do with the knowledge. How does it take you beyond simply recalling information?

Set 1. Explain the analogies that follow each knowledge statement.

Target Knowledge: Knows different ways in which living things can be grouped and purposes of different groupings (Science, Grades 3–5)

Kangaroo:marsupial::platypus:monotreme

Target Knowledge: Knows the defining characteristics of a variety of literary forms and genres (Language Arts, Grades 9–12)

Sonnet:poem::passion play:drama

Target Knowledge: Understands the properties of and the relationships among addition, subtraction, multiplication, and division (Mathematics, Grades 3–5)

Addition:subtraction::multiplication:division

Set 2. Complete the analogies that follow each knowledge statement.

Target Knowledge: Understands the characteristics and properties (e.g., order relations, relative magnitude, base-10 place values) of the set of rational numbers and its subsets (Mathematics, Grades 6–8)

2:4::4:x

x = _____ because _____

Target Knowledge: Understands similarities and differences among the characteristics of artworks from various eras and cultures (Visual Arts, Grades 5–8)

van Gogh:expressionism::_____:_____

Target Knowledge: Knows various people and groups who make, apply, and enforce rules and laws for others and who manage disputes about rules and laws (Civics, Grades 3–5)

President:United States::_____:_____

Target Knowledge: Knows the characteristics of a variety of regions (Geography, Grades 3–5)

_____:_____::grass:meadow

FIGURE 4.4 (CONTINUED)

Checking My Understanding—Analogies

Think about your answers to the following questions:

Describe the process you used to explain the analogies in Set 1.

Describe the process you used to complete the analogies in Set 2. How was this process different from the process you used to explain the analogies in Set 1?

Considering the processes you described above, how would you prepare students to work on similar analogy activities?

FIGURE 4.5
Rubrics for Analogies

Creating Analogies Rubric

4   The student concisely and accurately states the general pattern of the relationship between the first pair of elements and explains how it applies to the second pair of elements. The explanation shows a complete and detailed understanding of the analogy.

3   The student states the general pattern of the relationship between the first two elements and explains how it applies to the second pair of elements. The explanation shows an understanding of the analogy.

2   The student states the general pattern of the relationship between the first two elements in a way that reveals some misconceptions about how the elements in the first pair are related. Or, the student has some misconceptions about how the relationship applies to the second pair of elements.

1   The student identifies trivial information and has misconceptions about how the elements in the first pair are related. The student has misconceptions about how the relationship applies to the second pair of elements.

0   Not enough information to make a judgment.

Creating Analogies Rubric for Younger Students

4   The student correctly tells how the first two things are connected. The student tells how the general pattern applies to the second pair of things. The student uses details to completely explain the analogy.

3   The student correctly tells how the first two things are related. The student tells how the general pattern applies to the second pair of things.

2   The student makes mistakes explaining how the first two things are connected. Or, the student make mistakes telling how the general pattern applies to the second pair of things.

1   The student tells information that is not important. The explanation has some big mistakes. Or, the student cannot explain how the relationship applies to the second pair of elements.

0   The student does not try to do the task.

FIGURE 4.6

Planning for Analogies Worksheet

What knowledge will students be learning?

Do I need to set aside time to teach students the process of creating analogies? How will I teach them the process?

Will I ask students to use a graphic organizer?

How much guidance will I provide students?

How will students explain their work and communicate their conclusions?

How will I monitor how well students are creating and using analogies?

What will I do to help students who are not creating and using analogies effectively?

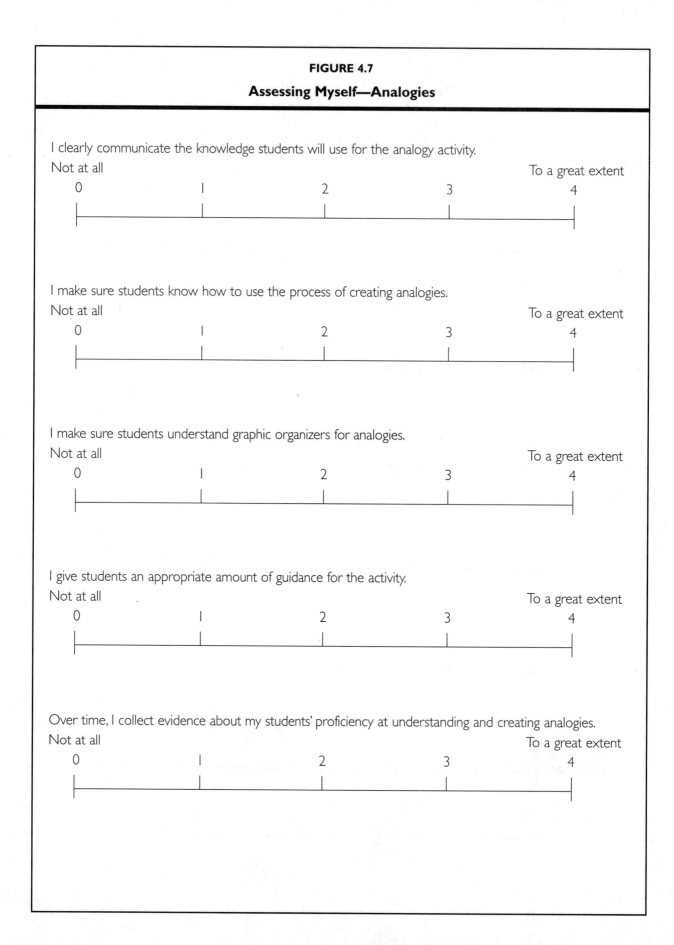

FIGURE 4.7

Assessing Myself—Analogies

I clearly communicate the knowledge students will use for the analogy activity.

Not at all   To a great extent

0   1   2   3   4

I make sure students know how to use the process of creating analogies.

Not at all   To a great extent

0   1   2   3   4

I make sure students understand graphic organizers for analogies.

Not at all   To a great extent

0   1   2   3   4

I give students an appropriate amount of guidance for the activity.

Not at all   To a great extent

0   1   2   3   4

Over time, I collect evidence about my students' proficiency at understanding and creating analogies.

Not at all   To a great extent

0   1   2   3   4

Module Reflection

Review your responses to the questions in the Figure 4.1, Reflecting on My Current Beliefs and Practices—Analogies worksheet (p. 43). How has this module affected your thinking about teaching and learning? Use the space provided to record your thoughts.

- Reading this information affirms some of what I already knew about analogies

- Now, I better understand some things about analogies

- I think I will change how I use analogies in my classroom

Modules 5–6

Summarizing and Note Taking

Study Group Tip

If you are using this handbook in a study group, your group might want to read and discuss the research summaries about summarizing and note taking in the companion book, *Classroom Instruction That Works.*

Summarizing and note taking require students to distill information. These processes seem straightforward, but they are quite complex. To summarize information, we must decide which parts of it are important, which trivial, which repetitive. We must delete some information, reword some ideas, and reorganize information. Similarly, with note taking we must synthesize material, prioritize pieces of data, restate some information, and organize concepts, topics, and details. Summarizing and note taking involve many mental processes.

Research tells us that effective summaries involve deleting, substituting, and keeping some information, and that to carry out these processes well, students must analyze the information they are working with in a complex way. Research also shows that understanding the explicit structure of information helps students to summarize. Note taking is similar to summarizing because students need to think about and shape the information they are recording. Research indicates that simply recording information verbatim is not an effective technique. On the other hand, research also says that the more notes students take, the better. Further, students need to consider their notes a work in progress; they should revise and review their notes. In these modules, we offer strategies and suggestions for using what research tells us works in the classroom. We encourage you to use these and other approaches to using summarizing and note taking to enhance students' learning.

List of Figures

SUMMARIZING

Summarizing is a process we do almost automatically. When we read, hear, or see information, we don't take it in exactly as we experience it. We pick and choose what is most important and then restate that information in a brief, synthesized fashion. In a sense, we find the main pattern running through the story or event and make connections among important pieces of information. Summarizing involves at least two highly related elements: (1) filling in missing parts and (2) translating information into a synthesized form. The first aspect of summarizing (filling in the missing information) can be illustrated using this scenario:

> Two card players stared at each other from across the table. Both appeared tense, although the man smoking the cigar seemed to have a slight smile on his face. He laid down his cards in a fanning motion that displayed one card at a time. When each new card was shown, his opponent in the silk shirt seemed to sink lower and lower into his chair. When the cigar-smoking antagonist finally had shown all of his cards, the silk-shirted man got up and left the table without showing his cards and without saying a word.

As you read these sentences, your mind naturally fills in many unstated elements. For example, you probably inferred that both men had bet substantial amounts of money on the hand; the cigar-smoking man knew he had a winning hand as soon as it was dealt him; the silk-shirted man lost the hand; and so on. Inferences like these might be thought of as *default inferences*. Unless explicitly stated otherwise, we expect certain things to occur in certain situations.

A few hours from now, if you were asked to retell what you had read in the passage, you would most likely engage in the second aspect of summarizing—translating information into a synthesized form. In your retelling, you probably would not give a verbatim account of the passage. Rather, you might provide a brief, synthesized version like the following:

> Two men had a large bet on a single hand of poker. As soon as the cards were all out, one of the men knew he had won the hand. After he showed his hand, his opponent silently got up and left, knowing he had lost.

The synthesized version of information we read or hear is sometimes referred to as a *macrostructure* (see Kintsch, 1979; van Dijk, 1980). Human beings tend to generate macrostructures for information they read, hear, or even see. This tendency explains why we are likely to remember the gist of movies we see rather than a scene-by-scene account.

Before reading "Recommendations for Classroom Practice," take some time to reflect on your current practices and beliefs related to using summarizing by completing the Reflecting on My Current Beliefs and Practices—Summarizing worksheet in Figure 5.1 (p. 59). This will give you a basis of comparison as you read about the strategies in the module.

Recommendations for Classroom Practice

We summarize all the time—the weather report on the morning news, a conversation with a colleague in the hallway, the happenings at the afternoon staff meeting, Thursday night's episode of our favorite show. Although we engage in summarizing daily, much of the mental processing involved is unconscious. We are not deliberately applying a summarizing strategy to Thursday night's episode. But we do not need to systematically summarize the information because we are not writing an essay about the plot intricacies in that episode or answering questions about heart surgery in class the next day. When we want students to summarize important elements of a lecture or a chapter from a reading assignment, we should give them specific summarizing strategies to help them apply this complex process to classroom content. In this module, we discuss several approaches to use in the classroom:

- teaching students the rule-based summarizing strategy,
- using summary frames, and
- teaching students reciprocal teaching and the group-enhanced summary.

Teach Students the Rule-Based Summarizing Strategy

Many students understand the basic idea of summarizing: you take a lot of information, pick out the main points, and make it shorter. Drawing from their understanding of the summarizing process, an effective summarizing strategy you can teach students is the *rule-based summarizing strategy* (Brown, Campione, & Day, 1981). The strategy involves a set of rules or steps that students use to construct a summary (Figure 5.2, p. 60).

To make these rules come alive for students, you can demonstrate them in some detail. You might present students with a passage such as the sample in Figure 5.3 (p. 61), and then walk them through the rules by thinking aloud as you summarize the passage.

Think Aloud As Presented by the Teacher. "I'll think aloud as I use the rules of the strategy. See if my thinking makes sense to you.

"The rules say to 'delete trivial material, delete redundant material, and substitute superordinate terms for more specific terms.'

"Let's see, the comment in parentheses, 'and maybe a bit of their childhood left in them,' seems trivial, so I can delete that. I'll also delete 'when you think about it, it is easy to understand the importance of models in science' because it doesn't give me any new information. Neither does the very last sentence, 'you may think of additional reasons why it would be necessary for scientists to develop models as they probe the secrets of nature,' so I'll get rid of that sentence too. Now, I see some lists. 'Models' covers 'model cars, tinker toys, model houses, and so on,' so I can delete that list. The list 'gravity, magnetism, or energy' seems important, and I can't think of a term that encompasses all three, so I'll leave that list. But, it's repeated, so I can delete the list once. Now here's my first paragraph: (see p. 60)

FIGURE 5.1

Reflecting on My Current Beliefs and Practices—Summarizing

In what situations is it important for my students to summarize?

What does summarizing help my students do?

What do I do to help students understand and use the process of summarizing?

What questions do I have about using summarizing in my classroom?

Most children like to play with models, ~~including model cars, tinker toys, model houses, and so on.~~ Likewise, most scientists interact with models. However, their model interaction is out of necessity ~~(and maybe a bit of their childhood left in them!)~~, as the forging of new science is frequently dependent on the development of models. ~~When you think about it, it is easy to understand the importance of models in science.~~ Many times the objects of a scientist's attention are too small to be observed directly, or they may be inaccessible for direct visual study, as would be the case for the center of the Earth or the surface of a distant galactic object. Other topics of study, such as gravity, magnetism, or energy, can be studied through their effects on matter. But ~~gravity, magnetism, and energy~~ [they] cannot be seen directly, so they too are modeled. ~~You may think of additional reasons why it would be necessary for scientists to develop models as they probe the secrets of nature.~~

"Those changes leave me with the following paragraph:

> Most children like to play with models. Likewise, most scientists interact with models. However, their model interaction is out of necessity, as the forging of new science is frequently dependent on the development of models. Many times the objects of a scientist's attention are too small to be observed directly, or they may be inaccessible for direct visual study, as would be the case for the center of the Earth or the surface of a distant galactic object. Other topics of study, such as gravity, magnetism, or energy, can be studied through their effects on matter, but they cannot be seen directly, so they too are modeled.

"Now I'll apply the rules to the second paragraph. A few phrases seem trivial to me—'in such a way as,' 'nothing more than,' 'in an effort,' 'often often used by beginning chemistry students,' and 'in great detail.' Since they don't add anything to my understanding of the content, I'll

---

FIGURE 5.2

Model for Summarizing

Steps for Rule-Based Summarizing

1. Delete trivial material that is unnecessary to understanding.
2. Delete redundant material.
3. Substitute superordinate terms for more specific terms (e.g., use fish for rainbow trout, salmon, and halibut).
4. Select a topic sentence, or invent one if it is missing.

Steps in Rule-Based Summarizing for Younger Students

1. Take out material that is not important for your understanding.
2. Take out words that repeat information.
3. Replace a list of things with a word that describes the things in the list (e.g., use trees for elm, oak, and maple).
4. Find a topic sentence. If you cannot find a topic sentence, make one up.

Adapted from Brown, Campione, & Day (1981).

FIGURE 5.3

Summarizing Strategy—Sample Passage

Most children like to play with models, including model cars, tinker toys, model houses, and so on. Likewise, most scientists interact with models. However, their model interaction is out of necessity (and maybe a bit of their childhood left in them!), as the forging of new science is frequently dependent on the development of models. When you think about it, it is easy to understand the importance of models in science. Many times the objects of a scientist's attention are too small to be observed directly, or they may be inaccessible for direct visual study, as would be the case for the center of the Earth or the surface of a distant galactic object. Other topics of study, such as gravity, magnetism, or energy, can be studied through their effects on matter. But gravity, magnetism, and energy cannot be seen directly, so they too are modeled. You may think of additional reasons why it would be necessary for scientists to develop models as they probe the secrets of nature.

The models that scientists develop take many different forms. In some cases they are actual physical constructions. A good example of this kind of model would be one that represents the Earth, moon, and sun as small wooden spheres that are mechanically moved in such a way as to illustrate the phases of the moon, eclipses, and so forth. Other models may be nothing more than mental images that are developed in an effort to picture something unseen. A good example would be the Bohr solar system model of the atom that is often used by beginning chemistry students. In this model the nucleus is imagined to be like the sun and the electrons are visualized as whirling around the nucleus analogous to the planets orbiting the sun. Other models are mathematical in nature and depend on algebraic or other kinds of statements to describe a phenomenon or object. Rays of light are good examples, as these can be treated as waves and equations can be developed that describe the properties of waves in great detail.

Models usually evolve and are improved as scientific advances are made. Not infrequently, a model is thrown out completely based on new findings that prove it to be misleading or fatally incorrect. It is also the case that different models often are used to describe the same thing, and the choice of models depends on the goal of the scientific investigation or perhaps the scientific sophistication of the individual conducting the work. A good example once again is models of the atom. The solar system model is adequate for many purposes, but a highly mathematical model based on the field of quantum mechanics is necessary for rationalizing other aspects of an atom's behavior. In a fundamental way, models are developed in an effort to explain how things work in nature.

Source: From "Models in Science: Student Text" in *The Sun and Solar Wind*, by Bogner, D., McCormick, B. J., & Fox, L. R., 2001 [Online]. http://www.genesismission.org/educate/scimodule/topics.html

---

delete these phrases. I don't see any lists, but there is some redundant material. I can delete 'a good example of this kind of model would be one that.' Then I'll reword what's left of the third sentence and combine it with sentence two like this: 'In some cases they are actual physical constructions, such as small wooden spheres representing the Earth, moon, and sun that are mechanically moved to illustrate the phases of the moon, eclipses, and so on.'

"Now I think I'll delete the last part of the sentence that begins 'Other models are mathematical.' 'In nature' doesn't add anything to my understanding and 'depend on algebraic or other kinds of statements to describe a phenomenon or object' is really covered by the very last sentence that provides an example. Now, my second paragraph reads like this:

> The models that scientists develop take many different forms. In some cases they are actual physical constructions, [such as small wooden spheres representing the Earth, moon, and sun that are mechanically moved] ~~A good example of this kind of model would be one that represents the Earth, moon, and sun as small wooden~~

spheres that are mechanically moved in such a way as to illustrate the phases of the moon, eclipses, and so forth. Other models may be nothing more than mental images that are developed in an effort to picture something unseen. A good example would be the Bohr solar system model of the atom that is often used by beginning chemistry students. In this model the nucleus is imagined to be like the sun and the electrons are visualized as whirling around the nucleus analogous to the planets orbiting the sun. Other models are mathematical in nature and depend on algebraic or other kinds of statements to describe a phenomenon or object. Rays of light are good examples, as these can be treated as waves and equations can be developed that describe the properties of waves in great detail.

"My new paragraph is as follows:

The models that scientists develop take many different forms. In some cases they are actual physical constructions, such as small wooden spheres representing Earth, moon, and sun that are mechanically moved to illustrate the phases of the moon, eclipses, and so forth. Other models may be mental images that are developed to picture something unseen. A good example would be the Bohr solar system model of the atom. In this model the nucleus is imagined to be like the sun and the electrons are visualized as whirling around the nucleus analogous to the planets orbiting the sun. Other models are mathematical in nature. Rays of light are good examples, as these can be treated as waves and equations can be developed that describe the properties of waves in great detail.

"Now for the last paragraph. This paragraph contains a lot of important information, but I'll still try to apply the rules. Does anything seem trivial? I can delete 'It is also the case that,' 'perhaps,' and 'once again.' Since I know we are talking about science here, I can delete 'scientific' in two places in the third sentence. I'll also replace 'the individual conducting the work' with 'scientist.' There are no lists, so now my paragraph reads:

Models usually evolve and are improved as scientific advances are made. Not infrequently, a model is thrown out completely based on new findings that prove it to be misleading or fatally incorrect. It is also the case that different models often are used to describe the same thing, and the choice of models depends on the goal of the scientific investigation or perhaps the scientific sophistication of the individual conducting the work [scientist]. A good example once again is models of the atom. The solar system model is adequate for many purposes, but a highly mathematical model based on the field of quantum mechanics is necessary for rationalizing other aspects of an atom's behavior. In a fundamental way, models are developed in an effort to explain how things work in nature.

"My results are as follows:

Models usually evolve and are improved as scientific advances are made. Not infrequently, a model is thrown out completely based on new findings that prove it to be misleading or fatally incorrect. Different models often are used to describe the same thing, and the choice of models depends on the goal of the investigation or the sophistication of the scientist. A good example is models of the atom. The solar system model is adequate for many purposes, but a highly mathematical model based on the field of quantum mechanics is necessary for rationalizing other aspects of an atom's behavior. In a fundamental way, models are developed in an effort to explain how things work in nature."

Using a think-aloud process gives students a model for the rule-based summarizing strategy and helps them to understand how each step in the process works. Modeling the process in this way also prepares students to practice the rule-based strategy in less structured situations.

Use Summary Frames

A summary frame is another powerful tool that students can use to help them summarize information. A summary frame is a series of questions designed to highlight the important elements of specific patterns commonly found in text. We will present common patterns and their accompanying frames:

- narrative or story
- topic-restriction-illustration (T-R-I)
- definition
- argumentation
- problem or solution
- conversation

You are probably familiar with the basic structure of all of these patterns because they commonly occur in a variety of texts, including fiction, textbooks, and editorial pieces. A summary frame requires that we consider the specific elements found in each pattern and create

a set of questions to guide students as they summarize a text. In other words, you build the summary frame around the pattern of the text students are reading. To illustrate, consider Figures 5.4, 5.5, 5.6, 5.7, 5.8, and 5.9.

The following example shows the use of the narrative summary frame described in Figure 5.4 (p. 64).

The Narrative Frame Illustration. The passage is the story "Jack and the Beanstalk."
Frame Questions
1. Who are the main characters? What are their characteristics? *A little boy named Jack, his mother who is a widow, the mean Giant, and the Giant's wife.*
2. When and where did the story take place? What were the circumstances? *A long time ago in a little cottage. Jack and his mother have suffered through a long winter, and they are very poor. Jack's mother is sick.*
3. What prompted the action in the story? *Jack's mother asks him to take their cow to the market to sell.*
4. How do the main characters react emotionally to what happens at the start of the story? *Jack really enjoyed going to the market, so he was looking forward to taking the cow.*
5. What did the main characters decide to do? Did they set a goal? What was it? *Jack will take the cow to the market to sell so that he and his mother can buy food.*
6. How did the main characters try to accomplish their goals? *On his way to the market, Jack runs into a butcher who has some beans. The butcher tells Jack that the beans are magic, so Jack trades the cow for the beans. When he gets home, his mother is very upset and throws the beans out the door. The next morning, Jack finds that the*

FIGURE 5.4

Narrative Frame

The narrative or story pattern

Stories and other narratives commonly include the following elements:

1. Characters: the characteristics of the main characters in the story.
2. Setting: the time, place, and context in which the story took place.
3. Initiating event: the impetus that starts the action rolling in the story.
4. Internal response: how the main characters react emotionally to the initiating event.
5. Goal: what the main characters decide to do as a reaction to the initiating event (sometimes this is the goal they set).
6. Consequence: how the main characters try to accomplish the goal.
7. Resolution: how the goal turns out.

Note: Elements 3–7 are sometimes repeated to create an *episode*.

The narrative frame

Guiding questions for the narrative or story frame:

1. Who are the main characters? And what distinguishes them from other characters?
2. When and where did the story take place? What were the circumstances?
3. What prompted the action in the story?

4. How did the characters express their feelings?

5. What did the main characters decide to do? Did they set a goal? What was it?

6. How did the main characters try to accomplish their goals?
7. What were the consequences?

---

beans have grown up over night into a thick, tall stalk. Jack climbs the beanstalk and finds himself in a beautiful countryside with a castle.

7. How does the story turn out? Did the main characters accomplish their goals? *Jack learns that a Giant who killed Jack's father, a good knight, now lives in the castle. On different trips to the castle, the Giant's wife lets Jack in and he takes some gold coins, a hen that lays golden eggs, and a harp that plays beautiful music. The last time, the giant chases Jack. When Jack gets to the bottom of the beanstalk, he chops it down and kills the Giant.*

Summary: *Jack and his mother lived a long time ago in a little cottage. Jack trades their cow for some magic beans, which grow into a giant beanstalk. Jack climbs the beanstalk and takes some gold coins, a hen that lays golden eggs, and a harp that plays music from the Giant who had killed his father. Jack chops down the beanstalk and kills the Giant. Then Jack and his mother return to the castle where they once lived.*

The example on page 64 illustrates the Topic-Restriction-Illustration Frame. See also Figure 5.5 (p. 65).

Topic-Restriction-Illustration (T-R-I) Frame Illustration. The passage is about mammals. *Mammals are a group of vertebrate animals—animals with backbones. Mothers nourish baby mammals with milk. Mammals are warm-blooded, which means that they keep their body temperature within a narrow range despite changes in the environment. One sub-group of mammals is the marsupial group. Marsupials give birth to live young, but the babies are still very undeveloped when they are born. Baby marsupials live inside a special pouch on the mother's stomach and feed on milk supplied by her nipples. Kangaroos are one type of marsupial. They live in Australia and on islands close by. Kangaroos use their large back legs and tails for hopping. Another marsupial is the opossum. The Virginia opossum is the only marsupial that lives in North America. Long, shiny, white hair and an undercoat of soft, woolly fur cover the Virginia opossum. An opossum has 50 teeth. It sleeps during the day and hunts food at night.*

Frame Questions
Topic (T): What is the general statement or topic? *Mammals*
Restriction (R): What information does the author give that narrows or restricts the general statement or topic? *Marsupials are one sub-group of mammals.*
Illustration (I): What examples does the author present to illustrate the restriction? *Kangaroos are one kind of marsupial that live in Australia. The Virginia opossum is the only marsupial that lives in North America.*

<u>Summary:</u> *Mammals are warm-blooded animals with backbones. Mothers feed their young with milk. Marsupials are a category of mammals. Two examples of marsupials are the kangaroo and opossum.*

The next example illustrates the definition frame presented in Figure 5.6 (p. 66).

FIGURE 5.5

Topic-Restriction-Illustration (T-R-I) Frame

The Topic-Restriction-Illustration pattern
Expository texts that fit this pattern commonly include the following elements:
Topic: a general statement about the topic to be discussed
Restriction: statements that limit the information in some way

Illustration: statements that exemplify the topic or restriction

The Topic-Restriction-Illustration frame
Guiding questions for the T-R-I frame:

Topic: What is the general statement or topic?

Restriction: What information does the author give that narrows or restricts the general statement or topic?
Illustration: What examples does the author give to illustrate the topic or restriction?

The T-R-I pattern can have several restrictions and additional illustrations.

FIGURE 5.6

Definition Frame

The definition pattern

Text that follows this pattern typically describes a particular concept and identifies subordinate concepts. This pattern commonly includes the following elements:

Term: the subject to be defined

Set: the general category to which the term belongs

Gross characteristics: those characteristics that separate the term from other elements in the set

Minute differences: the different classes of objects that fall directly beneath the term

The definition frame

Guiding questions for the definition frame:

What is being defined?
To which general category does the item belong?

What characteristics separate the item from other things in the general category?

What are some different types or classes of the item being defined?

The Definition Frame Illustration. The passage is about sonnets.

Sonnets are lyric poems with 14 lines that follow a formal rhyme scheme. The two major types of sonnets are the Petrarchan (Italian) and the Shakespearean (English).

The Petrarchan sonnet, named for the Italian poet Petrarch, consists of an octave, or eight-line stanza, with two quatrains that rhyme a b b a, a b b a. The first quatrain introduces the theme of the sonnet, and the second quatrain develops the theme. The last six lines form a sestet and rhyme c d e c d e, or c d c d c d, or c d e d c e. The first three lines of the sestet illustrate the theme; the last three lines bring closure to the whole poem. Sir Philip Sidney's Astrophel and Stella *(1591) exemplifies the Petrarchan sonnet written in English. In the 17th century, John Milton also wrote sonnets based on the Petrarchan form in both English and Italian.*

The Shakespearean sonnet, named for the English poet and playwright William

Shakespeare, consists of three quatrains, each rhymed differently—a b a b, c d c d, e f e f—and a closing couplet rhymed g g. English sonnets written in the 16th century dealt primarily with love, but in the 17th century, writers such as John Donne wrote sonnets that dealt with other subjects. In the 18th century, Romantic poets such as William Wordsworth, Samuel Taylor Coleridge, and Percy Bryce Shelley revitalized the form. Elizabeth Barrett Browning and Dante Gabriel Rossetti wrote sonnets during the Victorian period.

Frame Questions
1. What is being defined? *The sonnet*
2. To which category of things does the item belong? *The genre poems*
3. What characteristics separate the item from other things in the general category? *Sonnets consist of 14 lines and follow rhyming schemes.*
4. What are some types or classes of the thing being defined? *Petrarchan and Shakespearean sonnets.*

Summary: A sonnet is a lyric poem with 14 lines that follows a rhyming scheme. The Petrarchan or Italian sonnet consists of an octave and a sestet. The Shakespearean or English sonnet consists of three quatrains and a couplet.

The next illustration refers to the argumentation summarizing technique shown in Figure 5.7.

The Argumentation Frame Illustration. The passage is about multistate lotteries.

State and local parks, recreation facilities, wildlife habitats, and open-space initiatives benefit from the proceeds of our state lottery games. Multistate lotteries involve more players than our state's current lottery games, so they offer potentially bigger pay-offs. They also offer additional funding for state parks, wildlife habitats, and open space. Our state should join a multistate lottery.

Joining a multistate lottery will increase lottery revenues and help our state continue to support our parks, recreation facilities, wildlife habitats, and open space. Further, because a multistate lottery has the potential to generate even more money than the current state lottery, the state will have a source of revenue to spend on health and safety problems in public schools.

Now people drive out of state to purchase tickets. The money that our states' citizens spend on lottery games should stay in our state. Also, these multistate lotteries are the only way for people in smaller states, like ours, to win really big jackpots. Tickets for the big lottery games are usually cheap, typically only one dollar, but they give players the potential to win millions of dollars.

FIGURE 5.7

Argumentation Frame

The argumentation pattern

Texts that fit the argumentation frame attempt to support a claim. The argumentation pattern commonly includes the following elements:

Evidence: information that leads to a claim

Claim: the assertion that something is true (identify the claim that is the focal point of the argument)

Support: examples of or explanations for the claim

Qualifier: a restriction on the claim or evidence counter to the claim

The argumentation frame

Guiding questions for the argumentation frame:

Evidence: What information does the author present that leads to a claim?

Claim: What does the author assert is true? What basic statement or claim is the focus of the information?

Support: What examples or explanations support the claim?

Qualifier: What restrictions on the claim, or evidence counter to the claim, are presented?

We do have opportunities to participate in lottery games in our state, but joining a multistate lottery would give citizens more choices.

Frame Questions
1. What information does the author present that leads to a claim? *The state benefits from state lottery games, and multistate lottery games offer more money for state programs.*
2. What does the author assert is true? What basic statement is the focus of the information? *Our state should join a multistate lottery.*
3. What examples or explanations does the author present to support the claim? *Multistate lotteries will give the state a source of revenue to spend on health and safety problems in public schools. People drive out of state to purchase tickets for big, multistate lottery games, but that money should stay in our state. Multistate lotteries are the only way for people in smaller states to win really big jackpots. Tickets for the big lottery games are usually cheap, but they give players the potential to win millions of dollars.*
4. What restrictions on the claim, or evidence counter to the claim, does the author present? *Our state already has lottery games.*

<u>Summary:</u> *Although our state already has lottery games, joining a multistate lottery would provide more benefits to the state. Joining a multistate lottery would keep more money in the state and allow players to win bigger jackpots.*

Using the topic of fossil fuels, the next illustration employs the problem or solution summary framework presented in Figure 5.8 (p. 69).

The Problem or Solution Frame Illustration. The passage is on fossil fuels.

Humans are consuming fossil fuels at much faster rates than they are produced in the Earth's crust. Eventually, we will use up these nonrenewable resources. We don't know for certain when the Earth's fossil fuels will be depleted, but we have already seen evidence that certain fossil fuels are being depleted in some regions. For example, the United States's production of crude petroleum was at its highest in 1970. Since that time, the United States has begun importing a higher percentage of petroleum.

Reducing the world's dependence on fossil fuels is problematic. However, there are several alternative energy sources, including nuclear energy, hydroelectric energy, solar energy, and wind energy. These energy sources currently account only for about 14 percent of the world's energy consumption; therefore, we need to focus efforts on developing these viable alternatives.

Different types of nuclear reactors that use different types of fuel, moderators, and coolants have been built throughout the world to produce electric power. However, public concerns about the safety of nuclear power, risks of accidents, high construction costs, high waste-disposal costs, and strict regulations have hindered the growth of nuclear power as an energy source. In fact, many countries have opted to phase out nuclear power plants altogether.

Falling water is another source of energy used to generate electric power. Hydroelectric power is renewable because of the recurring nature of the hydrologic cycle, and it produces neither thermal nor particulate pollution; however, geography limits the use of hydroelectricity. Large dams are typically used to take advantage of falling water to create hydroelectric power. Countries with mountains that lie close to industrial areas and experience heavy rainfall, such as Norway,

---

FIGURE 5.8

Problem or Solution Frame

The problem or solution pattern	**The problem or solution frame**
Text that fits this pattern introduces a problem and then identifies one or more solutions. This pattern commonly includes the following elements:	Guiding questions for the problem or solution frame:
Problem: a statement of something that has happened or might happen that is problematic	What is the problem?
Solution: a description of one possible solution	What is a possible solution?
Solution: a statement of another possible solution	What is another possible solution?
Solution: a statement of another possible solution	What is another possible solution?
Solution: identification of the solution with the greatest chance of success	Which solution has the best chance of succeeding?

Sweden, Canada, and Switzerland, can rely heavily on hydroelectricity. A number of other countries, including the United States, Russia, China, India, and Brazil, also use hydroelectricity, but on a much smaller scale.

Solar energy has enormous potential. Each day, the Earth receives solar energy that is almost 200,000 times the total world electrical-generating capacity. Solar energy itself is free, but collecting, converting, and storing it has limited its use.

Wind energy can be converted into mechanical energy to perform work such as pumping water or grinding grain. Modern wind turbines convert wind energy into electrical energy. Wind is a clean and renewable source of energy, so many countries, such as Germany, Denmark, India, China, and the United States, are expanding their use of modern wind turbines. Clusters of individual wind turbines are grouped to form wind power plants, sometimes called "wind farms." Typically the electricity produced from these "wind farms" supplements more traditional sources of electric power, such as burning coal. Wind energy technology has improved so that modern wind turbines produce electric power as efficiently as other power-generating technologies. Widespread use of wind energy faces obstacles such as suitable terrain, wind conditions, and environmental concerns such as the visual alteration of the landscape, noise from spinning turbine rotors, and impact on wildlife.

There is no clear answer to the diminishing supply of fossil fuels available for energy production. Given the intricacies and limitations of alternative energy sources, the solution for each nation depends on a variety of factors, including geography, citizen concerns, and environmental issues.

Frame Questions

1. What is the problem? *Depletion of fossil fuels*
2. What is a possible solution? *Alternative energy sources, such as nuclear energy*
3. What is another possible solution? *Hydroelectric energy*
4. What is another possible solution? *Solar energy*
5. What is another possible solution? *Wind energy*
6. Which solution has the best chance of succeeding? *The best solution depends on a number of factors, such as geography, resource availability, and environmental concerns.*

<u>Summary:</u> *Humans are consuming fossil fuels at much faster rates than they are produced in the Earth's crust. We need to find ways to use alternative energy sources more efficiently. Nuclear energy, hydroelectric energy, solar energy, and wind energy are all possible sources for supplementing and eventually replacing the use of fossil fuels. Development of any of these alternatives faces obstacles and concerns. There is not one correct answer; rather, the solution will be different for different countries.*

The Conversation Frame Illustration. See Figure 5.9 to examine how conversations are framed. The following passage is excerpted from *Bailey's Café:*

We've got no menus.

All right, give me a hamburger. Hold the fries.

Hamburgers only on Tuesday.

Some roast beef, then. Make it lean. And . . .

No roast beef till the weekend.

So what can I get *today?*

What everybody else is having.

I don't eat corned-beef hash.

That's what we got. And warm peach cobbler.

I'm not eating no hash. How's the peach cobbler?

Divine. (Naylor, 1992)

Frame Questions

1. How did the members of the conversation greet each other? *A worker in a restaurant told a customer they had no menus.*
2. What question or topic was insinuated, revealed, or referred to? *Ordering something to eat.*
3. How did the discussion progress?

Did either person state facts? *The restaurant worker said hamburgers were available only on Tuesday, roast beef was only available on the weekend, and the customer could have what everyone else was eating.*

Did either person make a request of the other? *The customer asked for a hamburger, then some roast beef.*

Did anyone demand a specific action of the other? *No, but the customer stated he would not eat corned-beef hash.*

Did anyone threaten specific consequences if a demand was not met? *No, but the restaurant worker implied that if the customer did not want corned-beef hash, he could go somewhere else to eat. The restaurant worker said that they were serving corned-beef hash and warm peach cobbler.*

FIGURE 5.9

Conversation Frame

The conversation pattern

Conversations commonly include the following elements:

Greeting: some acknowledgment that the parties have not seen each other for a while

Inquiry: a question about some general or specific topic

Discussion: an elaboration or analysis of the topic. Commonly included in the discussion are one or more of the following:

    Assertions: statements of facts by the speaker

    Requests: statements that solicit actions from the listener

    Promises: statements that assert that the speaker will perform certain actions

    Demands: statements that identify specific actions to be taken by the listener

    Threats: statements that specify consequences to the listener if commands are not followed

    Congratulations: statements that indicate the value the speaker puts on something done by the listener

Conclusion: the conversation ends in some way

The conversation frame

Guiding questions for the conversation frame:

How did the members of the conversation greet each other?

What question or topic was insinuated, revealed, or referred to?

How did their discussion progress?

Did either person state facts?

Did either person make a request of the other?

Did either person make a promise to perform a certain action?

Did either person demand a specific action of the other?

Did either person threaten specific consequences if a demand was not met?

Did either person indicate that he valued something that the other had done?

How did the conversation conclude?

Did either person indicate that he/she valued something that the other had done? *The customer asked about the peach cobbler, suggesting that he might want to order some.*

4. How did the conversation conclude? *The restaurant worker told the customer the peach cobbler is "divine."*

Summary: A worker in a restaurant tells a customer that the restaurant has no menus. The restaurant apparently serves only specific foods on certain days of the week. The customer tries to order a hamburger and then roast beef, but is told he can only have corned-beef hash or warm peach cobbler. Finally, the customer asks about the warm peach cobbler.

Teach Students Reciprocal Teaching and Group-Enhanced Summary

Reciprocal teaching (Palinscar & Brown, 1984, 1985) incorporates the process of summarizing and engages students in other thinking processes. In this module we present an adaptation of this process, which we refer to as "group-enhanced summarization." To use group-enhanced summarizing effectively, students need to understand the various roles they can play in the process. You can guide students using a set of steps:

1. Summarizing—After students have silently or orally read a short section of a passage, a single student acting as the student leader summarizes what has been read, heard, or seen. Other students, with guidance from the student leader, may add to the summary. If students have difficulty summarizing, the teacher might point out clues (e.g., important items or obvious topic sentences) that aid in the construction of good summaries.

2. Questioning—The student leader asks some questions to which the class responds. The questions are designed to help students identify important information in the passage. For example, the student leader might look back over the selection and ask questions about specific pieces of information. The other students then try to answer these questions based on their recollection of the information.

3. Clarifying—Next, the student leader tries to clarify confusing points in the passage. She might point these out or ask other students to point them out. For example, the student leader might say, "The part about the baseball player who was really an alien was confusing to me.

Can anyone explain this?" Or, the student leader might ask students to ask clarification questions. The group then attempts to clear up the confusing parts. This process might involve rereading parts of the passage.

4. Predicting—The student leader asks for predictions about what will happen in the next segment of the text. The leader can write the predictions on the blackboard or on an overhead, or all students can write them in their notebooks.

The summary statement that begins the reciprocal teaching strategy might be considered a first draft of a summary. The other phases of reciprocal teaching—questioning, clarifying, and predicting—help students to analyze the information, providing for a group-enhanced summary. Group-enhanced summarizing works very well because the process involves multiple analyses and interactions with the summary, as shown in the Reciprocal Teaching Illustration.

Reciprocal Teaching Illustration. Students in Ms. Hood's class were studying how computers work. After students had read a long passage about computers, Ms. Hood asked several students to serve as student leaders for a reciprocal teaching task. Ms. Hood had taught her students the steps for reciprocal teaching, and they had practiced, so they knew their roles and what each step required. After the reading, Chantelle, one of the student leaders, summarized the first passage:

> The operating system is the software that makes a computer work. It does three big things. Number one, it tells the computer hardware, like the mouse, printers, the monitor, and the computer memory, what

to do. Two, it deals with hardware errors and data loss. And, three, it organizes the files you store on the hard drive, a floppy disk, a CD, or a Zip disk. Today's operating systems, like Windows or Mac or UNIX, can do several things at one time. That's called 'multitasking.'

Finn added, "Windows 98 and the Mac operating system use a GUI—a graphical user interface with pictures called icons that represent various commands. Examples of icons are folders and the trash can."

To begin the ***questioning*** phase of the process, Chantelle asked questions about specific information: (1) When an operating system is multitasking, what is it actually doing? (2) What is virtual memory?

After students answered the questions, Chantelle asked if anyone had questions they wanted to ask to ***clarify*** confusions they had. Craig said he was confused about how a multitasking operating system created the illusion of processes running simultaneously. Lissa answered, "On computers with only one CPU, a multitasking OS (the operating system) runs each process individually for a set period of time. If the process doesn't finish in the given time, the OS puts it on hold and runs another process according to its schedule. Short processes run quickly and our sense of time is much slower, so processes appear to be running simultaneously."

Finally, Chantelle asked students to ***predict*** the content of "Computer Memory." Kara said, "I think the next section will talk about how a computer stores data. And it will probably explain RAM and ROM, as well as other ways of storing data like floppy disks and CD-Roms."

Tools to Facilitate Summarizing in the Classroom

Before using our recommendations in your classroom practice, consider a hypothetical situation or problem. It will give you an opportunity to apply what you have learned in the previous discussion. If you find it difficult to complete the exercise in Figure 5.10 (pp. 74–76), Checking My Understanding—Summarizing, we suggest you reread "Recommendations for Classroom Practice." The other assessment and planning tools that follow will help you guide your students in summarizing activities.

Assessing the Impact on Students

Rubrics are one tool you can use to gauge students' progress. Sample rubrics are provided in Figure 5.11 (p. 77) for evaluating students' progress in using summarizing. These rubrics can be revised for students to use as part of the self-assessment process.

Planning Classroom Activities and Assessing Myself

Answering a series of questions will help you discover how you might use the strategies for summarizing presented in this module. You can use the Planning for Summarizing Worksheet, Figure 5.12 (p. 78), to guide your thinking when planning summarizing activities for your students.

Rubrics help assess student learning. You can also use a tool to assess yourself—how effectively you are using summarizing strategies. Use Figure 5.13 (p. 80) to evaluate your effectiveness in using summarizing with your students.

FIGURE 5.10

Checking My Understanding—Summarizing

The following passage is taken from a science module entitled, "Heat: An Agent of Change."

Heat and Thermodynamics

Heat can move in three ways: conduction, convection, and radiation. Conduction is movement of heat that occurs either when two objects are touching each other or within an object. This is the most common way heat travels between two solids, for example two pieces of metal touching each other. The molecules in the warmer solid are more active than the molecules in the cooler solid. They are bumping into and colliding with each other more than the cooler molecules are. At the place where the two solids touch, the faster molecules in the warmer solid jostle and nudge the slower moving molecules in the cooler solid. This bumping and pushing slows down the faster molecules, but speeds up the slower ones. The jostling and pushing spreads through all the molecules in both objects until all are moving at about the same speed. Enough heat energy has been conducted from the warmer object to the cooler one so that they are now both at the same temperature and conduction stops.

In liquids and gases, heat moves most often by convection. Convection is a movement of warmer material through cooler material that would not be possible in the more tightly packed arrangement of a solid. When a portion of the liquid or gas becomes hotter than its surroundings, those molecules move around more and become less densely packed. The less dense material starts to rise upward through the surrounding material. People say, "Hot air rises." This is an example of convection. You can sometimes see convection currents in warm liquids, such as coffee, tea, or the hot water in which oatmeal is cooking.

As the warmer, less densely packed molecules rise through their cooler surroundings, they lose some of their heat energy to neighboring molecules. This is according to the Second Law of Thermodynamics, which states that heat moves from warmer material to cooler material. As the warmer molecules rise in the convection currents, they cool off until they are the same temperature as their surroundings. But the heat energy that they acquired somewhere else has moved to a different place in the liquid or gas.

The third type of movement of heat does not have to occur in matter. It has nothing to do with molecules. Radiation of heat as waves of energy can even occur in a vacuum. There are many types of radiation. If you look at the electromagnetic spectrum of the sun, you will notice several types of radiation that can travel to the Earth through space. Infrared radiation is the heat energy that the Sun puts out. Visible light accounts for most of the heat energy put out by the Sun.

Scientists have studied heat for many years. Learning about the theories scientists use to describe the movement of heat at the molecular level is important in an engineer's education. Engineers often take a course called Thermodynamics, in which they study the properties of various materials and how heat moves through and between them. They later put this information to use designing materials for space missions.

Source: Adapted from Heat and Thermodynamics: Student Text in *Heat: An Agent of Change*, by Rawls, G., Henry, M., & Krueger, A. , 2001 [Online]. http://www.genesismission.org/educate/scimodule/topics.html

---

FIGURE 5.10 (CONTINUED)

Checking My Understanding—Summarizing

Using the Rule-Based Strategy

Use the rule-based summarizing strategy to summarize the passage.

1. Delete trivial material that is unnecessary to understanding.

2. Delete redundant material.

3. Substitute superordinate terms for more specific terms (e.g., "fish" for "rainbow trout, salmon, and halibut").

4. Select a topic sentence, or invent one if it is missing.

Using Summary Frames

Now use the definition frame questions to summarize the passage about heat.

Definition Frame Worksheet

What is being defined?

To which general category does the item belong?

What characteristics of the item separate it from other things in the general category?

What are some different types or classes of the item being defined?

(continued on p. 76)

FIGURE 5.10 (CONTINUED)

Checking My Understanding—Summarizing

Now use the T-R-I (Topic-Restriction-Illustration) frame questions to summarize the first paragraph of the article.

Topic-Restriction-Illustration Worksheet

Topic: What is the general statement or topic?

Restriction: What information does the author give that narrows or restricts the general statement or topic?

Illustration: What examples does the author give to illustrate the topic or restriction?

FIGURE 5.11

Rubrics for Summarizing

Summarizing Rubric

4   The student identifies the main pattern running through the information along with minor patterns.

3   The student identifies the main pattern running through the information.

2   The student addresses some of the features of the main pattern running through the information, but excludes some critical aspects.

1   The student does not address the main pattern running through the information.

0   Not enough information to make a judgment.

Summarizing Rubric for Younger Students

4   The student finds the most important pattern in the information. The student also finds other less important patterns.

3   The student finds the most important pattern in the information.

2   The student finds some parts of the most important pattern in the information. The student misses some important parts.

1   The student does not find the most important pattern in the information.

0   The student does not try to do the task.

FIGURE 5.12

Planning for Summarizing Worksheet

What knowledge will students be learning?

What specific information will I ask students to summarize?

- ☐ film or video
- ☐ chapter
- ☐ lecture
- ☐ story
- ☐ article
- ☐ event
- ☐ other_____

What strategy will I ask students to use?

- ☐ Rule-Based Summarizing Strategy
- ☐ Summary Frames
  - ☐ Narrative or Story
  - ☐ Topic-Restriction-Illustration (T-R-I)
  - ☐ Definition
  - ☐ Argumentation
  - ☐ Problem or Solution
  - ☐ Conversation
- ☐ Reciprocal Teaching with Group-Enhanced Summary Activity
- ☐ other_____

FIGURE 5.12 (CONTINUED)

Planning for Summarizing Worksheet

Do I need to set aside time to teach them the strategy I want them to use? How will I teach them the strategy?

How much guidance will I provide students?

How will students explain their work and communicate their conclusions?

How will I monitor how well students are doing with summarizing?

How will I respond if some students are not summarizing effectively?

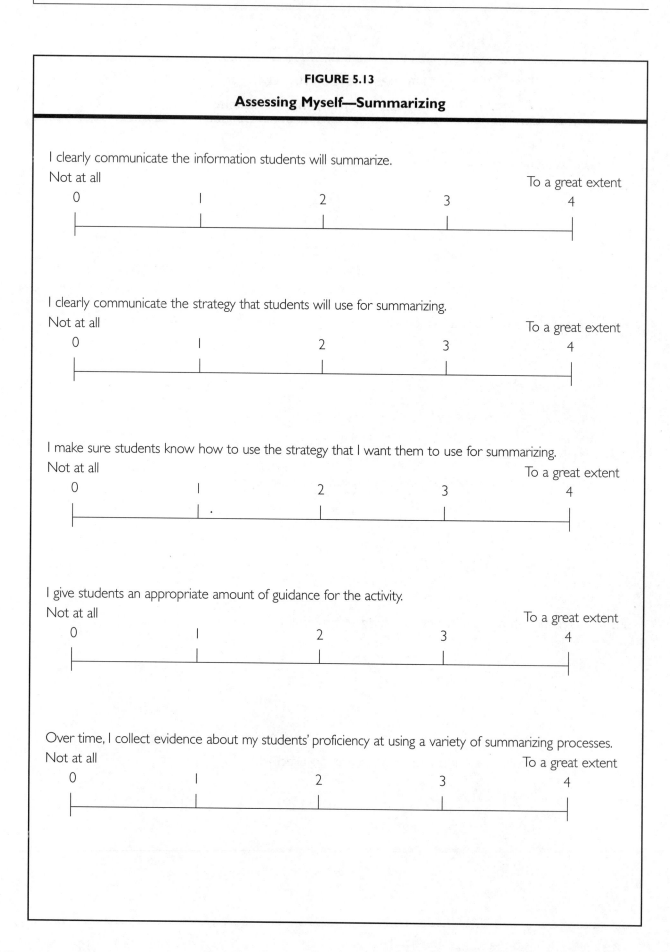

FIGURE 5.13

Assessing Myself—Summarizing

I clearly communicate the information students will summarize.

Not at all   To a great extent
0   1   2   3   4

I clearly communicate the strategy that students will use for summarizing.

Not at all   To a great extent
0   1   2   3   4

I make sure students know how to use the strategy that I want them to use for summarizing.

Not at all   To a great extent
0   1   2   3   4

I give students an appropriate amount of guidance for the activity.

Not at all   To a great extent
0   1   2   3   4

Over time, I collect evidence about my students' proficiency at using a variety of summarizing processes.

Not at all   To a great extent
0   1   2   3   4

Module Reflection

Review your responses to the questions in Figure 5.1, Reflecting on My Current Beliefs and Practices—Summarizing (p. 59). How has this module affected your thinking about teaching and learning? Use the space provided to record your thoughts.

- Reading this information affirms some of what I already knew about summarizing

- Now, I better understand some things about summarizing

- I think I will change how I use summarizing in my classroom

NOTE TAKING

Note taking and summarizing are closely related. Both processes require students to identify what is most important about the knowledge they are learning and then state that knowledge in their own words. Although note taking is one of the most useful study skills a student can cultivate, often teachers do not explicitly teach note-taking strategies in the classroom. Maybe you have never thought about teaching students to take notes. We all have our own personal style for taking notes with arrows and bullets, capitals and indentations, underlines and double underlines, flowcharts and doodles. Ultimately, students construct their own personal note-taking systems. As educators, we can give them research-based strategies to use to design their own systems.

Before reading "Recommendations for Classroom Practice," take some time to reflect on your current practices and beliefs related to using note taking with your students by completing the worksheet in Figure 6.1, Reflecting on My Current Beliefs and Practices—Note Taking (p. 83).

Recommendations for Classroom Practice

In this module, we discuss several approaches to use in the classroom:

- teaching students a variety of note-taking formats,

- giving students teacher-prepared notes, and
- reminding students to review their notes.

Teach Students a Variety of Note-Taking Formats

There is no one correct way to take notes. In fact, different students will prefer different note-taking formats, so it's a good idea to present a variety of methods. Here we show three different formats for taking notes: informal outline, web, and combination notes.

Informal Outline. One common note-taking format is the informal outline, Figure 6.2 (pp. 84–85). The informal outline uses indentation to indicate major ideas and their related details. Students simply indent ideas that are more subordinate.

Web. Another common format for notes is to use a web, Figure 6.3 (p. 86). Webbing uses the relative size of circles to indicate the importance of ideas and lines to indicate relationships. More important ideas are in larger circles than less important ideas. Lines from one circle to another indicate that the concepts in the connected circles are related in some way. Webbing gives students a visual representation of the relationships between and among ideas or elements. The disadvantage of the strategy is that it limits the amount of information a

FIGURE 6.1

Reflecting on My Current Beliefs and Practices—Note Taking

What is the purpose of taking notes?

What is my personal style for taking notes?

What do I do in the classroom to help students take notes?

What questions do I have about note taking?

FIGURE 6.2

Informal Outline Notes

Jazz

Origins

    Multiple influences

      Banjo music of minstrel shows

      Black-influenced Latin American music

      18th and 19th century European popular and light classical music

      ragtime

      blues

Turn of 20th century—New Orleans Jazz

    Trumpet or cornet—melody

    Improvisation focused on ensemble sound

    Musicians

      Original Dixieland Jazz Band

      New Orleans Rhythm Kings (1922)

      Creole Jazz Band (1923)

        King Oliver—leader

      Jelly Roll Morton

    Louis Armstrong

      Brought soloist to prominence

      Started scat singing—no words

1920s—Chicago, New York City

    Experimentation, soloists, added saxaphone

    Musicians in Chicago

      Jack Teagarden (trombone)

      Gene Krupa (drums)

      Benny Goodman (clarinet)

      Bix Beiderbecke (cornet)

FIGURE 6.2 (CONTINUED)

Informal Outline Notes

1920s—Chicago, New York City (continued)

    Jazz Piano

        New York City Harlem District

        Stride Piano

            James Johnson

            Fats Waller

    Boogie Woogie

        Left hand repeats bass pattern, right plays free

        Meade Lux Lewis

        Pete Johnson

        Pine Top Smith

    Chicago—innovative Earl "Fatha" Hines

1930s to 1940s: Swing Era

    Big Band—groups of jazz musicians

    Rhythmic change—2 beats to 4 beats per bar

    Riffs in call—response pattern

    Musicians

        Duke Ellington (Cotton Club)

        Fletcher Henderson

        Jimmie Lunceford

        Chick Webb

        Cab Calloway

    Kansas City—Count Basie

    Jazz Singing

        Billie Holiday

        Ella Fitzgerald

        Mildred Bailey

FIGURE 6.3

Webbing Notes—Number Theory

Understands basic number theory concepts (e.g., prime and composite numbers, factors, multiples, odd and even numbers, divisibility) (Math, 3–5)

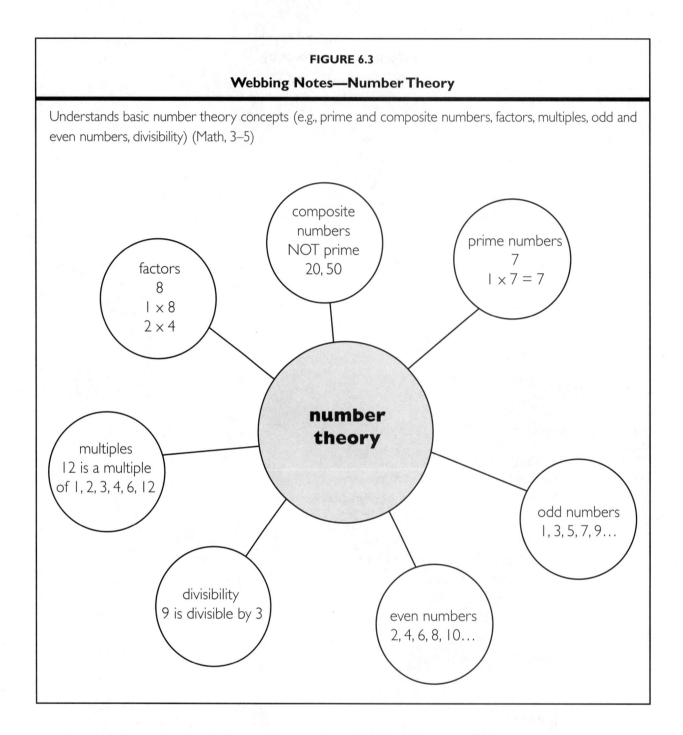

student can record simply because the circles themselves can hold only so many words.

Combination Notes. A very flexible note-taking strategy that uses both the informal outline and pictures or graphic representations is referred to as combination notes, Figure 6.4

(p. 87). Each page of notes is divided into two parts by a line running down the middle of the page. On the left-hand side of the page, students take notes using some variation of informal outlining. On the right-hand side of the page, students use graphic representations to organize the new information. Finally, in a

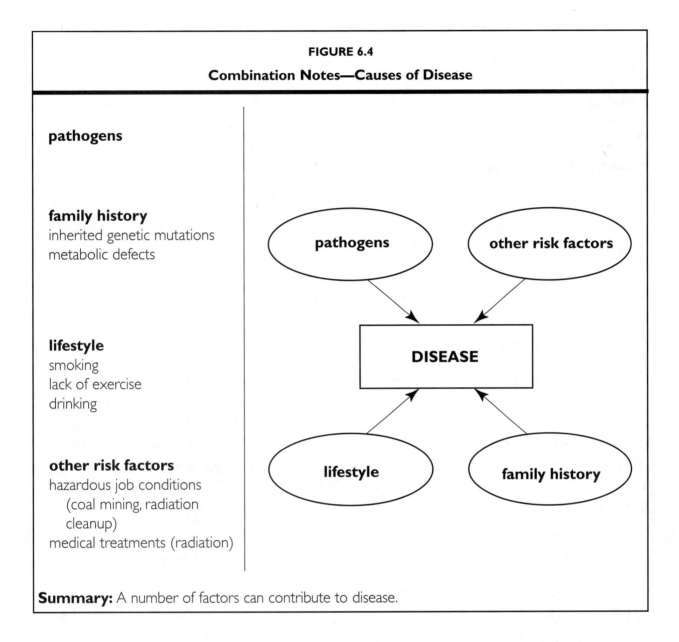

FIGURE 6.4

Combination Notes—Causes of Disease

pathogens

family history
inherited genetic mutations
metabolic defects

lifestyle
smoking
lack of exercise
drinking

other risk factors
hazardous job conditions
(coal mining, radiation
cleanup)
medical treatments (radiation)

pathogens

other risk factors

DISEASE

lifestyle

family history

Summary: A number of factors can contribute to disease.

strip across the bottom of the page, students write a summary statement for the notes.

This note-taking method takes extra time, but is useful because students review the information several times—first, as they record their notes; second, as they create drawings or other graphics for their notes; and third, as they construct summary statements of what they have learned from the information.

If students are using the combination notes technique, they need to take occasional breaks from recording written notes so they can make a graphic representation of their notes or portray the information in some visual way. Also, when they have finished taking notes, or periodically throughout the process, students must record summary statements of what they have learned at the bottom of the page.

Give Students Teacher-Prepared Notes

Providing students with notes before exposing them to new content is a powerful way to introduce students to note taking. Teacher-prepared notes give students a clear idea of what you think is important and help them focus their learning. Teacher-prepared notes also give students a good model for how they can organize content. To illustrate, Figure 6.5 shows notes that a teacher might give students at the beginning of a lesson on the life cycle.

Remind Students to Review Notes

Reviewing their notes before tests is one of the most powerful uses students can make of their notes. If notes have been well designed and students have systematically elaborated on them, they are perfect tools for test preparation. Before a quiz or a test, remind students to look over their notes.

Tools to Facilitate Note Taking in the Classroom

Before using our recommendations in your classroom practice, consider a hypothetical situation or problem to check your understanding of the previous discussion. The other assessment and planning tools that follow will help you guide your students in learning how to take notes in the classroom.

Checking My Understanding

You might have started out using a note-taking strategy similar to one of the formats we describe in this module, but over time you have adapted and shaped your note-taking technique to fit your personal style and needs. To stimulate your thinking about teaching students to take notes, try a couple of the formats described in this module. Take notes while watching a news broadcast, participating in a professional development workshop, or during a video or reading assignment that your students are doing. After you try a strategy, ask yourself these questions: (1) What worked well about taking notes this way? (2) What would I change the next time to adapt or modify this technique?

Assessing the Impact on Students

Rubrics are one tool you can use to gauge students' progress. Sample rubrics are provided in Figure 6.6 (p. 90) for evaluating students' progress in taking notes. These rubrics can be revised, when appropriate, for students to use as part of the self-assessment process to help them reflect on their work.

Planning Classroom Activities and Assessing Myself

Answering a series of questions will help you discover how you might use the strategies for note taking presented in this module. You can use the Planning for Note Taking worksheet, Figure 6.7 (p. 91), to guide your thinking when planning note-taking activities for your students.

Rubrics help assess student learning. You can also use a tool to assess yourself—how effectively you are using note-taking strategies. Use Figure 6.8 (p. 92) to help evaluate your effectiveness in teaching and reinforcing note taking in the classroom.

FIGURE 6.5

Teacher Prepared Notes—Life Cycle

Plants and animals go through a life cycle that includes the stages of

- **Birth**
- **Growth and development**
- **Reproduction**
- **Death**

This general pattern is the same for all plants and animals. The details of the life cycle are different for individual organisms.

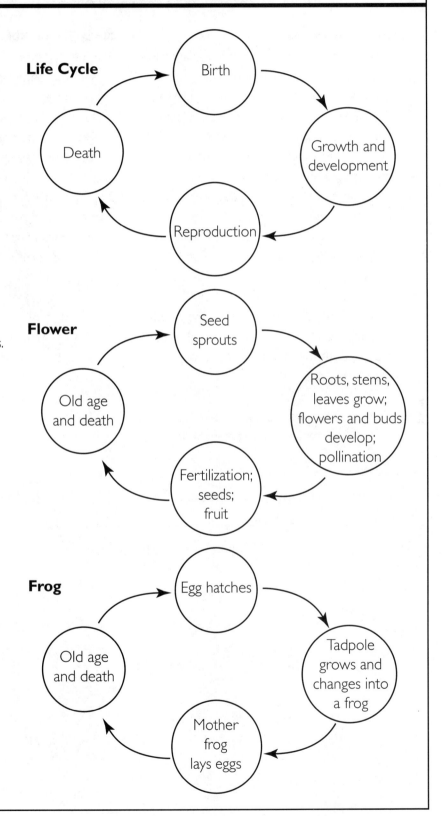

Life Cycle

Birth → Growth and development → Reproduction → Death →

Flower

Seed sprouts → Roots, stems, leaves grow; flowers and buds develop; pollination → Fertilization; seeds; fruit → Old age and death →

Frog

Egg hatches → Tadpole grows and changes into a frog → Mother frog lays eggs → Old age and death →

FIGURE 6.6

Rubric for Note Taking

Note-Taking Rubric

4 The student's notes contain the relevant information presented in the learning experience and are organized in a way that captures the main ideas and any important supporting ideas. In addition, the format of the student's notes makes it easy to see relationships among the information.

3 The student's notes contain the relevant information presented in the learning experience and are organized in a way that captures the main ideas and any important supporting ideas.

2 The student's notes are missing some important information or are not organized in a way that captures the main ideas and important supporting ideas.

1 The student's notes do not contain the relevant information presented in the learning experience.

0 Not enough information to make a judgment.

Note-Taking Rubric for Younger Students

4 The student's notes include the important information presented. The student organizes the notes to show the main ideas and important supporting ideas. The way the student organizes the notes makes it easy to see relationships among the pieces of information.

3 The student's notes contain the important information presented. The student organizes the notes to show the main ideas and important supporting ideas.

2 The student's notes are missing some important information. The student's notes do not show the main ideas.

1 The student's notes do not include the important information presented.

0 The student did not try to take notes.

FIGURE 6.7

Planning for Note Taking Worksheet

What knowledge will students be learning?

What partial or complete notes will I provide students?

What note taking strategy will I ask students to use?

☐ Informal outline
☐ Web
☐ Combination notes
☐ Teacher-prepared notes
☐ Reviewing their notes
☐ Other_____

Do I need to set aside time to teach them the note-taking strategy that I want them to use?

How will I teach them the strategy?

How will I provide students time to revise and review their notes?

How will I monitor how well students are taking notes?

What will I do to help students who are not taking notes effectively?

FIGURE 6.8

Assessing Myself—Note Taking

I clearly communicate the knowledge about which students will take notes.

Not at all   To a great extent

0   1   2   3   4

When appropriate, I provide students clear and accurate notes in a variety of formats.

Not at all   To a great extent

0   1   2   3   4

I clearly communicate the strategy that students will use to take notes.

Not at all   To a great extent

0   1   2   3   4

I make sure students know how to use the strategy that I want them to use for taking notes.

Not at all   To a great extent

0   1   2   3   4

I provide class time for students to review and revise their notes.

Not at all   To a great extent

0   1   2   3   4

Over time, I collect evidence about my students' proficiency at using a variety of processes for taking notes.

Not at all   To a great extent

0   1   2   3   4

Module Reflection

Review your responses to the questions in Figure 6.1, Reflecting on My Current Beliefs and Practices —Note Taking (p. 83). How has this module affected your thinking about teaching and learning? Use the space provided to record your thoughts.

- Reading this information affirms some of what I already knew about note taking

- Now, I better understand some things about note taking

- I think I will change how I use note taking in my classroom

3

REINFORCING EFFORT AND PROVIDING RECOGNITION

Study Group Tip

If you are using this handbook in a study group, your group might want to read and discuss the research summaries about reinforcing effort and providing recognition in the companion book, *Classroom Instruction That Works.*

Effective instruction deals with more than knowledge and skills. In this section, we address two activities that focus on student motivation: reinforcing effort and providing recognition. Most people know intuitively that student motivation plays a critical role in the learning process. However, it's only recently that research has demonstrated the roles reinforcing effort and providing recognition have in the process of motivating students.

Research shows that students may not realize the influence effort has on their success in school, but they can learn that effort helps them succeed. Simply teaching students that added effort pays off in terms of enhanced achievement actually increases student achievement. In fact, one study (Van Overwalle & De Metsenaere, 1990) found that students who were taught about the relationship between effort and achievement achieved more than students who were taught techniques for time management and comprehension of new material.

Research also shows that rewards do not necessarily decrease student motivation and that reward is most effective when contingent on successfully completing a specific level of performance. We also know that symbolic recognition is more powerful than tangible rewards. In this module, we offer strategies and suggestions for using what research tells us works in the classroom. We encourage you to use these and other approaches for using reinforcing effort and providing recognition to enhance students' learning.

List of Figures

REINFORCING EFFORT

People generally attribute success on any given task to one of four causes—ability, effort, other people, or luck. Believing in the power of effort tends to improve achievement, whereas belief in ability, other people, or luck ultimately inhibits achievement. A belief in ability seems useful—if you believe you have ability, you can tackle anything. But, no matter how much ability you think you have, inevitably you will encounter tasks that you believe exceed your abilities. This belief may influence your desire to try. Belief in other people or luck as the primary cause of success also has drawbacks. What if you find yourself alone? Or, what if your luck runs out? Belief that hard work and determination—effort—will lead to success has the greatest effect on achievement. Believing in effort can serve as a powerful motivational tool that students can apply to any situation.

Before reading "Recommendations for Classroom Practice," take some time to reflect on your current practices and beliefs about reinforcing student effort by completing the Reflecting on My Current Beliefs and Practices—Reinforcing Effort worksheet, Figure 7.1 (p. 98).

Recommendations for Classroom Practice

You can use a variety of strategies to reinforce student effort in your classroom. In this module, we discuss two approaches to use in the classroom:

- teaching students that effort can improve achievement, and
- asking students to chart effort and achievement.

Teach Students That Effort Can Improve Achievement

Explicitly teaching students the importance of effort is one way to help them understand it. You might share personal examples of times that you succeeded because you continued to try even when a task was hard or when a solution was not immediately apparent. For example, you might tell students about how you learned to snowboard even though your first efforts were disastrous: you cut your chin, got seven stitches, cracked your tailbone, and could barely sit down for a month, much less stand up on a snowboard on the mountain. You might share stories about how effort helped you to succeed in school—for example, how you taught yourself the multiplication tables, how you learned to write a good thesis sentence, how you finally came to understand the quadratic equation, or how you learned to read a topographic map.

Teachers might also seek out and share examples of well-known athletes, educators, or political leaders who succeeded mainly because they simply didn't give up (e.g., Daniel "Rudy" Ruettiger, the Notre Dame student whose unwavering commitment to play on the

FIGURE 7.1

Reflecting on My Current Beliefs and Practices—Reinforcing Effort

How do I reinforce students' effort in my classroom?

What is my purpose when I reinforce effort in the classroom?

What makes reinforcing effort effective or ineffective?

What questions do I have about reinforcing effort?

university's football team was the subject of the inspiring movie "Rudy"). You might also share examples from stories that are familiar to students, such as "The Little Engine That Could."

Finally, you might ask students to recall and describe personal examples of times that they succeeded because they didn't give up. Reflecting on their personal experiences in this way helps make the rewards that can come from effort more real and attainable to students.

Ask Students to Chart Effort and Achievement

Keeping track of effort and achievement is a good way to demonstrate their interdependence. Students can use the rubrics in Figures 7.2 and 7.3 (p. 100) for particular assignments and then complete a graph so they can readily see the relationship between their effort and achievement.

Charting their effort and achievement will reveal patterns and help students see the connection between the two. You can ask students to use a simple chart to keep track of effort and achievement (Figure 7.4, p. 101).

Students might also create a graph to better see the relationship between their effort and their achievement on tasks (Figure 7.5, p. 102).

In addition to charting the relationship between the two variables, you might ask students to describe what they learned from the experience. For example, you might periodically ask students to describe what they

---

FIGURE 7.2

Rubrics for Effort

Effort Rubric

4   The student works on tasks until completed and continues working on the task even when difficulties arise or a solution is not immediately evident. The student views difficulties that arise as opportunities to strengthen understanding.

3   The student works on tasks until completed and continues working on the task even when difficulties arise or a solution is not immediately evident.

2   The student puts some effort into the task but stops working when difficulties arise.

1   The student puts very little effort into the task.

0   Not enough information to make a judgment.

Effort Rubric for Younger Students

4   The student works on the task until she finishes it. The student keeps working even when she has trouble and cannot find an answer at first. The student uses problems as chances to learn more.

3   The student works on the task until she finishes it. The student keeps working even when she has trouble and cannot find an answer at first.

2   The student tries to do the task but stops working when she has problems.

1   The student does not try very hard.

0   The student does not try at all.

FIGURE 7.3

Rubrics for Achievement

Achievement Rubric

4 The student exceeded the objectives of the task or lesson.

3 The student met the objectives of the task or lesson.

2 The student met a few of the objectives of the task or lesson but did not meet others.

1 The student did not meet the objectives of the task or lesson.

0 The student did not do the task.

Achievement Rubric for Younger Students

4 The student did more than the task asked.

3 The student did everything the task asked.

2 The student did some of the things the task asked him to do, but the student did not do all of the things the task asked.

1 The student did not do what the task asked.

0 The student did not do the task.

---

noticed about the relationship between the effort they put into a project or task and their achievement. Reflecting on their experiences in this way heightens students' awareness of the power of effort.

Tools to Facilitate Effort in the Classroom

Before using our recommendations in your classroom practice, consider a hypothetical situation or problem to check your understanding of the previous discussion. The other assessment and planning tools that follow will help you guide your students to exert effort and achieve goals in the classroom.

Checking My Understanding

Here is one example of how a teacher might use a personal story about the power of effort to teach her students about the connection between effort and achieving goals. When Ms. Parsley reads "The Little Engine That Could" with her 1st graders, she always tries to tell them a personal story that made a connection about the value of effort. One day she told them a story about how she learned to snowboard.

"The first time I went snowboarding, my brothers took me to the top of the mountain, told me not to 'catch my front edge,' and took off. Well, I spent about two hours falling down the mountain. Once when I fell, I cut my chin. I had to get seven stitches, and I was so sore I could barely sit down for about three weeks.

"But I didn't give up. Two months later I went again. Only this time I took a lesson. We practiced on a small slope where I learned how to stand up on the board and how to stop myself. I still fell, but no stitches this time.

"I fell a lot my first year of snowboarding, but I kept practicing. I've been snowboarding now for three years. Sometimes you have to keep telling yourself, 'I can do it,' just like the Little Engine in the story.

FIGURE 7.4
Effort and Achievement Chart

Student: *Gabriela Szabo* Date:	Assignment	Effort	Achievement
Fri., Oct. 20	Homework: *Practice solving linear functions*	2	1
Wed., Oct. 25	Quiz: *Graphs of linear functions*	4	2
Thurs., Oct. 26	In-class practice: *Solving linear equations*	4	3
Tues., Oct. 31	Quiz: *Solving linear equations*	4	4
Wed., Nov. 1	Homework: *Properties of linear equations*	3	2
Fri., Nov. 3	In-class assignment: *Properties of linear equations*	2	2
Tues., Nov. 7	Homework: *Solving linear equations*	2	2

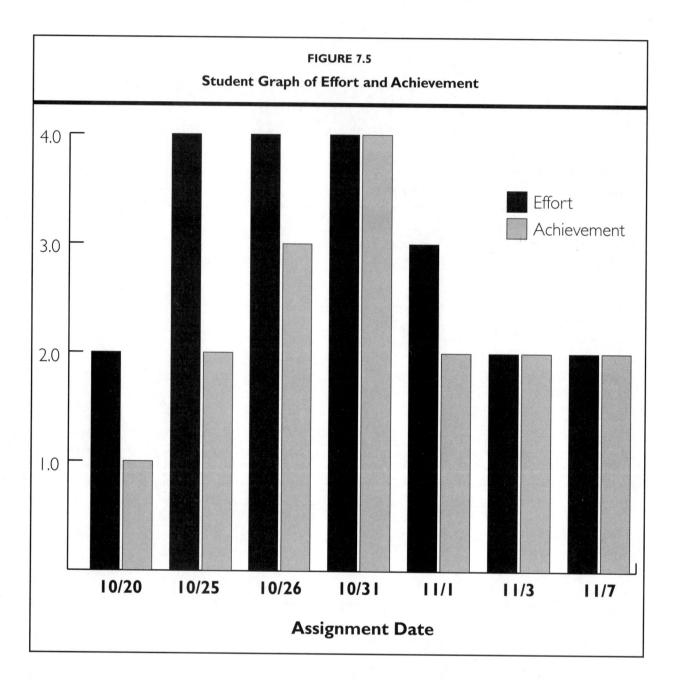

FIGURE 7.5

Student Graph of Effort and Achievement

Assignment Date

You'll find that effort like this also pays off in your schoolwork. When we begin to learn subtraction next week, whenever you are frustrated, remember to keep trying and see what happens."

Think about your experiences with effort and success. Write a personal story about a time that effort helped you achieve a goal, or, choose an inspirational story about someone you know, an athlete, a political figure, or a student you once taught. Explain how this story connects to what you have just read about the relationship between effort and achievement.

Assessing the Impact on Students

Rubrics are one tool you can use to gauge students' progress. Sample rubrics are provided in

Figure 7.2 (p. 99) for evaluating students' progress in effort. These rubrics can be revised, when appropriate, for students to use as part of the self-assessment process to help them reflect on their work.

Planning Classroom Activities and Assessing Myself

Answering a series of questions will help you discover how you might use the strategies for encouraging effort presented in this module. You can use the Planning for Reinforcing Effort Worksheet, Figure 7.6 (p. 104), to guide your thinking about reinforcing students' effort.

Rubrics help assess student learning. You can also use a tool to assess yourself—how effectively you use strategies to encourage student effort. Use Figure 7.7 (p. 105) to evaluate your effectiveness in reinforcing student effort in your classroom.

FIGURE 7.6

Planning for Reinforcing Effort Worksheet

What strategy will I use to teach students about effort?

    ☐ Share a personal story.

    ☐ Ask students to share a personal story.

    ☐ Tell them what the research shows.

    ☐ Ask students to chart effort and achievement.

    ☐ Other_____

What will I do to acknowledge the efforts students make?

How will I monitor the extent to which students believe that effort can lead to achievement?

What will I do to help students who do not believe that effort will lead to achievement?

FIGURE 7.7

Assessing Myself—Reinforcing Effort

I teach my students about the relationship between effort and achievement.

Not at all · To a great extent

0 · · · · · · · · · 1 · · · · · · · · · 2 · · · · · · · · · 3 · · · · · · · · · 4

I reinforce the importance of effort.

Not at all · To a great extent

0 · · · · · · · · · 1 · · · · · · · · · 2 · · · · · · · · · 3 · · · · · · · · · 4

I monitor the extent to which students believe effort will lead to achievement.

Not at all · To a great extent

0 · · · · · · · · · 1 · · · · · · · · · 2 · · · · · · · · · 3 · · · · · · · · · 4

Over time, I collect evidence about the effect that reinforcing effort has on my students' achievement.

Not at all · To a great extent

0 · · · · · · · · · 1 · · · · · · · · · 2 · · · · · · · · · 3 · · · · · · · · · 4

Module Reflection

Review your responses to the questions in the Reflecting on My Current Beliefs and Practices—Reinforcing Effort worksheet, Figure 7.1 (p. 98). How has this module affected your thinking about teaching and learning? Use the space provided to record your thoughts.

- Reading this information affirms some of what I already knew about reinforcing effort

- Now, I better understand some things about reinforcing effort

- I think I will change how I reinforce students' effort in my classroom

PROVIDING RECOGNITION

Varying reports on the effects of reward have led many educators to believe that *any* form of reward has a negative effect on learning. However, rewards can be powerful motivators if they are contingent on attaining a stated goal or standard, and if they are symbolic. We have all had the experience of being motivated by some form of recognition for accomplishing a specific goal. Some of us have tried harder to get good grades so we could make the honor roll at school, or played harder to earn a sticker for the back of our football helmet, or trained diligently to earn another patch for our scouting achievements.

The lack of understanding about the effects of praise and rewards, and the negative opinions associated with them, have caused us to believe the best way to think about symbolic, contingency-based rewards is as "recognition" for specific accomplishments. However, providing recognition is not a simple matter of saying, "Job well done." As this module illustrates, recognition can take many forms.

Before reading "Recommendations for Classroom Practice," take some time to reflect on your current practices and beliefs about providing recognition to your students by completing the worksheet in Figure 8.1, Reflecting on My Current Beliefs and Practices— Providing Recognition (p. 108). This will give you a basis of comparison as you read about the strategies in the module.

Recommendations for Classroom Practice

You can use a variety of strategies to enhance the effect recognition has on students. In this module, we discuss several approaches to use in the classroom:

- establishing a rationale for recognition;
- following guidelines for effective and ineffective praise;
- using recognition tokens; and
- using the pause, prompt, and praise technique.

Establish a Rationale for Recognition

It is a good idea to establish a rationale for the types of recognition that you use in class. You might explain to students that you will recognize them for their accomplishments, but that recognition is not automatic. Students need to understand that you will give recognition when they have accomplished an identified level of performance for a particular task, such as accurately balancing and explaining an oxidation-reduction reaction in chemistry, developing a sound argument with examples and expert opinion, or learning the multiplication tables to 10 x 10. Students also need to understand that if they do not receive recognition, it does not mean that they have failed.

FIGURE 8.1

Reflecting on My Current Beliefs and Practices—Providing Recognition

What does providing recognition mean to me?

What do I do in my classroom to provide recognition for students?

What makes providing recognition effective or ineffective?

What questions do I have about providing recognition in my classroom?

Follow Guidelines for Effective and Ineffective Praise

When used properly, praise is highly effective. Generally, it is best to provide recognition for specific elements of an accomplishment. For example, if a student has been having trouble performing two-column addition, you might praise her when she remembers to "carry 10" or when she reaches a specified level of automatic skill.

Just as recognition should be specific to particular accomplishments, praise should be specific to particular students. Global praise does not give individual students information about their knowledge or abilities. The research as depicted in Figure 8.2 (p. 110) gives a more detailed look at the characteristics of effective and ineffective recognition.

Use Recognition Tokens

Symbolic tokens, such as stickers or certificates, can be effective tools to recognize the successful completion of specific learning goals. However, to keep students from losing their intrinsic motivation, teachers should avoid rewarding students for simply completing an activity. Connecting a token to the attainment of an identified performance standard makes the recognition concrete and contingent on achieving a goal. For example, a teacher might give certificates to students who achieve their goals on spelling tests, or give out different colors of string that can be tied to students' musical instruments when they have performed music at specific levels of difficulty.

Use the Pause, Prompt, and Praise Technique

Teachers and tutors can adapt and use the "pause, prompt, and praise" technique to give students immediate, specific, and contingent praise (Merrett & Thorpe, 1996). This strategy works well with students who are struggling with a challenging task.

Many times when a student encounters difficulty, he will look immediately to the teacher for help. In the "pause" phase of this strategy, rather than responding immediately, the teacher "pauses" when the student makes an error or hesitates while performing a task. The pause gives the student an opportunity to identify and correct his mistake. The teacher might also use this pause to discuss the difficulties the student is experiencing.

The next phase of this strategy is the "prompt," during which the teacher gives a specific suggestion for improvement based on the type of error the student made. The "praise" element provides a further opportunity for feedback based on the student's success. The praise is not just an opportunity to say "good job" or "well done." Rather, praise should be based on the student's specific achievement. The praise is contingent on the student correcting his error or improving his achievement.

Tools to Facilitate Recognition in the Classroom

Before using our recommendations in your classroom practice, consider a hypothetical situation or problem to check your understanding of the previous discussion about providing

FIGURE 8.2

Guidelines for Praise

Effective Praise	Ineffective Praise
1. Is delivered contingently	1. Is delivered randomly or unsystematically
2. Specifies the particulars of the accomplishment	2. Is restricted to global positive reactions
3. Shows spontaneity, variety, and other signs of credibility; suggests clear attention to the student's accomplishment	3. Shows a bland uniformity, which suggests conditioned response made with minimal attention
4. Rewards attainment of specified performance criteria (which can include effort criteria)	4. Rewards mere participation, without consideration of performance processes or outcomes
5. Provides information to students about their competence or the value of their accomplishments	5. Provides no information at all or gives students information about their status
6. Orients students toward better appreciation of their own task-related behavior and thinking about problem solving	6. Orients students toward comparing themselves with others and thinking about competing
7. Uses students' own prior accomplishments as the context for describing present accomplishments	7. Uses the accomplishments of peers as the context for describing students' present accomplishments
8. Is given in recognition of noteworthy effort or success at difficult (for this student) tasks	8. Is given without regard to the effort expended or the meaning of the accomplishment (for this student)
9. Attributes success to effort and ability, implying that similar successes can be expected in the future	9. Attributes success to ability alone or to external factors such as luck or easy task
10. Fosters endogenous attributions (students believe that they expend effort on the task because they enjoy the task and/or want to develop task-relevant skills)	10. Fosters exogenous attributions (students believe that they expend effort on the task for external reasons—to please the teacher or win a competition or reward)
11. Focuses students' attention on their own task-relevant behavior	11. Focuses students' attention on the teacher as an external authority who is manipulating them
12. Fosters appreciation of and desirable attributions about task relevant behavior after the process is completed	12. Intrudes into the ongoing process, distracting attention from task relevant behavior

Source: From "Teacher Praise: A Functional Analysis," by J. Brophy, 1981, *Review of Educational Research, 51*(1), p. 26. Copyright 1981 by the American Educational Research Association. Reprinted with permission.

recognition. The additional assessment and planning tools that follow will help you guide your students in their learning by providing effective recognition in the classroom.

Checking My Understanding

Read the following hypothetical examples of providing recognition in a classroom. Evaluate each example in terms of the Guidelines for Praise, Figure 8.2 (p. 110). For each example, consider whether the recognition the teacher provides is likely to be effective or ineffective. Assign each sample specific criteria from the list provided in the guidelines and explain your thinking.

Example 1. Dana was unable to make any connections among the elements using a table of characteristics. Mr. Mulder suggests she focus on one characteristic and look for connections. When he returns later, Dana explains how she has figured out a way to group the elements according to boiling point. Mr. Mulder congratulates her on finding a valid connection.

Example 2. Mr. Mulder circulates as students are working in small groups. He pauses at Station 1 and comments, "Nice work on your calculations." At Station 2, he says, "Nice work on your graphs." At Station 3, he says, "Nice work on your calculations."

Example 3. "You really did a good job working through all of the steps and checking your answers for this problem. I know you've had difficulties with multistep calculations before and sometimes settled for getting any answer

down on paper, even if it wasn't correct. Your determination with this task really showed."

Example 4. "Good job, Jackson. Keep it up."

Think about a recent time when you provided recognition to students. Describe what occurred in as much detail as possible. Analyze this example of providing recognition and see if you can identify why it was effective or ineffective.

Assessing the Impact on Students

Rubrics are one tool you can use to gauge students' progress. Sample rubrics are given in Figure 8.3 (p. 112) for evaluating students' progress in demonstrating motivation and using recognition. These rubrics can be revised, when appropriate, for students to use as part of the self-assessment process to help them reflect on their work.

Planning Classroom Activities and Assessing Myself

Answering a series of questions will help you discover how you might use the strategies for providing recognition presented in this module. You can use the Planning for Providing Recognition Worksheet, Figure 8.4 (p. 113), to guide your thinking when planning how to go about recognizing students.

Rubrics help assess student learning. You can also use a tool to assess yourself—how effectively you use strategies to recognize your students. Use Figure 8.5 (p. 114) to evaluate your effectiveness in providing recognition for students in your classroom.

FIGURE 8.3

Rubrics for Recognition

Recognition Rubric

4   The student consistently demonstrates a motivation to achieve and strives to achieve when there is no promise of reward. The student regularly and spontaneously uses recognition effectively in peer groups. The student feels acknowledged and understands why he is being recognized.

3   The student consistently demonstrates a motivation to achieve. The student uses recognition effectively in peer groups. The student feels acknowledged.

2   The student inconsistently demonstrates a motivation to achieve. The student sometimes uses recognition in peer groups. The student feels acknowledged.

1   The student rarely demonstrates a motivation to achieve. The student does not use recognition in peer groups. The student does not feel acknowledged.

0   Not enough information to make a judgment.

Recognition Rubric for Younger Students

4   The student is motivated to do well on tasks, even when no one promises a reward. On a regular basis, the student recognizes other students for accomplishments. The student feels recognized for accomplishments and understands why he is being recognized.

3   The student is motivated to do well on tasks. The student recognizes other students for accomplishments. The student feels recognized for accomplishments.

2   The student is sometimes motivated to do well on tasks. The student sometimes recognizes other students for accomplishments. The student feels acknowledged.

1   The student is hardly ever motivated to do well on tasks. The student does not recognize others for accomplishments. The student does not feel acknowledged.

0   The student does not show any motivation.

FIGURE 8.4

Planning for Providing Recognition Worksheet

What is my rationale for providing recognition in the classroom?

How will I share this rationale with students?

What strategies for providing recognition do I want to use in the upcoming weeks?
- ☐ Following effective praise guidelines
- ☐ Using symbolic tokens or recognition
- ☐ Using the pause, prompt, and praise technique
- ☐ Other_____

What will I do to ensure that I provide recognition systematically?

How will I monitor the impact on students of my approaches to providing recognition?

What will I do to make my approaches to providing recognition more effective?

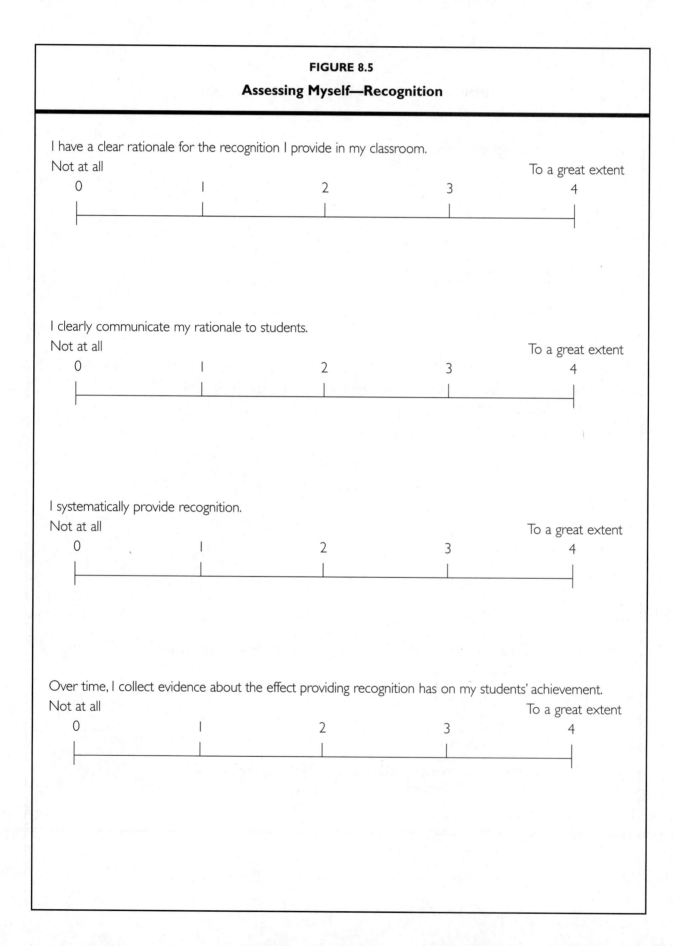

FIGURE 8.5

Assessing Myself—Recognition

I have a clear rationale for the recognition I provide in my classroom.

Not at all   To a great extent

0   1   2   3   4

I clearly communicate my rationale to students.

Not at all   To a great extent

0   1   2   3   4

I systematically provide recognition.

Not at all   To a great extent

0   1   2   3   4

Over time, I collect evidence about the effect providing recognition has on my students' achievement.

Not at all   To a great extent

0   1   2   3   4

Module Reflection

Review your responses to the questions in the Reflecting on My Current Beliefs and Practices—Providing Recognition worksheet, Figure 8.1 (p. 108). How has this module affected your thinking about teaching and learning? Use the space provided to record your thoughts.

- Reading this information affirms some of what I already knew about providing recognition

- Now, I better understand some things about providing recognition

- I think I will change how I provide recognition in my classroom

4

HOMEWORK AND PRACTICE

Study Group Tip

If you are using this handbook in a study group, your group might want to read and discuss the research summaries about homework and practice in the companion book, *Classroom Instruction That Works*.

Homework and practice are staples of the K–12 classroom. Both homework and practice give students opportunities to deepen their understanding and proficiency with content they are learning. We can even think of homework as a time for students to practice their skills, although students also practice apart from homework.

Research on homework tells us some things about homework and practice. First, in general, teachers should assign less homework to younger students than to older students. Second, parents should be minimally involved in their children's homework. Third, teachers should communicate the purpose of homework and comment on it. And fourth, when learning a skill, students need a great deal of practice in order to achieve mastery. Students also need time to shape and adapt the skill so they can use it effectively. In this section, we offer strategies and suggestions for using what research tells us works in the classroom. We encourage you to use these and other approaches for using homework and practice to enhance student's learning.

List of Figures

HOMEWORK

By the time students reach the middle grades, homework has become part of their lives. The usual reason for giving homework makes good sense: Homework extends learning opportunities beyond the confines of the school day. Studies show that students are in school a relatively short amount of time (Fraser, Walberg, Welch, & Hattie, 1987); thus, homework seems to be a good idea. Although homework can be a great asset, it can be a liability, depending on how we approach it.

Before reading "Recommendations for Classroom Practice," take some time to reflect on your current practices and beliefs about homework by completing the worksheet in Figure 9.1 (p. 120). This will give you a basis of comparison as you read about the strategies in the module.

Recommendations for Classroom Practice

In this module, we discuss several approaches to use in the classroom:

- establishing and communicating a homework policy,
- clarifying the purpose of homework,
- asking students to use homework assignment sheets, and
- commenting on homework.

Establish and Communicate a Homework Policy

Students and their parents need to understand expectations for homework. What is the purpose of homework? How much homework will be assigned? What are the consequences for missing or late homework assignments? How should parents be involved in their child's homework? A district, school, or teacher can establish and communicate a homework policy to answer such questions and to set feasible and defensible expectations of students and their parents. A clearly articulated homework policy can decrease tensions about homework that arise among parents, teachers, and students. Further, following explicit homework policies can enhance student achievement.

A note of caution is needed here. Research indicates that when parents help their children with homework, they can interfere with students' learning. Parents should know what homework their children are responsible for completing, and they certainly can facilitate the homework process, but they should not solve problems for their children. You can clarify these issues with parents in your written homework policy or at parent-teacher conferences.

If your school or district does not have a written homework policy, you might create one for your classroom. (See the sample in Figure 9.2, p. 121.) Your homework policy

FIGURE 9.1

Reflecting on My Current Beliefs and Practices—Homework

What are the purposes of homework?

What kind of homework do I assign my students?

What makes homework effective, and how do I know it has been effective?

What questions do I have about using homework?

FIGURE 9.2

Sample Homework Policy

This letter explains the homework policy for my classroom. Please read the policy with your child so that you understand the expectations of students and parents with regard to homework. Following these guidelines can help decrease tension associated with homework and increase your child's learning.

For your child to be successful with homework, he needs:

A place to do homework. If possible, your child should do his homework in the same place (an uncluttered, quiet space to study).

A schedule for completing homework. Set a homework schedule that fits in with each week's particular activities.

Encouragement, motivation, and prompting. It is not a good idea to sit with your child and do homework with him. Your child needs to practice independently and to apply what he has learned in class. If your child consistently cannot complete homework assignments alone, please contact me.

Understanding of the knowledge. When your child is practicing a skill, ask which steps he finds difficult and easy and how he plans to improve speed and accuracy with the skill. If your child is working on a project, ask what knowledge he is using to complete the work. If your child consistently cannot answer these questions, please contact me.

Reasonable time expectations. If your child seems to be spending too much time each night on homework, please contact me.

A bedtime. When it is time to go to bed, please stop your child, even if he has not finished the homework.

Grading: I will grade each homework assignment for content and timeliness. If your child turns in an assignment late, the score for "timeliness" will reflect the lateness.

Please return this policy with the appropriate signatures, acknowledging that you have read and discussed the policy with your child. If you have any questions about homework expectations, please contact me.

_____   _____

Parent's (or Guardian's) Signature   Student's Signature

should include information about your expectations for students and parents.

Clarify the Purpose of Homework

Just as a news reporter knows the purpose of his interview, so your students should know the purpose of homework assignments. Are they focusing on increasing their speed at long division? Are they accessing prior knowledge for tomorrow's introduction to the general theory of relativity? Are they extending what they have learned about food webs? Many times, students do not understand the purpose of homework assignments. When students don't know why they are doing an assignment, homework can seem like "busy work"—they simply want to get through it. Therefore, connecting homework assignments to a meaningful purpose is a powerful instructional practice. Here, we discuss three possible purposes for assigning homework: (1) to give students opportunities to practice skills, (2) to prepare students for a new topic, or (3) to elaborate on introduced material.

Homework assigned to provide practice is usually associated with learning a skill as opposed to learning information. When practice is the purpose of homework, it is imperative that students first reach a level of self-sufficiency in performing the skill. It makes little sense to assign practice homework when students are not capable of engaging in unsupervised practice. Homework assigned as practice commonly increases students' speed and accuracy relative to the skill they are learning. Practicing a skill requires a different kind of assignment and a different focus from the student than is required to learn new information.

To increase speed and accuracy on a particular skill, a student might break an assignment into chunks and time herself as she completes each section. If she's focused on increasing speed, a student is less likely to make a peanut butter sandwich or call her best friend in the middle of a problem set. Also, knowing that she is practicing to reach a goal gives the assignment meaning. Homework is no longer just busy work. Rather, the student is working toward improving speed and internalizing a skill.

When you assign homework to introduce a topic, the goal is to help students access prior knowledge about the topic. This type of homework assignment requires a different focus from the student than is required to practice a skill to improve speed and accuracy. These homework assignments might ask students to reflect on what they have learned from other classes, from reading, and from their experiences. When using homework to introduce a topic, you might also ask students to think about what they want to learn.

A homework assignment that asks students to elaborate on a topic might require them to engage in activities that extend their knowledge, such as conducting research, comparing items, constructing support for an argument, or representing knowledge in a graphic organizer.

All three of these purposes for homework are legitimate. The key is to identify a purpose for each homework assignment and communicate the purpose to students.

Ask Students to Use Homework Assignment Sheets

Students can use an assignment notebook to keep track of their daily assignments. You might provide students with assignment sheets that are similar to the pages found in a business day planner or a teacher's daily planner (Figure 9.3, p. 124). At the beginning of the year, explain the purpose of assignment sheets and show students how to complete them. Filling out an assignment sheet clarifies for students what they are supposed to do and why they are supposed to do it. The process also helps students see the relationship between the homework assignment and the information and skills they are learning. Even students who think they understand a given homework assignment might realize they have questions when they fill out an assignment sheet.

Comment on Homework

If you assign homework, comment on it. Timely and specific feedback on homework can improve student achievement. Teachers do not have enough time to provide extensive feedback on every homework assignment, so make this task more practicable by using different methods to comment on homework. For example, you might set up opportunities for students to share their work with each other and offer feedback. This approach works well when students are preparing for new information because they can share ideas and broaden their knowledge base before they dig in to the new information. When students are practicing a skill for homework, you might ask them to keep track of their accuracy or speed. As students record and watch their progress over time, they can identify areas where they need more work. Students might also keep a homework portfolio that you collect and comment on once a week.

Tools to Facilitate Effective Use of Homework

Before using our recommendations about homework in your classroom practice, consider a hypothetical situation to check your understanding of the previous discussion by completing the homework worksheet, Figure 9.4 (p. 125). The other assessment and planning tools that follow will help you guide your students in effective homework methods.

Assessing the Impact on Students

Rubrics are one tool you can use to gauge students' progress. Sample rubrics are provided in Figure 9.5 (p. 126) for evaluating students' progress in homework. These rubrics can be revised, when appropriate, for students to use as part of the self-assessment process to help them reflect on their work.

Planning Classroom Activities and Assessing Myself

Answering a series of questions will help you discover how you might use the strategies related to homework presented in this module. You can use the Planning for Homework Worksheet, Figure 9.6 (p. 127), to guide your thinking when planning homework for your students.

You assess student learning with the help of rubrics. You can use a tool to assess yourself, too—to determine how effectively you use strategies related to homework. Use Figure 9.7, (p. 128), to evaluate your effectiveness in using homework in the classroom and with your students.

FIGURE 9.3

Homework Assignment Sheet

Subject: _____   Date due: _____

Homework assignment

Purpose of the assignment

Information I need to know or skills I need to be able to do so I can complete the assignment

FIGURE 9.4

Checking My Understanding—Homework

Think about a class or subject area that you teach. Identify two homework assignments that you recently gave to students. Use the worksheet to analyze each assignment.

Homework Worksheet

Is the purpose of the homework clear?

What knowledge were students learning?

Did students understand the purpose? How do you know?

What kind of comments did you make on students' homework?

FIGURE 9.5

Rubrics for Homework

Homework Rubric

4   The student completes homework and meets or exceeds the expectations of the assignment. The student seeks clarification when she does not understand the purpose of the assignment. The student uses comments on homework to improve future work.

3   The student completes homework and meets all expectations for the assignment. The student seeks to understand the purpose of the assignment.

2   The student's homework is incomplete. The student does little to understand the purpose of the assignment.

1   The student does little to complete or turn in homework. The student does not try to understand the purpose of the assignment.

0   Not enough information to make a judgment.

Homework Rubric for Younger Students

4   The student finishes homework and does everything the assignment requires. The student also does more than the assignment requires. If the student does not understand the purpose of the assignment, she asks questions. The student uses comments to make her work better.

3   The student finishes homework and does everything the assignment requires. The student tries to understand the purpose of the assignment.

2   The student does not finish all the requirements of the assignment. The student does not really try to understand the purpose of the assignment.

1   The student starts homework, but does very little of the assignment. The student does not understand the purpose of the assignment.

0   The student does not try to do the homework.

FIGURE 9.6

Planning for Homework Worksheet

What is my homework policy?

How will I communicate my policy to students and parents?

What knowledge will students be learning?

What is the purpose of the assignment?

How will I communicate the purpose of the assignment to students?

How will I comment on the homework assignment?

How will I monitor the impact of homework assignments on students' learning?

What will I do to help students who are not doing homework assignments effectively?

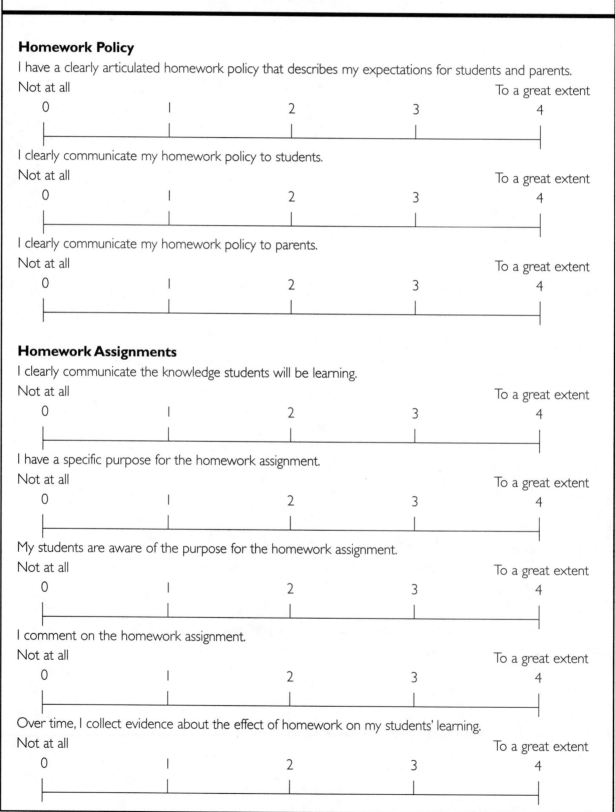

FIGURE 9.7

Assessing Myself—Homework

Homework Policy

I have a clearly articulated homework policy that describes my expectations for students and parents.

Not at all / To a great extent

0   1   2   3   4

I clearly communicate my homework policy to students.

Not at all / To a great extent

0   1   2   3   4

I clearly communicate my homework policy to parents.

Not at all / To a great extent

0   1   2   3   4

Homework Assignments

I clearly communicate the knowledge students will be learning.

Not at all / To a great extent

0   1   2   3   4

I have a specific purpose for the homework assignment.

Not at all / To a great extent

0   1   2   3   4

My students are aware of the purpose for the homework assignment.

Not at all / To a great extent

0   1   2   3   4

I comment on the homework assignment.

Not at all / To a great extent

0   1   2   3   4

Over time, I collect evidence about the effect of homework on my students' learning.

Not at all / To a great extent

0   1   2   3   4

Module Reflection

Review your responses to the questions in the Reflecting on My Current Beliefs and Practices—Homework worksheet, Figure 9.1 (p. 120). How has this module affected your thinking about teaching and learning? Use the space provided to record your thoughts.

- Reading this information affirms some of what I already knew about homework

- Now, I better understand some things about homework

- I think I will change how I use homework in my classroom

PRACTICE

Everyone knows the old saying, "Practice makes perfect." Practice may not always make perfect, but it is certain that without practice, little learning occurs. You might be surprised by the number of practice sessions students need before they can use new knowledge effectively. We can represent the relationship between practice sessions and learning as a curved line as depicted in Figure 10.1 (p. 131), where the vertical axis shows improvement in learning and the horizontal axis represents the number of practice sessions the student has engaged in.

The graph shows that when students first begin practicing a skill, their learning progresses rapidly. However, students probably need at least 20 practice sessions before you can be reasonably sure they grasp the new skill enough to use it effectively on their own. Although the more students practice, the smaller the learning increment, practice always enhances learning. Only after a great deal of practice can students perform a skill with speed and accuracy.

Before you read "Recommendations for Classroom Practice," take some time to reflect on your current practices and beliefs related to using practice by completing the worksheet in Figure 10.2 (p. 132), Reflecting on My Current Beliefs and Practices—Practice. This will give you a basis of comparison as you read about the strategies in the module.

Recommendations for Classroom Practice

Students need to practice skills and processes before they can use them effectively. In this module, we discuss several approaches to use in the classroom:

- determining which skills are worth practicing,
- scheduling massed and distributed practice,
- asking students to chart speed and accuracy, and
- helping students shape a skill or process.

Determine Which Skills Are Worth Practicing

One of the most significant decisions a teacher makes is to identify which skills are important enough to practice. Since practice takes a great deal of time and effort, your students probably can't afford to practice every skill they encounter. This time constraint means that students will not master all the skills that you teach. There is nothing wrong with that. But, if students do not have time to master everything, then you must distinguish between content they will practice in depth and content they will simply be introduced to. If you do not make this distinction, students will spend too much time on some skills and too little time on others.

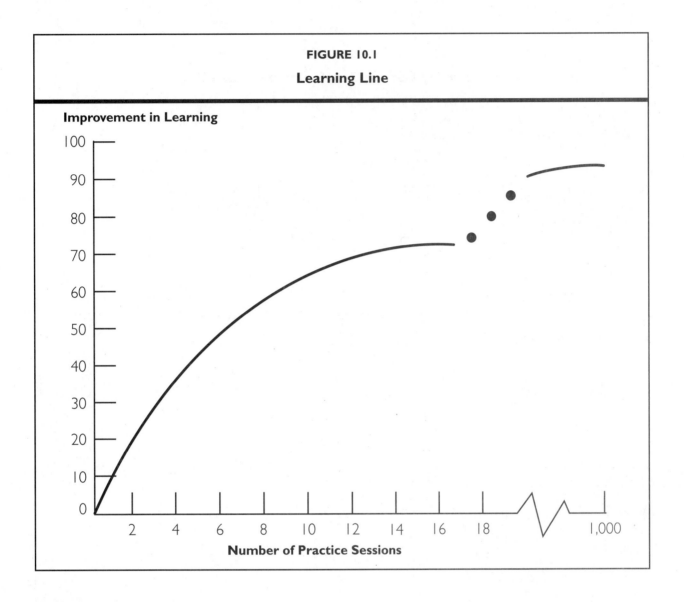

FIGURE 10.1

Learning Line

Improvement in Learning

Number of Practice Sessions

Schedule Massed Practice and Distributed Practice

At first, practice sessions should be close together—*massed practice*. Over time, you can space them apart—*distributed practice*. The relationship between massed and distributed practice can be represented graphically (Figure 10.3, p. 133).

When students are first learning a new skill or process, they should practice it immediately and often. That is, they should engage in *massed practice*. For example, in a computer technology class, pairs of students might work at the computer and practice using a spreadsheet program as many times as possible before the end of a period. The teacher might also provide time for students to practice the next day—perhaps not as long as at first, but for a substantial amount of time. The teacher should gradually increase the interval of time between practice sessions. Instead of practicing every day, students should practice every other day, then every third day, and so on. Lengthening the intervals of time between practice sessions involves students in *distributed practice*. Over time, students will internalize the new skill.

FIGURE 10.2

Reflecting on My Current Beliefs and Practices—Practice

What kind of skills do I ask my students to practice?

How do I decide which skills students need to practice a great deal and which skills they can just have a basic proficiency in?

What makes skills practice effective?

What questions do I have about using skills practice in my classroom?

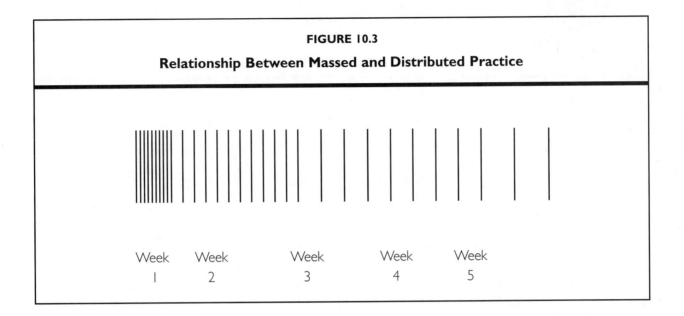

FIGURE 10.3

Relationship Between Massed and Distributed Practice

Week 1   Week 2   Week 3   Week 4   Week 5

Ask Students to Chart Speed and Accuracy

When developing some skills, the emphasis is on accuracy; with others, it's on accuracy and speed. For example, speed *and* accuracy are probably important when learning to tell time. If it takes you two minutes to figure out what time it is, Elvis may have left the building. Students need speed *and* accuracy when participating in conversations in a foreign language or estimating the cost of their purchases while standing in line at the store. However, speed is probably not so important when learning how to convert between English standard and metric units. When you're running that marathon, you have plenty of time to convert 26.2 miles to kilometers. Accuracy is probably more important than speed when students are learning the scientific method, how to write a good descriptive paragraph, or indirect measurement.

If students are working on accuracy, they can divide a series of problems into several clusters, and then chart the number they solved correctly for each cluster. If students are working on accuracy and speed, they might create a chart that indicates how many problems they solved correctly in a given period of time, and then try to beat that time for the next cluster. If accuracy suffers when speed increases, they can decide if they should slow down again to achieve accuracy, as illustrated below in the Speed and Accuracy Worksheet, Figure 10.4 (p. 134).

Help Students Shape a Skill or Process

It's easy for errors to creep into a skill when students are first learning it. Consequently, one aspect of shaping skills or processes—procedural knowledge—is to point out errors and pitfalls to students. You might demonstrate common mistakes or point out errors as students make them. A teacher in a woodshop class, for example, might demonstrate all the incorrect ways of using a lathe. Or she might walk around the classroom as students were using the lathe and point out incorrect uses to individual students. In geography class, a teacher might show students the steps for reading a contour map and then illustrate some

---

FIGURE 10.4

Speed and Accuracy Worksheet

Name: Jackson Harwood

Number of items in my practice set	Number of items performed correctly	Number of minutes to finish the practice set
5	4	4½
5	4	4
5	3	3½
5	4	4
5	5	4
5	5	3½
10	10	8
10	10	7½

---

common errors. Specifically, he might show how easy it is to misinterpret the altitudes for each contour layer and to make incorrect assumptions about specific types of contours. After demonstrating the proper way to eat a formal dinner in Japan, a foreign language teacher might demonstrate some common errors Americans make when visiting Japan.

Helping students shape a new skill or process involves illustrating important variations. Every skill or process has variations, and students must understand them in order to use the skill or process successfully. To perform three-column addition well, you must understand variations in that process: what to do when you have to carry from the first column to the second, what to do when you don't have to carry from the first column to the second, and so on. To shape the process of three-column addition, a teacher might use a single problem but keep changing it to illustrate all the variations. To highlight the variations, the teacher

might ask questions like the following: "What would happen if the 4 were a 7? How many ones and how many tens would I have? Now suppose in the tens column I carry two tens from the ones column. What would happen?" In addition to working through one or two examples and asking *what-would-happen-if* questions, be sure to provide practice in all of the variations. For example, you might give students problems to work out that exemplify all of the variations they have seen demonstrated.

Tools to Facilitate Practice in the Classroom

Before using our recommendations in your classroom practice, consider a hypothetical situation or problem to check your understanding of the previous discussion by completing the exercise in Figure 10.5 (p. 135). The other assessment and planning tools that follow will help you guide your students to practice effectively.

FIGURE 10.5

Checking My Understanding—Practice and Skills

Think of a skill or process that you can perform with fluency, almost automatically—like skiing, riding a horse, adding numbers in your head, or driving a car. How did you become so proficient? Think about the process you went through to learn this skill and answer the following questions.

How was this skill first introduced to you? How were you taught to perform the skill?

When did you first try the skill? How did you do?

How soon did you try the skill a second time? How did you do this time?

What kind of practice schedule did you follow to become adept at performing the skill?

How have you adapted or shaped the skill over time?

Assessing the Impact on Students

Rubrics are one tool you can use to gauge students' progress. Sample rubrics are provided in Figure 10.6 for evaluating students' progress in skills and processes. These rubrics can be revised, when appropriate, for students to use as part of the self-assessment process to help them reflect on their work.

Planning Classroom Activities and Assessing Myself

Answering a series of questions will help you discover how you might use the strategies for using practice in the classroom presented in this module. You can use the worksheet, Figure 10.7 (p. 137), to guide your thinking when planning practice activities for your students.

You assess student learning with the help of rubrics. A tool can help you assess yourself too—how effectively you use practice strategies. Use Figure 10.8 (p. 138) to evaluate your use of practice in the classroom.

FIGURE 10.6

Rubrics for Skills and Processes

Skills and Processes Rubric

4 The student performs the skill or process accurately and with fluency. The student understands the key features of the skill or process.

3 The student performs the skill or process accurately but not automatically.

2 The student makes some significant errors when performing the skill or process but can still do the basic steps.

1 The student makes so many errors when performing the skill or process that the student cannot actually do the skill.

0 Not enough information to make a judgment.

Skill Rubric for Younger Students

4 The student does the skill correctly and easily. The student understands the important parts of the skill.

3 The student does the skill correctly but not easily.

2 The student makes some big mistakes when he does the skill, but the student can still do the basic steps in the skill.

1 The student make so many big mistakes that he cannot do the skill.

0 The student does not try to do the skill.

FIGURE 10.7

Planning for Practice Worksheet

What skills will I only introduce?

How often will students perform or practice the skills I only introduce?

What are my expectations for student performance in those skills I only introduce?

What skills will I have students practice for mastery?

What will be the practice schedule?

How will I help students adapt or shape the skill or process?

What specific components or subcomponents of a process will I ask students to practice?

How will I monitor how well students are doing with the skill or process?

What will I do to help students who are not using the skill or process effectively?

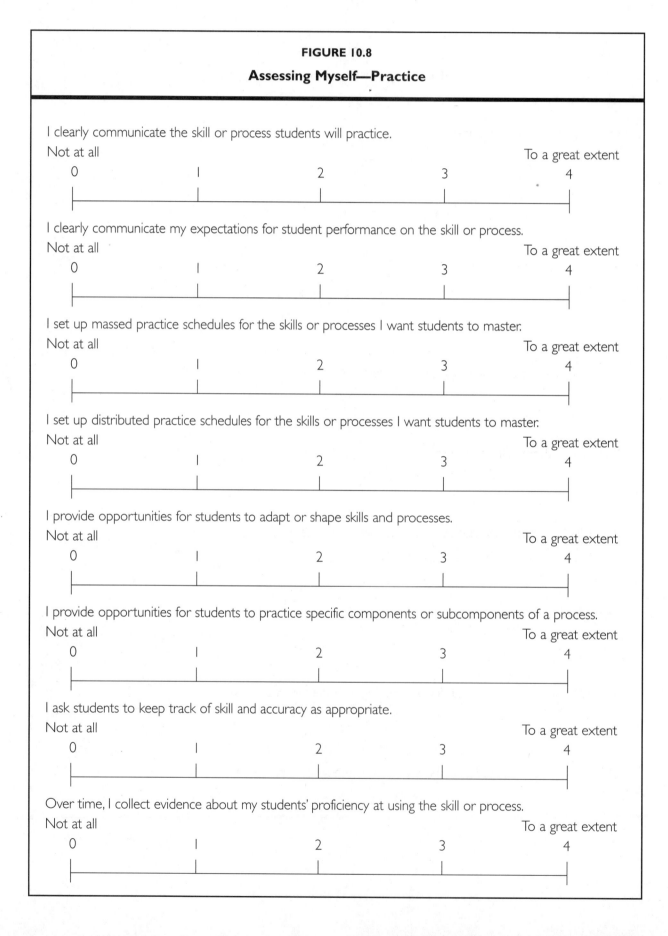

FIGURE 10.8

Assessing Myself—Practice

I clearly communicate the skill or process students will practice.

Not at all   To a great extent
  0   1   2   3   4

I clearly communicate my expectations for student performance on the skill or process.

Not at all   To a great extent
  0   1   2   3   4

I set up massed practice schedules for the skills or processes I want students to master.

Not at all   To a great extent
  0   1   2   3   4

I set up distributed practice schedules for the skills or processes I want students to master.

Not at all   To a great extent
  0   1   2   3   4

I provide opportunities for students to adapt or shape skills and processes.

Not at all   To a great extent
  0   1   2   3   4

I provide opportunities for students to practice specific components or subcomponents of a process.

Not at all   To a great extent
  0   1   2   3   4

I ask students to keep track of skill and accuracy as appropriate.

Not at all   To a great extent
  0   1   2   3   4

Over time, I collect evidence about my students' proficiency at using the skill or process.

Not at all   To a great extent
  0   1   2   3   4

Module Reflection

Review your responses to the questions in the Reflecting on My Current Beliefs and Practices—Practice worksheet, Figure 10.2 (p. 132). How has this module affected your thinking about teaching and learning? Use the space provided to record your thoughts.

- Reading this information affirms some of what I already knew about practice

- Now, I better understand some things about practice

- I think I will change how I use practice in my classroom

5

REPRESENTING KNOWLEDGE

Study Group Tip

If you are using this handbook in a study group, your group might want to read and discuss the research summary about representing knowledge in the companion book, *Classroom Instruction That Works.*

Many psychologists believe that we store knowledge in two ways: linguistically and nonlinguistically (Paivio, 1969, 1971, 1990). In other words, we store what we know in ways associated with words (the linguistic form) and with images (the nonlinguistic form). As a metaphor, the linguistic mode might be thought of as containing actual statements in long-term memory. In contrast, the imagery or nonlinguistic mode is expressed as mental pictures or even physical sensations, such as smell, taste, touch, kinesthetic association, and sound (Richardson, 1983).

Research tells us that we can use a variety of activities to help students represent knowledge in different ways. Research also indicates that nonlinguistic representations are more effective if they elaborate on or add to students' knowledge. In this module, we offer strategies and suggestions for using what research tells us works in the classroom. We encourage you to use these and other approaches for helping students represent knowledge.

List of Figures

NONLINGUISTIC REPRESENTATIONS

The more we use nonlinguistic representations while learning, the better we can think about and recall our knowledge. This is particularly relevant to the classroom, because studies have consistently shown that teachers primarily present new knowledge to students linguistically. They typically either talk to students about new content or have them read about the new content (Flanders, 1970). So, students are commonly left to their own devices to generate nonlinguistic representations for new knowledge. However, when teachers help students in this endeavor, the effects on achievement are strong. Explicitly engaging students in the creation of nonlinguistic representation actually stimulates and increases activity in the brain (Gerlic & Jausovec, 1999). Although students might not be likely to create nonlinguistic representations on their own, you can create opportunities for them to use this strategy.

Before reading "Recommendations for Classroom Practice," take some time to reflect on your current practices and beliefs about using nonlinguistic representations with your students by completing the worksheet in Figure 11.1 (p. 144), Reflecting on My Current Beliefs and Practices—Nonlinguistic Representation. This will give you a basis of comparison as you read about the strategies in the module.

Recommendations for Classroom Practice

In this module, we consider five strategies to use to help students represent the knowledge they are learning:

- graphic organizers,
- pictographic representations,
- mental images,
- physical models, and
- kinesthetic representations.

Use Graphic Organizers

Asking students to generate graphic representations of the knowledge they are learning is a straightforward way of representing knowledge. Graphic representations are typically used to organize declarative knowledge, or information. Declarative knowledge can be organized into patterns that help students see different relationships and connections among the pieces of information. Six common patterns used to organize information are descriptions, time sequences, process/cause-effect relationships, episodes, generalizations/principles, and concepts. Although there are many ways to construct graphic representations, using these organizational patterns provides a structure for teachers and students.

FIGURE 11.1

Reflecting on My Current Beliefs and Practices—Nonlinguistic Representation

What is the purpose of representing knowledge in different forms?

When do I ask students to represent knowledge using forms other than words?

What questions do I have about representing knowledge?

Using a graphic organizer might not come naturally to many students. Modeling how to use graphic organizers can help students understand how to use different types of organizers. This process does not need to be complicated. To demonstrate the use of a graphic organizer, you might give students a completed organizer that summarizes a film they have viewed or a set of information that you discussed in class. You might also give students a blank organizer and walk them through the process of organizing the information in different ways.

Descriptive Patterns. Descriptive patterns represent facts about specific persons, places, things, and events. The information organized into a descriptive pattern does not need to be in any particular order. Figure 11.2 shows how facts about a topic, Capital Resources, can be organized graphically.

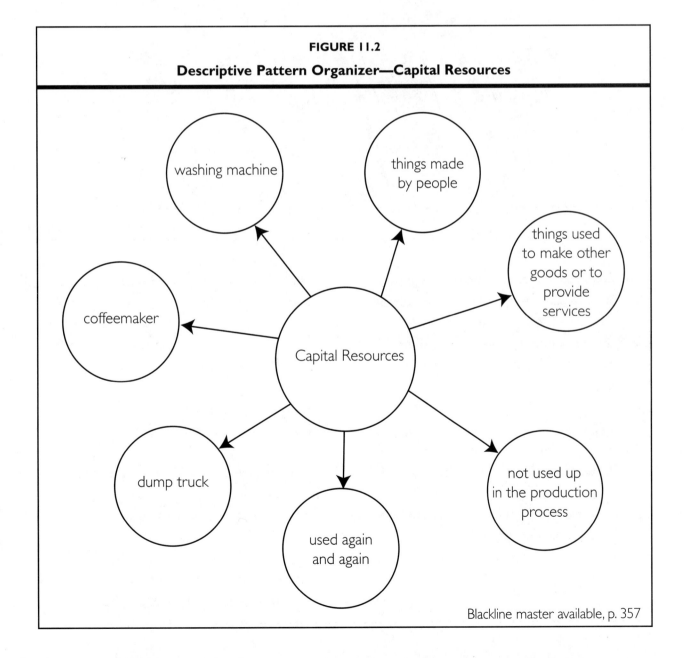

FIGURE 11.2

Descriptive Pattern Organizer—Capital Resources

washing machine

things made by people

things used to make other goods or to provide services

coffeemaker

Capital Resources

dump truck

used again and again

not used up in the production process

Blackline master available, p. 357

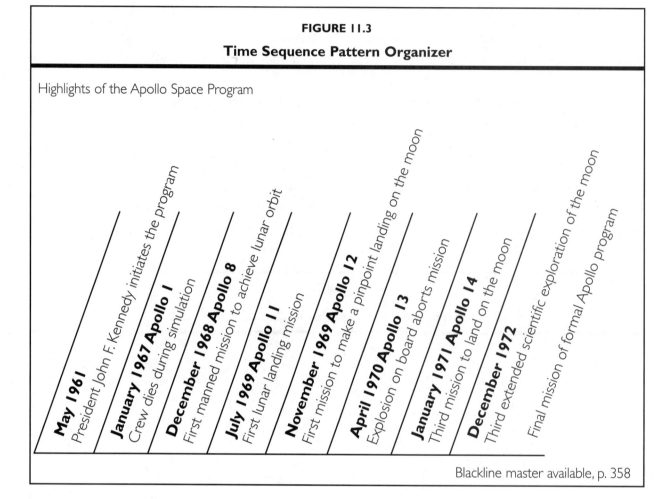

FIGURE 11.3

Time Sequence Pattern Organizer

Highlights of the Apollo Space Program

May 1961
President John F. Kennedy initiates the program

January 1967 Apollo 1
Crew dies during simulation

December 1968 Apollo 8
First manned mission to achieve lunar orbit

July 1969 Apollo 11
First lunar landing mission

November 1969 Apollo 12
First mission to make a pinpoint landing on the moon

April 1970 Apollo 13
Explosion on board aborts mission

January 1971 Apollo 14
Third mission to land on the moon

December 1972
Third extended scientific exploration of the moon

Final mission of formal Apollo program

Blackline master available, p. 358

Time Sequence Patterns. Time sequence patterns organize events in a specific chronological order. The timeline in Figure 11.3 shows how you can represent a time-sequence pattern graphically, using the Apollo space program as an example.

Process/Cause-Effect Patterns. Process/cause-effect patterns organize information into a causal network leading to a specific outcome or into a sequence of steps leading to a specific product. For example, the process of how a bill becomes a law can be organized as a pattern, such as shown in Figure 11.4 (p. 147).

Episode Patterns. Episode patterns organize information about specific events that include

- a setting (time and place),
- specific people,
- a specific duration,
- a specific sequence of events, and
- a particular cause and effect.

For example, you could organize the events involved in the Tiananmen Square Protest of 1989 into an episode pattern as shown in Figure 11.5 (p. 148).

Generalization/Principle Patterns.
Generalization/principle patterns organize information into general statements with

FIGURE 11.4

Process/Cause-Effect Pattern Organizer

How a Bill Becomes a Law in the United States

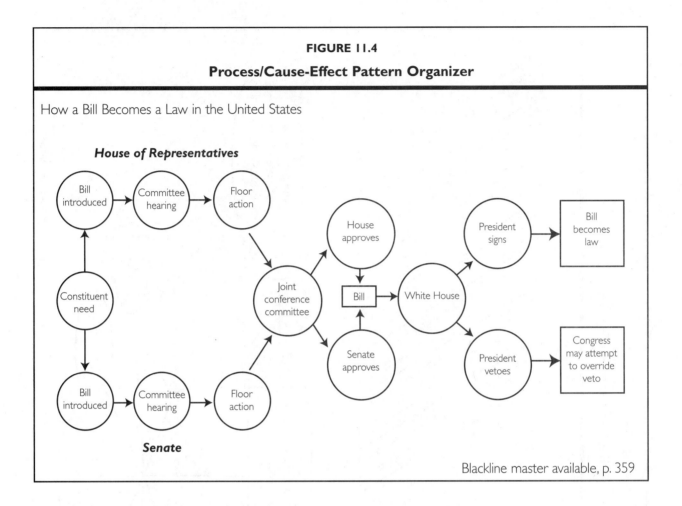

Blackline master available, p. 359

supporting examples. For example, the pattern organizer in Figure 11.6 (p. 149) begins with a statement for which students can provide examples—in this case fables.

Concept Patterns. Concept patterns, the most general of all patterns, organize information around a word or phrase that represents an entire class or category of persons, places, things, and events. The characteristics or attributes of the concept, along with examples of each, should be included in this pattern. The example in Figure 11.7 (p. 150) shows how the idea of modes of transportation can be organized this way.

Use Pictographic Representations

Drawing pictures or pictographs (e.g., symbolic pictures) to represent knowledge is a powerful way to generate nonlinguistic representations in the mind. For example, most students have either drawn or colored the human skeletal system or have seen a picture of one in the classroom. Similarly, most students have drawn or colored a representation of the solar system. A variation of a picture is the pictograph, a drawing that uses symbols or symbolic pictures to represent information. Pictographs can also use key words along with symbols. Figure 11.8 (p. 151) is a pictograph that a young student might draw to represent her community.

FIGURE 11.5

Episode Pattern Organizer—Tiananmen Square

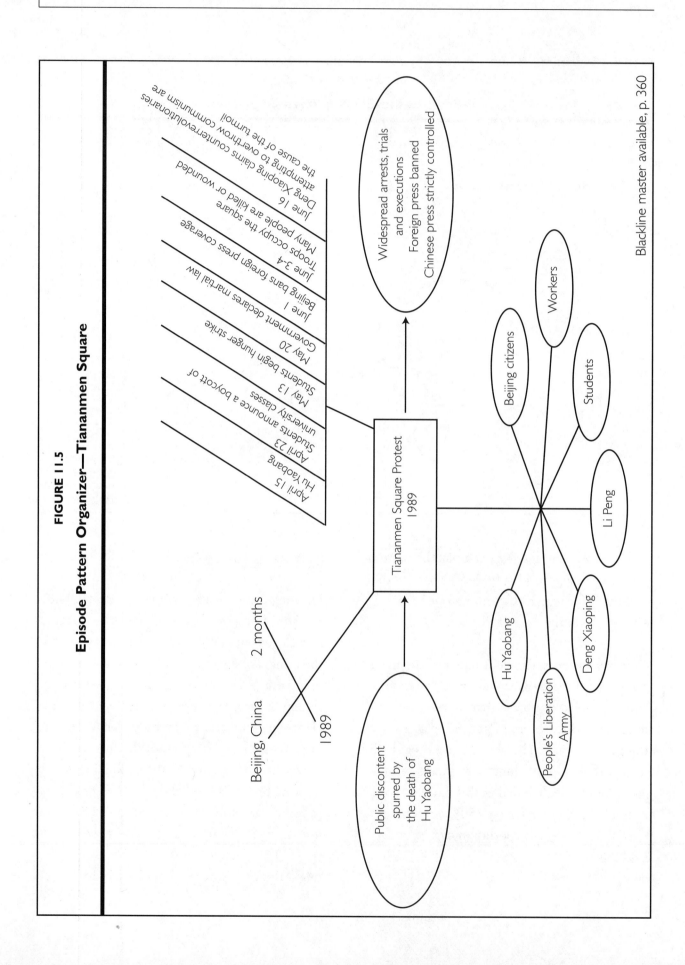

Blackline master available, p. 360

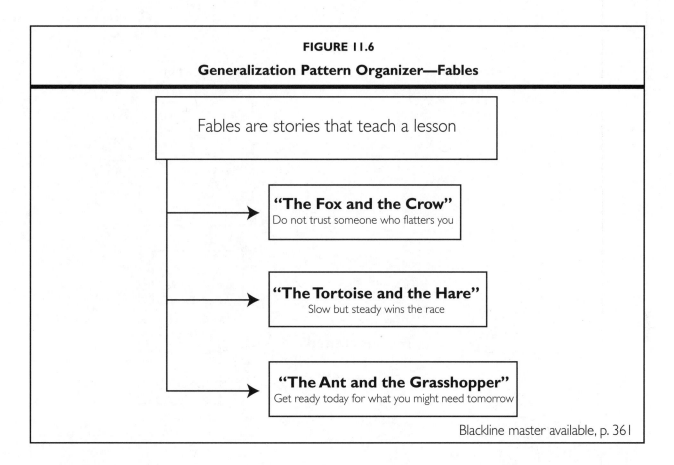

FIGURE 11.6

Generalization Pattern Organizer—Fables

Fables are stories that teach a lesson

"The Fox and the Crow"
Do not trust someone who flatters you

"The Tortoise and the Hare"
Slow but steady wins the race

"The Ant and the Grasshopper"
Get ready today for what you might need tomorrow

Blackline master available, p. 361

Use Mental Images

The most direct way to generate a mental representation is to simply construct or imagine a mental picture of knowledge you are learning. For abstract content, these mental pictures might be highly symbolic. To illustrate, psychologist John Hayes (1981) provides an example of how a student might generate a mental picture for the following physics equation:

$$F = \frac{(M_1 \times M_2)G}{r^2}$$

The equation states that force (F) is equal to the product of the masses of two objects (M_1 and M_2) times a constant (G) divided by the square of the distance between them (r^2). This information might be represented symbolically in a number of different ways. Hayes (1981) suggests an image of two large globes in space, with the learner in the middle trying to hold them apart:

> If either of the globes were very heavy, we would expect that it would be harder to hold them apart than if both were light. Since force increases as either of the masses (M_1 and M_2) increases, the masses must be in the numerator. As we push the globes further apart, the force of attraction between them will decrease as the force of attraction between two magnets decreases as we pull them apart. Since force decreases as distance increases, r must be in the denominator. (p. 126)

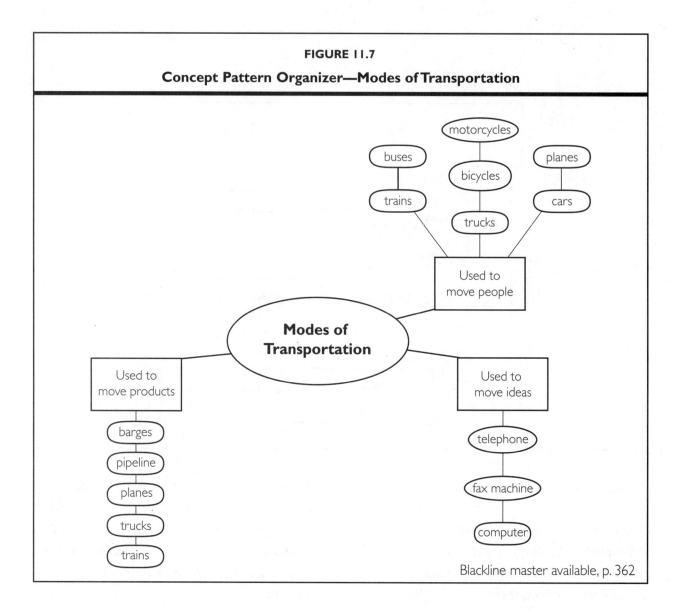

FIGURE 11.7

Concept Pattern Organizer—Modes of Transportation

Blackline master available, p. 362

Use Physical Representations

As the name implies, physical representations are models or concrete representations of the knowledge students are learning. Mathematics and science teachers commonly refer to concrete representations as "manipulatives." Young students might use math manipulatives to learn the processes of adding and subtracting. Older students might use geometric models to study a variety of attributes of three-dimensional figures.

You can also ask students to create physical representations. The very act of generating a concrete representation establishes an image of the knowledge in students' minds. If you ask students to create physical models, be sure the activity will extend students' understanding of the knowledge. What purpose does building a Berlin Wall out of sugar cubes serve? Besides the intricacies of *papier mâché*, what do students learn from building a volcano that erupts? The construction of the physical model should be closely tied to the knowledge

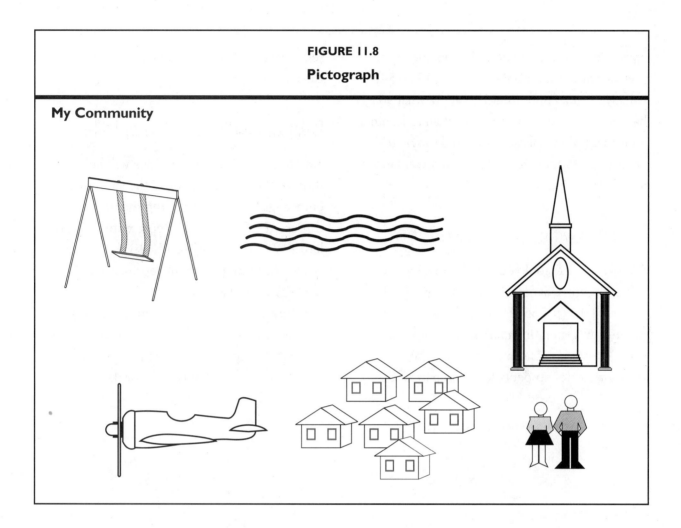

FIGURE 11.8
Pictograph

My Community

students are learning. For example, in a class where students are learning the concept of proportion and the relationship between two- and three-dimensional shapes, the teacher might ask students to choose an object from everyday life and create a scale model. Students would choose an object, identify a scale, draw a two-dimensional sketch, build the model, and write an explanation of the proportion and the process they used.

Use Kinesthetic Representations

Kinesthetic activities involve physical movement. Physical movement associated with specific knowledge generates a mental image of the knowledge in the mind of the learner. Many children find this an enjoyable way to express their knowledge. Students can role-play many processes or events in the classroom, such as how an electric circuit works, the way the planets move around the sun, the exchange of oxygen and carbon dioxide molecules in the body, adding and subtracting, or how a computer network operates.

Tools to Facilitate Nonlinguistic Representation in the Classroom

Before using our recommendations in your classroom practice, consider a hypothetical situation or problem to check your understanding of the previous discussion. Figure 11.9 (pp. 153–154) will give you an opportunity to apply what you have learned. The other assessment and planning tools that follow will help you guide your students in performing nonlinguistic representations in the classroom.

Assessing the Impact on Students

Rubrics are one tool you can use to gauge students' progress. Sample rubrics are provided in Figure 11.10 (p. 155) for evaluating students' progress in generating nonlinguistic representations. These rubrics can be revised, when appropriate, for students to use as part of the self-assessment process to help them reflect on their work.

Planning Classroom Activities and Assessing Myself

Answering a series of questions will help you discover how you might use the strategies for encouraging nonlinguistic representation. You can use the Planning for Representing Knowledge Worksheet, Figure 11.11 (p. 156), to guide your thinking about representing knowledge in your classroom.

Rubrics help assess student learning. You can also assess how effectively you encourage students to represent knowledge. Use Figure 11.12 (p. 157) to evaluate yourself.

FIGURE 11.9

Checking My Understanding—Graphic Organizers

Use a graphic organizer to represent the notes on kelp. Then answer the following questions.

What process did you go through to create the graphic organizer?

Does the graphic organizer make it easier to see any particular information or ideas than the page of notes does?

How would you use pictures to represent this information about kelp?

(continued on p. 154)

FIGURE 11.9 (CONTINUED)

Checking My Understanding—Graphic Organizers

Kelp

Large seaweed
Brown algae

Laminaria—
Abundant on Pacific Coasts and British
    Isles
Source of commercial iodine
3-10 ft. long

giant kelp
    produces algin

Macrocystis — GIANT KELP
    Can be 215 ft long
Biggest kelp
Large roots attach to ocean floor
Long branching stalk with blades that float

Rich in vitamins and minerals

Rock weed
Gulf weed—floats in Gulf
    Stream

Nereocystis
"sea otter's cabbage"
deep waters
130 ft. long

ALGIN
Used for making tires
A suspending agent emulsifier
Plastic, film, gel, rubber, linoleum
Cheese, pudding, ice cream

FIGURE 11.10

Rubrics for Nonlinguistic Representation

Nonlinguistic Representation Rubric

4 The student's representation indicates a detailed understanding of the information important to the topic.

3 The student's representation indicates a complete understanding of the information important to the topic.

2 The student's representation indicates an incomplete understanding of the topic or misconceptions about some of the information. However, the student shows a basic understanding of the topic.

1 The student's representation indicates an understanding of the topic that is so incomplete or has so many misconceptions that the student cannot be said to understand the topic.

0 Not enough information to make a judgment.

Nonlinguistic Representation Rubric for Younger Students

4 The student's picture shows that she understands all of the important information. The picture includes some details.

3 The student's picture shows that she understands the important information.

2 The student's picture shows that she does not really understand the topic. The picture shows some mistakes about the topic.

1 The student's picture shows that she does not understand the topic. The picture shows many mistakes about the topic.

0 The student did not try to create a picture.

FIGURE 11.11

Planning for Representing Knowledge Worksheet

What knowledge will students be learning?

Will I provide a representation for them or ask them to create their own?

What representing knowledge strategy will I ask students to use?
- ☐ Graphic organizer
- ☐ Pictograph
- ☐ Mental images
- ☐ Physical representation
- ☐ Kinesthetic activity
- ☐ Other_____

Do I need to set aside time to teach students the strategy I want them to use? How will I teach students the strategy?

How will I monitor students' creation and use of nonlinguistic representations?

What will I do to help students who are not using nonlinguistic representations effectively?

Figure 11.12
Assessing Myself—Nonlinguistic Representation

I clearly identify the knowledge students will use to generate representations.

Not at all   To a great extent

| 0 | 1 | 2 | 3 | 4 |

I clearly communicate the strategy that students will use to generate representations.

Not at all   To a great extent

| 0 | 1 | 2 | 3 | 4 |

I make sure students know how to use the strategy that I want them to use to represent knowledge.

Not at all   To a great extent

| 0 | 1 | 2 | 3 | 4 |

Over time, I collect evidence about my students' proficiency at using a variety of methods to represent knowledge.

Not at all   To a great extent

| 0 | 1 | 2 | 3 | 4 |

Module Reflection

Review your responses to the questions in the Reflecting on My Current Beliefs and Practices—Nonlinguistic Representation worksheet, Figure 11.1 (p. 144). How has this module affected your thinking about teaching and learning? Use the space provided to record your thoughts.

- Reading this information affirms some of what I already knew about representing knowledge

- Now, I better understand some things about representing knowledge

- I think I will change how I ask my students to represent knowledge.

MODULE 12

LEARNING GROUPS

6

Study Group Tip

If you are using this handbook in a study group, your group might want to read and discuss the research summary about cooperative learning in the companion book, *Classroom Instruction That Works*.

Organizing students into groups is an instructional strategy teachers have used for decades. In this section we focus on a particular grouping strategy referred to as cooperative learning, which has a strong research base to support its use.

Hundreds of studies support the effectiveness of cooperative learning (Johnson et al., 1981; Walberg, 1999). In general, research indicates that students who work in cooperative groups consistently outperform students who don't. We also know that adding competition to the mix does not enhance achievement. You gain nothing by asking cooperative groups to compete against one another. Finally, we know that cooperative groups should be small and that different types of groups should be organized for different purposes. Here we offer strategies and suggestions for using what the research tells us works in the classroom. We encourage you to use these and other approaches for using cooperative learning to enhance students' learning.

List of Figures

COOPERATIVE LEARNING

Cooperative learning is one of the most popular instructional innovations in U.S. education. Teachers use some form of cooperative learning at every grade level in all subject areas for all types of students. This module focuses on the approach developed by researchers David and Roger Johnson (1999). It is important to realize that cooperative learning involves more than simply placing students in groups and asking them to work cooperatively. Students must learn and master specific skills for working in groups.

Before reading "Recommendations for Classroom Practice," take some time to reflect on your current practices and beliefs about cooperative learning by completing the worksheet in Figure 12.1 (p. 162), Reflecting on My Current Beliefs and Practices. It will give you a basis of comparison as you read about the strategies in the module.

Recommendations for Classroom Practice

In this module, we discuss several approaches to use in the classroom:

- using elements of cooperative learning,
- varying grouping criteria, and
- managing group size.

Use Elements of Cooperative Learning

Most of us have participated in a group project where some of the team members did not pull their weight, where conflict reigned, where everyone wanted to be the leader, and no one wanted to be the leader—where working in a group was not enjoyable or productive. You can bet that many of your students dread the words "group work" because of similar experiences. But group work doesn't have to be chaotic and unproductive. We can use specific strategies to ensure that cooperative learning has a positive effect on learning.

Roger Johnson and David Johnson (2001), recognized leaders in the field of cooperative learning, define five elements of cooperative learning that distinguish it from other forms of group work:

1. **positive interdependence** (a sense of sink or swim together)
2. **face-to-face promotive interaction** (helping each other learn, applauding success and efforts)
3. **individual and group accountability** (each of us has to contribute to the group achieving its goals)
4. **interpersonal and small group skills** (communication, trust, leadership, decision making, and conflict resolution)

FIGURE 12.1

Reflecting on My Current Beliefs and Practices—Cooperative Learning

What is my purpose for using cooperative learning in the classroom?

What kind of cooperative learning activities do I use with my students?

I can think of a time when I used cooperative learning, and I was pleased with the results. Why did it work well?

I can think of a time when I used cooperative learning, and I was not pleased with the results. Why did it not work well?

What questions do I have about using cooperative learning in my classroom?

5. group processing (reflecting on how well the team is functioning and how to function even better)

(From "What is Cooperative Learning?" Johnson and Johnson, Cooperative Learning Center at the University of Minnesota [Online: http://www.clcrc.com/index.html#essays].)

Using the five elements of cooperative learning can decrease tension and make group work more constructive. You can design activities to emphasize each element as you introduce it. For example, you might emphasize group processing by asking students to periodically describe in writing how the group is performing. These periodic analyses might be handed in as part of the overall assignment. Once students become familiar with the five elements, these elements can become a more regular part of any cooperative learning situation.

Vary Grouping Criteria

Teachers can use a variety of criteria to group students (interests, birthday month, first letter of their first names, or color of their shirts). Students might also be grouped randomly by drawing names from a hat. Varying the tactics you use to group students will ensure that different students have the opportunity to work together.

Using informal, formal, and base groups (Johnson & Johnson, 1999) is one way to vary grouping patterns and activities. *Informal groups*, such as pair-share or turn-to-your-neighbor, are formed for specific or immediate needs and can last for a few minutes or an entire class period. You can use informal groups "on the fly" when and where you need them—for example, to check students' understanding of new content, to clarify expectations about an assignment, to review a skill, to check homework, to provide an opportunity for students to process information, or to provide closure on an activity.

Formal groups are perhaps the most structured of the three types of groups. In formal groups, students work on an extended academic assignment, perhaps for several days or even several weeks. For formal groups, the teacher designs tasks that encompass all of the defining elements of cooperative learning: positive interdependence, group processing, appropriate use of social skills, face-to-face promotive interaction, and individual and group accountability (Johnson & Johnson, 1999). Although these cooperative learning situations take time to create and to carry out in the classroom, they actively involve students in a variety of learning opportunities.

Base groups are long-term groups that last throughout a school year or a grading period. These groups are designed to give students a support system, to build camaraderie, and to create a sense of teamwork. Base groups are suitable for many different situations in all grades. Middle or high school science students might form base groups for the lab experiments they will conduct during the year. With younger students, you might use base groups to help with daily tasks, such as keeping track of homework assignments. Base groups also work well when students are learning and practicing a complicated, multistep process, such as the writing process, graphing complex functions, or analyzing historical perspectives and events. Working in base groups allows students to give each other feedback, identify strengths and weaknesses, practice for oral presentations, or clarify misconceptions with students they have come to know and trust.

Manage Group Size

Research indicates that cooperative groups should be small. Many teachers follow the rule of thumb "the smaller the better." Even though a particular task may seem to have enough work to occupy a large group, students may not have the skills needed to work effectively in larger groups. If resources allow, groups of three to five students are recommended.

Tools to Facilitate Cooperative Learning in the Classroom

Before using our recommendations in your classroom practice, consider a hypothetical situation or problem to check your understanding of the previous discussion. The worksheet in Figure 12.2 (p. 165) gives you an opportunity to apply what you learned in the previous discussion. The other assessment and planning tools that follow will help you guide your students in cooperative learning activities in the classroom.

Assessing the Impact on Students

Rubrics are one tool you can use to gauge students' progress. Sample rubrics are provided in Figures 12.3 (p. 166), 12.4 (p. 167), and 12.5 (p. 168) for evaluating students' progress in working in cooperative groups. These rubrics can be revised, when appropriate, for students to use as part of the self-assessment process to help them reflect on their work.

FIGURE 12.2

Checking My Understanding

Think about a time when you worked in a cooperative group. How did it go? Reflecting on what you have just read, use the following questions to analyze your experience.

Cooperative Learning Worksheet

What was the purpose of the cooperative learning activity?

Did the activity involve members in a way in which they
- Felt a sense of "sink or swim" together?

- Were responsible for contributing to the group achieving its goal?

- Engaged in communication, trust, leadership, decision making, and conflict resolution?

Were opportunities provided to reflect on how well the team functioned and how they might improve?

Was the group size manageable?

What would have made the group work better together?

FIGURE 12.3

Rubrics for Group Goals

Rubric for Working Toward Achievement of Group Goals

4   The student communicates commitment to group goals and works hard to carry out assigned roles. The student actively helps identify group goals.

3   The student communicates commitment to group goals and effectively carries out assigned roles.

2   The student communicates a commitment to group goals but does not carry out assigned roles.

1   The student does not communicate commitment to group goals and does not carry out assigned roles.

0   Not enough information to make a judgment.

Rubric for Working Toward Achievement of Group Goals for Younger Students

4   The student promises to work on the group goals. The student works hard to do her jobs. The student actively helps identify group goals.

3   The student promises to work on the group goals. The student effectively does her jobs.

2   The student promises to work on the group goals, but the student does not do her jobs.

1   The student does not work on the group goals, and the student does not do her job.

0   The student does not work in the group.

FIGURE 12.4

Rubrics for Effective Interpersonal Skills

Rubric for Effective Interpersonal Skills

4   The student actively promotes effective group interaction and participates in group interaction without prompting. The student expresses ideas and opinions in a way that is sensitive to the feelings and knowledge base of others.

3   The student participates in group interaction without prompting. The student expresses ideas and opinions in a way that is sensitive to the feelings and knowledge base of others.

2   The student participates in group interaction with prompting or expresses ideas and opinions without considering the feelings and knowledge base of others.

1   The student does not participate in group interaction, even with prompting, or expresses ideas and opinions in a way that is insensitive to the feelings or knowledge base of others.

0   Not enough information to make a judgment.

Rubric for Effective Interpersonal Skills for Younger Students

4   The student actively helps the group work together. The student joins group activities without being asked. The student says what he thinks in a way that respects what others feel and know.

3   The student joins group activities without being asked. The student says what he thinks in a way that respects what others feel and know.

2   The student only joins group activities when someone asks. Sometimes the student says what he thinks in a way that hurts others' feelings.

1   The student does not join group activities, even when someone asks. Or, the student says what he thinks in a way that hurts others' feelings.

0   The student does not work in the group.

FIGURE 12.5

Rubrics for Group Maintenance

Rubric for Contributing to Group Maintenance

4 The student takes initiative to identify changes or modifications necessary in the group process and works toward carrying out those changes.

3 The student helps identify changes or modifications necessary in the group process and works toward carrying out those changes.

2 When prompted, the student helps identify changes or modifications necessary in the group process, or is only minimally involved in carrying out those changes.

1 The student does not attempt to identify changes or modifications necessary in the group process, even when prompted, or refuses to work toward carrying out those changes.

0 Not enough information to make a judgment.

Rubric for Contributing to Group Maintenance for Younger Students

4 The student acts as a leader to help the group decide on changes about how to work together. The student works hard to make those changes.

3 The student helps the group decide on changes and about how to work together. The student works to make those changes.

2 When someone asks, the student helps the group decide on changes and about how to work together. The student only does a little to help make those changes.

1 The student does not try to help the group decide on changes and how to work together, even when someone asks. The student does not do things to make those changes.

0 The student does not work in the group.

Planning Classroom Activities and Assessing Myself

Answering a series of questions will help you discover how you might use the strategies for cooperative learning presented in this module. You can use the Planning for Cooperative Learning Worksheet, Figure 12.6 (pp. 169–170), to guide your thinking about cooperative learning in your classroom.

Rubrics help assess student learning. You can assess yourself too—how effectively you use strategies to encourage cooperative learning with your students. Use Figure 12.7 (p. 171) to evaluate your effectiveness regarding the use of cooperative learning in the classroom.

FIGURE 12.6

Planning for Cooperative Learning Worksheet

What knowledge will students be learning?

What type of group will I use?

☐ Informal group

☐ Formal group

☐ Base group

☐ Other_____

What criteria will I use to group students?

What size will the groups be?

Will students use a particular element of cooperative learning for the activity?

☐ Positive interdependence

☐ Face-to-face promotive interaction

☐ Individual and group accountability

☐ Interpersonal and small group skills

☐ Group processing

☐ Other_____

Do I need to set aside time to teach students about the role? How will I teach them about the role?

(continued on p. 170)

FIGURE 12.6 (CONTINUED)

Planning for Cooperative Learning Worksheet

How will I monitor how well students are working in the group?

How will I monitor the effects of the cooperating learning activity on students' learning?

What will I do to help students who are not working well in the group?

What will I do to improve the effects of the cooperative learning experience on students' learning?

FIGURE 12.7

Assessing Myself—Cooperative Learning

I clearly communicate the knowledge students will be learning.

Not at all   To a great extent

  0   1   2   3   4

Over time, I vary the criteria I use to group students.

Not at all   To a great extent

  0   1   2   3   4

Over time, I vary the types of groups I use.

Not at all   To a great extent

  0   1   2   3   4

I keep group size manageable.

Not at all   To a great extent

  0   1   2   3   4

I make sure students understand the elements of cooperative learning they are supposed to be using.

Not at all   To a great extent

  0   1   2   3   4

Over time, I collect evidence about my students' proficiency at using a variety of roles in a cooperative learning situation.

Not at all   To a great extent

  0   1   2   3   4

Over time, I collect evidence about the impact of cooperative learning activities on my students' learning.

Not at all   To a great extent

  0   1   2   3   4

Module Reflection

Review your responses to the Reflecting on My Current Beliefs and Practices—Cooperative Learning worksheet, Figure 12.1, (p. 162). How has this module affected your thinking about teaching and learning? Use the space provided to record your thoughts.

- Reading this information affirms some of what I already knew about cooperative learning

- Now, I better understand some things about cooperative learning

- I think I will change the way I use cooperative learning in my classroom

SETTING OBJECTIVES AND PROVIDING FEEDBACK

Study Group Tip

If you are using this handbook in a study group, your group might want to read and discuss the research summaries about setting objectives and providing feedback in the companion book, *Classroom Instruction That Works.*

Setting objectives and providing feedback engage the metacognitive thinking of students. In other words, objectives and feedback give students direction and help them think about their own learning. Some people differentiate between goals and objectives, but in this section we use the terms interchangeably.

Research shows that instructional goals narrow students' focus. Educators should set flexible learning goals and encourage students to personalize them. In terms of providing feedback, we know feedback should explain to students what they are doing correctly and incorrectly. Also, feedback should be timely and refer to a specific level of performance. Further, studies show that students can give feedback to each other. In this module, we offer strategies and suggestions for using what research tells us works in the classroom. We encourage you to use these and other approaches for setting objectives and providing feedback to enhance student learning.

List of Figures

SETTING OBJECTIVES

Students learn most efficiently when they know the goals or objectives of a specific lesson or learning activity. This makes intuitive sense. If students are aware of an intended outcome, they know what to focus on. When setting objectives, the teacher simply gives students a target for their learning. However, as we discuss in this module, objectives can be written in a number of formats and used in different ways.

Before reading "Recommendations for Classroom Practice," take some time to reflect on your current practices and beliefs about setting objectives for your students by completing the worksheet in Figure 13.1, Reflecting on My Current Beliefs and Practices—Setting Objectives (p. 176). It will give you a basis for comparison as you read about the strategies in the module.

Recommendations for Classroom Practice

In this module, we discuss several approaches to use in the classroom:

- setting objectives that are not too specific,
- personalizing objectives,
- communicating objectives, and
- negotiating contracts.

Set Objectives That Are Not Too Specific

Research suggests that learning goals that are too specific might actually constrain students' learning. When students engage in a rich learning experience, a clear, concise learning objective can help them focus on what to learn from the experience. If the knowledge in the objective is too narrow, however, or if the objective focuses the students too much on a specific skill, students might not attend to all of the learning that could result from the rich experience. Although it might be appropriate for some objectives to be very specific, teachers should review their objectives and decide if student learning could be enhanced with broader objectives.

Personalize Objectives

Objectives become powerful learning tools when they give direction to students but allow them some flexibility to further define their own interests within a topic. To build in flexibility, you can identify knowledge at a fairly general level so that students can then identify more specific knowledge that interests them. For example, you might set as a learning goal "understands basic ideas about networked computers." Students can use this broad learning goal as a guide for creating more specific learning targets, such as "I want to know how a modem works," or "I want to know how our computer at home uses the telephone line to connect to the Internet," or "What's the difference between the Internet and an Intranet?"

FIGURE 13.1

Reflecting on My Current Beliefs and Practices—Setting Objectives

What is the purpose of setting objectives in the classroom?

How do I set objectives in my classroom now?

What do I do to communicate classroom objectives to my students?

What questions do I have about setting objectives in my classroom?

You might need to help students construct their specific personal learning goals because they often set broad goals that are difficult to measure. For example, how would a student know if he had reached a goal to "become a better writer"? You might help students define more concrete, measurable goals, such as "I want to write more effective introductions with clear, concise thesis statements" or "I want to use good paragraph form in my writing and use strong supporting details." You might also give students sentence stems to help them set learning goals. These stems might be presented in the context of a "learning goals sheet." To illustrate, in a 5th grade social studies class studying the basic purposes of government in the United States, the teacher might give students a learning goals sheet, such as shown in Figure 13.2. Students would fill in the information that is underlined.

Communicate Objectives

Communicating objectives effectively is probably just as important as designing them. Of course, students must understand the objectives so that they can work with the teacher to achieve the desired level of performance. Both short-term and long-term goals need to be clearly visible to students and in language that they can understand. To ensure that students are aware of the long-term objectives, some teachers post the learning goals for the grading period on the walls of the classroom so students can always see them. You can give students goals for units of study or individual lessons in a handout, or you can set aside time for students to copy the objectives you provide.

Learning goals should also be communicated to parents. If parents, especially those of younger students, understand the learning

---

FIGURE 13.2

My Learning Goals

Our learning goal for this unit:
Understanding the basic purposes of government in the United States

Complete the following sentences to set your personal learning goals.
I know _one purpose of our government is to protect individual rights,_

but I want to know _what does the common good mean?_

I want to know more about _what laws the president makes and what laws our governor makes._

objectives, they can provide appropriate support to students. One effective and simple method of communicating learning goals to parents is a letter. To illustrate, Figure 13.3 (p. 179) is a letter written to parents that communicates the learning objectives for a grading period, as well as the criteria for grading.

Negotiate Contracts

Contracting with students to attain specific goals is a variation on goal setting. A contract gives students a great deal of control over their learning. In brief, contracts individualize goals for learning so that students have some "say so" about what they will work on and the grade they will receive for their work.

For example, in a language arts class, the teacher might contract with students for reading and vocabulary goals. In the contract, students might agree to spend 20 minutes per day reading. Students might individualize their contracts with books that are appropriate for their reading ability, agree to identify 10 words per week from their reading, and define these words in their vocabulary journals. The teacher might then meet individually with students every other week to discuss their progress and update their reading lists.

Tools to Facilitate Setting Objectives in the Classroom

Before using our recommendations in your classroom practice, consider a hypothetical sit-

uation or problem to check your understanding of the previous discussion. Completing the worksheet in Figure 13.4 (p. 180) will give you an opportunity to apply what you have learned. The other assessment and planning tools that follow will help you guide your students to set objectives in the classroom.

Assessing the Impact on Students

Rubrics are one tool you can use to gauge students' progress. Sample rubrics are given in Figure 13.5 (p. 181) for evaluating students' progress in setting and achieving objectives. These rubrics can be revised, when appropriate, for students to use as part of the self-assessment process to help them reflect on their work.

Planning Classroom Activities and Assessing Myself

Answering a series of questions will help you discover how you might use the strategies for setting objectives presented in this module. You can use the worksheet in Figure 13.6 (p. 182) to guide your thinking when planning for setting objectives in the classroom

Rubrics help assess student learning. You can assess yourself too—how effectively you set objectives with your students. Use Figure 13.7 (p. 183) to evaluate your effectiveness regarding setting objectives.

FIGURE 13.3

Letter to Parents About Learning Goals

Dear Parents:

During this grading period, we will be studying maps and the spatial organization of the Earth's surface. Specifically, we will be working so that your child will achieve the following objectives. Your child should be able to demonstrate that he

- Understands the concepts of absolute and relative location.
- Uses scale to determine distances.
- Understands and uses geographic databases
- Understands how topography influences the way people live and the extent to which they must depend on others.
- Understands how human activity influences the topography of regions.

In addition, students will continue to work on general abilities that are yearlong goals. Your child will be working to improve his

- Ability to compare, and
- Ability to communicate clearly.

Finally, your child will also be held accountable for the following two areas that are very important to his learning:

- Putting effort into work, even when it is difficult.
- Participating in a group to achieve a goal.

Students will receive feedback on these factors and will be able to share their progress with you. If you have any questions, please feel free to call.

Sincerely,

(Add teacher's signature line and name of class)

FIGURE 13.4

Checking My Understanding—Setting Objectives

Learning Goals Worksheet

1. Rewrite several of these learning objectives so that they allow for more flexibility for students.

   a. Students will demonstrate that they understand plot and character and are able to construct a narrative by writing a ghost story.

   b. Students will demonstrate that they know three causes of Word War I, World War II, and the Vietnam War.

   c. Students will demonstrate that they know the categories in the food pyramid by creating a menu for a restaurant.

   d. Students will demonstrate that they are able to use the Internet by finding three Web sites about whales.

2. Make a list of sample learning objectives for this module. Be precise, but try to write them in a way that would allow participants to personalize the goals.

FIGURE 13.5

Rubrics for Setting Objectives

Objectives Rubric

4   The student understands and achieves or exceeds the requirements of the learning objectives provided by the teacher. The student adapts the learning goals to her own interests.

3   The student understands and achieves the requirements of the learning objectives provided by the teacher.

2   The student has a partial understanding of the learning objectives provided by the teacher and does some work to complete the requirements of the objectives.

1   The student does not understand the objectives provided by the teacher and does little to achieve the objectives.

0   Not enough information to make a judgment.

Objectives Rubric for Younger Students

4   The student understands the requirement of the objectives. The student does everything she needs to meet the objectives. The student uses the teacher's objectives as a guide and makes her own learning goals.

3   The student understands the requirements of the learning objectives. The student does everything she needs to meet the objectives.

2   The student understands some things about the learning objectives. The student does some work to meet the objectives.

1   The student does not understand the objectives. The student does little to meet the objectives.

0   The student does not try to understand or meet the objectives.

FIGURE 13.6

Planning for Setting Objectives Worksheet

What knowledge will students be learning?

How will I state the objectives for this lesson?

How will I encourage students to personalize objectives?

How will I communicate my objectives to students and parents?

How will I use contracts with students?

How will I monitor how well students are meeting the learning objectives?

What will I do to help students who are not meeting objectives?

FIGURE 13.7

Assessing Myself—Setting Objectives

I provide students with objectives that are clear but provide enough flexibility for their input.

Not at all   To a great extent

0   1   2   3   4

I encourage students to personalize objectives.

Not at all   To a great extent

0   1   2   3   4

I clearly communicate the learning objectives to students.

Not at all   To a great extent

0   1   2   3   4

I clearly communicate the learning objectives to parents.

Not at all   To a great extent

0   1   2   3   4

I negotiate fair contracts with students that help clarify objectives and set expectations.

Not at all   To a great extent

0   1   2   3   4

I monitor how well students are progressing toward meeting the learning objectives.

Not at all   To a great extent

0   1   2   3   4

Over time, I collect evidence about how well students are progressing toward meeting the learning objectives.

Not at all   To a great extent

0   1   2   3   4

Module Reflection

Review your responses to the questions in the Reflecting on My Current Beliefs and Practices—Setting Objectives worksheet, Figure 13.1 (p. 176). How has this module affected your thinking about teaching and learning? Use the space provided to record your thoughts.

- Reading this information affirms some of what I already knew about setting learning objectives

- Now, I better understand some things about setting learning objectives

- I think I will change the way I set objectives in my classroom

PROVIDING FEEDBACK

Some education researchers believe providing feedback is the most powerful thing that a classroom teacher can do to enhance student achievement. After considering the findings from almost 8,000 studies, researcher John Hattie (1992) commented: "The most powerful single modification that enhances achievement is feedback. The simplest prescription for improving education must be "'dollops of feedback'" (p. 9). Yet for feedback to be most effective, it should be given specifically. In this module we consider the different forms feedback might take and factors that enhance the effectiveness of feedback regardless of its format.

Before reading "Recommendations for Classroom Practice," reflect on your current practices and beliefs about providing feedback for your students by completing the worksheet in Figure 14.1, Reflecting on My Current Beliefs and Practices—Providing Feedback (p. 186). It will give you a basis for comparison as you read about the strategies in the module.

Recommendations for Classroom Practice

Giving students effective feedback about their work can improve their learning. In this module, we discuss several approaches to use in the classroom:

- using criterion-referenced feedback and explanations,

- using feedback from assessments,
- engaging students in peer feedback, and
- asking students to self-assess.

Use Criterion-Referenced Feedback and Explanations

In general, the more specific feedback is, the better. When possible, teachers should try to focus their feedback on specific types of knowledge and skill, help students understand how well they are doing as compared to a performance standard, and give an explanation of why their work exceeds, meets, or misses the standard. Often referred to as "criterion-referenced," this type of feedback gives students more information about their learning than norm-referenced feedback, which tells them how their performance ranks relative to the performance of other students.

Rubrics are effective tools for providing students with criteria that describe specific levels of performance for declarative content (information) or procedural content (skills or processes). You can use the general rubrics for information and for processes and skills, provided in the section of this module entitled "Assessing the Impact on Students" to spell out the basic requirements for student performance on these types of knowledge. You can adapt these generic rubrics to meet the specific criteria of particular skills or concepts.

FIGURE 14.1

Reflecting on My Current Beliefs and Practices—Providing Feedback

What is the purpose of providing feedback in the classroom?

What kind of feedback do I provide my students?

What makes feedback useful to my students?

What questions do I have about providing feedback?

Rubrics aren't just for teachers. Rubrics let students know up front what they need to know or be able to do. They help take the surprise out of scores. Therefore, involving students in adapting generic rubrics to meet the specific criteria of particular skills or concepts is a powerful way to refine generic rubrics. When students help to identify the criteria for achievement on a specific skill or concept, they clarify the components necessary for each level of achievement. This process helps articulate levels of performance in terms students understand so they know exactly what they have to know or be able to do and encourages them to clear up misconceptions before they begin to work. Figure 14.2 is a rubric for students to use in solving a linear equation; Figure 14.3 (p. 188) is a rubric for consumer influences on health. Both of these figures were adapted from the generic rubrics for procedural and declarative knowledge.

Use Feedback from Assessments

Classroom assessments can be one primary vehicle that teachers use to give students feedback. Ideally, scores from assessments should be used to determine next steps students must take to improve their learning. Research suggests that certain practices render feedback on classroom assessments most effective:

- Give timely feedback. Stated negatively, if too much time (e.g., one week or more) elapses from the time students take a test until they receive feedback on it, what they learn from that assessment will be minimal.
- Explain what was correct and what was incorrect on an assessment. Everyone has seen students look at a score at the top of a test and then toss the paper aside. An assessment is much more likely to have a positive influence on students' learning if time is set aside to make sure students understand what they did well and what they did not do well.

FIGURE 14.2

Student Rubric for Solving a Linear Equation

4   I can perform the skills and processes important to solving a linear equation with no significant errors and with fluency. In addition, I understand the key aspects of solving a linear equation, such as isolating the variable, combining terms, and using the distributive property.

3   I can perform the process of solving a linear equation without making significant errors.

2   I make some significant errors when performing the process of solving a linear equation but still perform the process.

1   I make so many errors when performing the process of solving a linear equation that I cannot actually solve a linear equation.

0   I did not attempt to solve the linear equation.

FIGURE 14.3

Student Rubric for Consumer Influences on Health

---

4   I completely understand the information important to consumer influences, including
- media influences,
- information from school,
- family influences, and
- peer pressure.

I can give detailed examples about how those influences affect the decisions we make about health resources, products, and services. I can explain complicated connections and differences between these influences.

3   I completely understand the information important to consumer influences and how those influences affect decisions about health resources, products, and services. I can give detailed examples.

2   I understand some of the important information related to consumer influences and how those influences affect decisions about health resources, products, and services. I cannot give detailed examples.

1   I understand very little about the important information related to consumer influences and how those influences affect decisions about health resources, products, and services.

0   I did not try to do the task.

Engage Students in Peer Feedback

Peer feedback is underused, yet it is highly effective and quite flexible. Peer feedback doesn't mean that students actually "grade" each other or "score" each other's papers. Instead, the goal is for students to clarify for each other what was correct or incorrect in an assessment. This type of feedback can be as simple as a student who answered an item correctly explaining to a student who didn't answer it correctly what was lacking in his incorrect response.

Students can also be involved in a review process during longer projects, such as designing an experiment, writing a research paper, developing a mathematical model, or creating a Web site, as described in the Peer Feedback Illustration, Figure 14.4 (p. 189).

Ask Students to Self-Assess

Self-assessment is another effective form of peer review. Self-assessment can be as simple as asking students to score themselves on an assignment using rubrics or asking them to summarize their progress on learning goals at the end of a grading period. In combination with rubrics, self-assessment forms can be devised to help students gauge their own progress. The forms do not need to be complex or require a lot of work on the student's part. A simple form might ask students to score themselves using rubrics for processes or

FIGURE 14.4

Peer Feedback Illustration

Mr. Terrell's Build-Your-Own-Web-Site unit gave him the perfect opportunity to involve students in the feedback process. After the lesson on Web site usability, he explained to students how they were going to enact one of the key tenets of usability—the usability test. "We've learned about the importance of making your site easy for people to use and making it pleasing to the eye. As part of the design process, I want you to conduct tests with five users from the class. The feedback you receive from these tests will give you ideas for improving your design."

When Parker's site was almost ready to test, she scheduled five tests with different students at different times. She planned to get feedback from three students on her original design, make adjustments to the site based on their comments, and then test the new design with two more students.

Her plan worked well. Joe, her first test user, happened to have a red-green color deficiency, so he had problems using the navigation bar with purple lettering on top of a green background. Devon made some suggestions about how to make the text on the site more concise and informative. Her third test user, T. J., asked some questions about the purpose of an e-mail form and how it worked.

Using the feedback she received from the first round of usability tests, Parker revised the site before testing it again. To follow up on Joe's problem with her color scheme, she asked him to take another look at her revised site.

New feedback from Joe and the two new testers informed Parker that her color scheme worked and the form was much easier to use, but she still needed to improve the text on the site. Involving students in the feedback process provided Parker with immediate responses to her work and helped her monitor her own progress as she continued working on the Web site.

concepts and perhaps effort. Asking students to give some written response further encourages reflection on their level of skill and knowledge, as well as on how hard they are working toward meeting their learning goals. This type of self-assessment helps students to connect what they are doing in the classroom to their learning goals and, ultimately, to their grades. The Student Self-Assessment Illustration, Figure 14.5 (p. 190), describes how students and teachers might use self-assessment in a communications class.

Tools to Facilitate Providing Feedback in the Classroom

Before using our recommendations in your classroom practice, consider a hypothetical situation or problem to check your understanding of the previous discussion. Consider the scenario in Figure 14.6 (p. 191). It will give you an opportunity to apply what you have learned. The other assessment and planning tools that follow will help you guide your students in activities that provide feedback in the classroom.

FIGURE 14.5

Student Self-Assessment Illustration

Mr. Keller thought it was important for students in his theater arts class to assess their basic acting skills. Students chose specific rehearsal days to rate themselves on several factors, including the accuracy of their diction, the degree to which they used effective breathing control, the precision of their body alignment, and the depth of their concentration.

Mr. Keller passed out a self-assessment sheet for each student to use and demonstrated how to use it. The sheet had blank spaces where students could periodically rate themselves using 4-point scales to assess their understanding and skill. The sheet also had spaces where students could write specific comments about their progress. Mr. Keller told students that they should write freely about how well they thought they did after each performance.

Once every two weeks, Mr. Keller collected students' self-assessments and then met with them to give his feedback about their progress. During each conference, the student and Mr. Keller identified areas the student seemed to be doing well in, those that could be improved, and strategies for improvement.

Student: Nadine Fultz	**Rehearsal**	**Skill**
Wed., Nov. 1	A Raisin in the Sun	diction—3 concentration—4

Comments and Analysis: I'm really getting the hang of the language the characters use in the play. My concentration has been really solid and that has helped me improve my accuracy when speaking my lines.

Fri., Nov. 10	A Raisin in the Sun	diction—3 body alignment—2

Comments and Analysis: My diction is hitting the mark, but I could be stronger. I still need to work on the flow of my lines. I'm having a little trouble with my body alignment. I need to pay more attention to the placement and movement of other actors and to my audience.

FIGURE 14.6

Checking My Understanding—Providing Feedback

Mr. Bing and Mr. Kelly each gave their students a major test at the end of their unit on currents and waves. They both included multiple-choice, true-false, and short-answer test items, as well as an essay question.

Mr. Bing clustered the test items according to the type of item. The next day, he had students check each other's papers on the multiple-choice and true-false items so that students knew immediately how many answers were right in those sections of the test. Two weeks later he handed the papers back to students with scores on the short answer and essay questions, and a final point total. He dedicated a class period to discussing some of the common errors and why these errors were made.

Mr. Kelly had clustered the test items according to the type of knowledge that was being assessed. This included students' understanding of ecosystems, students' understanding of types of currents and waves, and students' ability to calculate length, height, and frequencies of waves. Four days after the test, he handed the tests back to students with a score for each cluster of items. The score was based on rubrics that had been given to students at the beginning of the unit. On the day that he handed back the papers, he reminded students to refer to the rubrics.

1. Identify the strengths and weaknesses of these two approaches to providing feedback. Try to refer to what research suggests about the potential for feedback to influences students' learning.

2. How could these teachers use peer and self-assessment to facilitate providing feedback in the classroom?

Assessing the Impact on Students

Rubrics are one tool you can use to gauge students' progress. Sample rubrics are given in Figures 14.7 and 14.8 (p. 193) for evaluating students' progress in understanding information and performing skills or processes. These rubrics can be revised, when appropriate, for students to use as part of the self-assessment process to help them reflect on their work.

Planning Classroom Activities and Assessing Myself

Answering a series of questions will help you discover how you might use the strategies for providing feedback presented in this module. You can use the worksheet in Figure 14.9 (p. 194) to guide your thinking when planning for providing feedback in the classroom

Rubrics help assess student learning. You can assess yourself too—how effectively you give feedback to your students. Use Figure 14.10 (p. 195) to evaluate your effectiveness regarding providing feedback to students in your classroom.

FIGURE 14.7

Rubrics for Generic Information

Rubric for Information

4   The student has a complete and detailed understanding of the information important to the topic.

3   The student has a complete understanding of the information important to the topic.

2   The student has an incomplete understanding of the topic or misconceptions about some of the information.

1   The student's understanding of the topic is incomplete, or he has so many misconceptions that he cannot be said to understand the topic.

0   Not enough information to make a judgment.

Rubric for Information for Younger Students

4   The student understands the important information completely. The student knows details about the information.

3   The student understands the important information.

2   The student does not completely understand the important information, or the student's thinking shows some mistakes about the information.

1   The student does not understand the important information. The student's thinking shows big mistakes about the information.

0   The student does not try to do the task.

FIGURE 14.8

Rubrics for Generic Procedures

Rubric for Processes and Skills

4   The student performs the skill or process accurately and with fluency. The student understands the key features of the skill or process.

3   The student performs the skill or process accurately but not automatically.

2   The student makes some significant errors when performing the skill or process but can do the basic steps.

1   The student makes so many errors when performing the skill or process that he cannot actually do the skill.

0   Not enough information to make a judgment.

Rubric for Processes and Skills for Younger Students

4   The student does the skill correctly and easily. The student understands the important parts of the skill.

3   The student does the skill correctly but not easily.

2   The student makes some big mistakes when he does the skill, but the student can still do the basic steps in the skill.

1   The student make so many big mistakes that he cannot do the skill.

0   The student does not try to do the skill.

FIGURE 14.9

Planning for Providing Feedback Worksheet

What knowledge will students be learning?

What will I do to ensure that students understand the rubrics?

What will I do to ensure that I provide feedback in a timely manner?

How will I engage students in the feedback process?

How will I monitor the impact of feedback on student learning?

What will I do to help students who are not responding well to feedback?

FIGURE 14.10

Assessing Myself—Providing Feedback

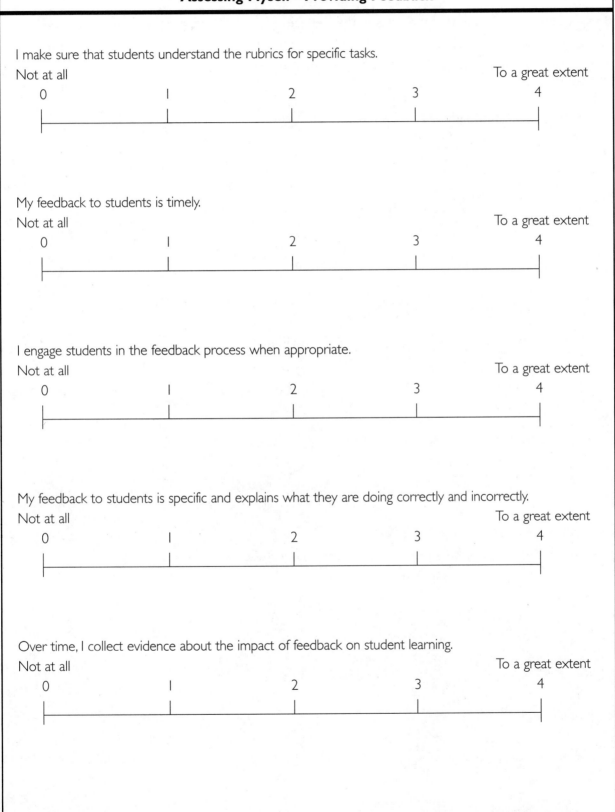

I make sure that students understand the rubrics for specific tasks.

Not at all   To a great extent

0   1   2   3   4

My feedback to students is timely.

Not at all   To a great extent

0   1   2   3   4

I engage students in the feedback process when appropriate.

Not at all   To a great extent

0   1   2   3   4

My feedback to students is specific and explains what they are doing correctly and incorrectly.

Not at all   To a great extent

0   1   2   3   4

Over time, I collect evidence about the impact of feedback on student learning.

Not at all   To a great extent

0   1   2   3   4

Module Reflection

Review your responses to the questions in the Reflecting on My Current Beliefs and Practices—Providing Feedback worksheet, Figure 14.1 (p. 186). How has this module affected your thinking about teaching and learning? Use the space provided to record your thoughts.

- Reading this information affirms some of what I already knew about providing feedback

- Now, I better understand some things about providing feedback

- I think I will change how I provide feedback to my students

8

GENERATING AND TESTING HYPOTHESES

Study Group Tip

If you are using this handbook in a study group, your group might want to read and discuss the research summary about generating and testing hypotheses in the companion book, *Classroom Instruction That Works.*

When students generate and test hypotheses, they are applying knowledge. The student who observes that a metal toy boat floats in water when a lighter piece of metal sinks, can apply his knowledge to hypothesize that the surface area of an object affects buoyancy. Next, he experiments with objects of various sizes, shapes, and weights to test his conjectures.

As with many thinking and reasoning skills, students generate and test hypotheses all the time. If I do this, what might happen? If that thing acts in this way, what might happen? Research shows that we generate and test hypotheses inductively or deductively. Inductive approaches require students first to discover the principles and then to generate hypotheses. Using the example of buoyancy, a teacher using an *inductive* approach would ask students to discover principles about buoyancy and then generate hypotheses based on these discovered principles. However, a teacher using a *deductive* approach would present students with a principle of buoyancy, such as the Archimedes Principle. With this knowledge as a basis, students would then generate and test hypotheses based on this principle.

Although we usually think of generating and testing hypotheses about the physical world, such as what allows a heavy ship to float, this process can be applied to psychological phenomena. For example, based on how people relate to specific types of visual stimuli, someone might generate and test a hypothesis about the effects of a specific type of advertisement.

Research shows that asking students to explain their hypotheses and conclusions enhances their learning. In this section we address six different types of tasks you can use with students to engage them in generating and testing hypotheses: systems analysis, problem solving, decision making, historical investigation, experimental inquiry, and invention. In the following modules, we discuss strategies that can help students understand how to apply the steps for each process.

List of Figures

SYSTEMS ANALYSIS

Across the disciplines, students study systems: computer network systems, the highway system, ecosystems, government systems, weather systems. One way to enhance and exercise students' understanding of these systems is to ask them to generate hypotheses that predict what might happen if an aspect of a system changes.

In some systems, such as a linear equation, the functional relationship is clearly defined; that is, as one part changes, another part changes a specific quantity, a specific direction, a specific period of time. In many systems, the functional relationship is not so clear and exactly how one part affects another is more complicated:

- If you add 3 parts of memory to a computer network system, does the productivity of that system increase by 3, or by some other factor?
- If we time the stoplights down 14th Avenue so that a car driving the speed limit doesn't have to stop for more than two miles, how does that affect traffic on the parallel 13th Avenue? How does that affect traffic on the streets that cross 14th Avenue?
- If the CEO of a company provides more information to all of her employees, does that always make the company run more smoothly?

Determining at what point the flow of resources, information, or energy begins to diminish the functioning of a system is complex, but these considerations help students push their understanding to new levels.

Before reading "Recommendations for Classroom Practice," take some time to reflect on your current practices and beliefs about systems analysis by completing the worksheet in Figure 15.1 (p. 200). This will give you a basis for comparison as you read about the strategies in the module.

Recommendations for Classroom Practice

Systems analysis is a complex process that students will need to learn about and practice. In this module, we discuss several approaches to use in the classroom:

- giving students a model for the process,
- using familiar content to teach students the steps for systems analysis,
- giving students graphic organizers for systems analysis,
- giving students guidance as needed, and
- asking students to explain their hypotheses and conclusions.

Give Students a Model for the Process

Systems analysis is a complicated reasoning process because in a system, all parts affect each other. When you think about how one

---

FIGURE 15.1

Reflecting on My Current Beliefs and Practices—Systems Analysis

---

What does it mean to do a systems analysis?

What is the purpose of asking students to do a systems analysis?

What kinds of activities do I use with my students to help them analyze systems?

What questions do I have about systems analysis?

FIGURE 15.2

Model for Systems Analysis

Steps in the Process of Systems Analysis

1. Explain the purpose of the system, the parts of the system, and the function of each part.
2. Describe how the parts affect one another.
3. Identify a part of the system, describe a change in that part, and then hypothesize what might happen as a result of this change.
4. When possible, test your hypothesis by actually changing the part or by using a simulation to change the part. Or, "test" your hypothesis by considering and describing the effects of the change on the system.

Steps in the Process of Systems Analysis for Younger Students

1. What are the parts of the system? How does each part work?
2. How do the parts affect one another?
3. Pick a part of the system. What might happen if that part did something differently?

4. Change the part to test your hypothesis. If you cannot change the part, use a pretend setup and act out the change to test your hypothesis. Or, think through and explain what might happen if you make the change.

---

part works, you also have to consider the 2 or 12 or 20 or 50 other things that the part affects. Identifying the parts of a system and describing how those parts affect one another can be a complicated endeavor. Imagine if we were discussing a quadratic equation, or a transportation system, or a computer network system, or a business. One part affects another part, which affects another part, and so on. To facilitate systems analysis activities with academic content, you can give students a model for the process. The model can be a set of steps for students to follow, as shown in Figure 15.2.

Use Familiar Content to Teach Steps for Systems Analysis

Students are familiar with many systems, but they might not be used to thinking about the parts and their interactions as systems. You might start with familiar, everyday examples of

systems that are easy to describe, such as an aquarium, a terrarium, a chemical reaction that takes place in a beaker, or a soccer match. It's easier to identify the parts of a contained system, such as an aquarium or a chemical reaction in a beaker, than it is in an open system, such as a school district or an ecosystem. Also, because the system is contained, interactions among the parts are likely fewer than in a larger, more open system, such as a weather system or a community. Thus, students will have an easier time if they initially work with familiar, contained systems.

Give Students Graphic Organizers for Systems Analysis

Graphic organizers are tools students can use as a visual guide to the systems analysis process. Figure 15.3 (p. 202) is one example of a graphic organizer.

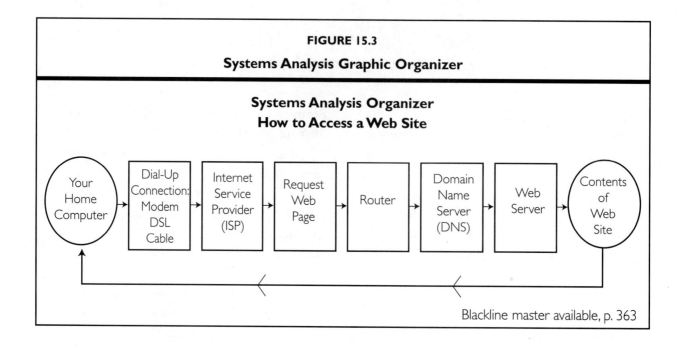

FIGURE 15.3

Systems Analysis Graphic Organizer

Systems Analysis Organizer
How to Access a Web Site

Blackline master available, p. 363

Give Students Guidance As Needed

When students are first learning to analyze systems, you might structure the activity by defining the system, its purpose, and parts. At first, you might also guide students as they explain how the parts affect one another and generate hypotheses. This structured systems analysis activity might be appropriate for students in many situations. For example, if you want students to think about certain parts of their community as a system, you might define those parts, thereby limiting the scope of the activity to the specific area of study.

After students have had some practice completing more structured systems analysis activities, you can ask them to do more of the work. In a less structured activity, students are responsible for defining the system's parts and purpose, as well as explaining the interactions, generating a hypothesis, and testing it.

Ask Students to Explain Hypotheses and Conclusions

Explaining their thinking helps students enhance their understanding of the systems analysis process and the steps involved. You can use several methods to help students explain their hypotheses and conclusions:

- Give students a results template (Figure 15.4, p. 203) that asks them to explain their work and what they learned from their experience.
- Use sentence stems to prompt students' thinking about the process: I think if I change_____ _____,then_____ _____ will happen.
- Let students use audiotapes to record their thinking as they go through the steps in the systems analysis process and to describe what they learned.

FIGURE 15.4

Results Template—Systems Analysis

My hypothesis about what will happen

I think this will happen because

After I completed the systems analysis, I found

As a result of doing this task, I learned

Tools to Facilitate Systems Analysis in the Classroom

Before using our recommendations in your classroom practice, consider a hypothetical situation or problem to check your understanding of the previous discussion by completing the exercise in Figure 15.5 (p. 204). It will give you an opportunity to apply what you have learned. The other assessment and planning tools that follow will help you guide your students in the process of analyzing systems in the classroom.

Assessing the Impact on Students

Rubrics are one tool you can use to gauge students' progress. Sample rubrics are provided in Figure 15.6 (p. 205) for evaluating students' progress in using the process of systems analysis.

These rubrics can be revised, when appropriate, for students to use as part of the self-assessment process to help them reflect on their work.

Planning Classroom Activities and Assessing Myself

Answering a series of questions will help you discover how you might use the strategies for analyzing systems presented in this module. You can use the Planning for Systems Analysis Worksheet, Figure 15.7 (p. 206), to guide your thinking when planning for asking students to use systems analysis.

Rubrics help assess student learning. You can assess yourself too—how effectively you use strategies to guide systems analysis in your classroom. Use Figure 15.8 (p. 207) to evaluate your use of systems analysis.

FIGURE 15.5

Checking My Understanding—Systems Analysis

Think about your classroom as a system. Define the system: the parts, the function of each part, and the purpose.

Write a paragraph that explains how the parts affect one another. For example, you might think about how your students interact, how you affect your students, and how an interruption affects the classroom system.

Now, imagine a change in the system: Starting next week, a teacher's assistant will be available to work with students in your classroom for half a day each day.

Make a hypothesis about what will happen as a result of this change.

Describe a possible scenario in which you "test" this hypothesis.

FIGURE 15.6

Rubrics for Systems Analysis

Systems Analysis Rubric

4   The student describes the system in great detail and generates and tests a valid hypothesis.

3   The student describes the system and generates and tests a valid hypothesis.

2   The student does not completely describe the system, or the student describes the system in a way that reveals some misconceptions. Or, the student's hypothesis does not fit the situation.

1   The student does not describe the system accurately and does not generate a valid hypothesis.

0   Not enough information to make a judgment.

Systems Analysis Rubric for Younger Students

4   The student tells what the parts of the system are and how they work. The student uses details when he tells about the system. The student makes a hypothesis and tests it.

3   The student tells what the parts of the system are and how they work. The student makes a hypothesis and tests it.

2   The student tells what some of the parts of the system are, but the student makes some mistakes when he tells how they work. Or, the student's hypothesis does not fit the situation.

1   The student tells what some of the parts of the system are. The student makes big mistakes when he tells how they work. The student's hypothesis does not fit the situation.

0   The student does not try to do the systems analysis.

FIGURE 15.7

Planning for Systems Analysis Worksheet

What knowledge will students be learning?

Do I need to set aside time to teach students the process of systems analysis? How will I teach them the process?

Will I ask students to use a graphic organizer?

How much guidance will I provide students?

How will students explain their hypothesis and communicate their conclusions?

How will I monitor how well students are doing with systems analysis?

What will I do to help students who are not using systems analysis effectively?

FIGURE 15.8

Assessing Myself—Systems Analysis

I clearly communicate the knowledge students will use for the systems analysis activity.

Not at all   To a great extent

0   1   2   3   4

I make sure students know how to use the process of systems analysis.

Not at all   To a great extent

0   1   2   3   4

I make sure students understand the graphic organizers for systems analysis.

Not at all   To a great extent

0   1   2   3   4

I give students an appropriate amount of guidance for the activity.

Not at all   To a great extent

0   1   2   3   4

Over time, I collect evidence about my students' proficiency at using systems analysis.

Not at all   To a great extent

0   1   2   3   4

Module Reflection

Review your responses to the questions in the Reflecting on My Current Beliefs and Practices—Systems Analysis worksheet, Figure 15.1 (p. 200). How has this module affected your thinking about teaching and learning? Use the space provided to record your thoughts.

- Reading this information affirms some of what I already knew about systems analysis

- Now, I better understand some things about systems analysis

- I think I will change how I use systems analysis in my classroom

PROBLEM SOLVING

Students encounter structured problems all the time—in textbooks, worksheets, and homework. These structured problems have clear-cut goals, and the available resources are specified. Like a puzzle, these problems typically have one correct answer—if you put all the pieces together in the correct way, you get the right picture. In this module, we discuss strategies for *unstructured problems*—problems that do not have clearly defined goals or constraints and that usually have more than one solution, the kind of messy problems that we face in everyday life.

Before reading "Recommendations for Classroom Practice," take some time to reflect on your current practices and beliefs about problem solving by completing the worksheet in Figure 16.1 (p. 210). This will give you a basis for comparison as you read about the strategies in the module.

Recommendations for Classroom Practice

Problem solving is a complex process that students will need to learn about and practice. In this module, we discuss several approaches to use in the classroom:

- giving students a model for the process,
- using familiar content to teach students the steps for problem solving,

- giving students graphic organizers for problem solving,
- giving students guidance as needed, and
- asking students to explain their hypotheses and conclusions.

Give Students a Model for the Process

By definition, problems involve obstacles and constraints. While solving problems, students must generate and test hypotheses related to the various solutions they predict might work. For example, a teacher might present students with a task that requires them to build a model car or a bridge under the constraint that they may use limited or specific materials only, such as balsa wood, a rubber band, or a mouse trap. Using their understanding of concepts related to the problem, such as *inertia*, *gravity*, *energy*, *force*, and *motion*, they must consider several different approaches to a solution and then generate and test their hypotheses about those solutions. To facilitate problem-solving activities with academic content, you can give students a model for the process as shown in Figure 16.2 (p. 211).

Problem solving is about finding the *best* solution, not just any solution. If mice invade my apartment, and I want to be rid of them, I can move. That's definitely one solution, but perhaps not the *best* one. Two of the steps in

FIGURE 16.1

Reflecting on My Current Beliefs and Practices—Problem Solving

What is the purpose of asking students to solve problems?

What kinds of problem-solving activities do I use with my students?

What questions do I have about problem solving?

FIGURE 16.2

Model for Problem Solving

Steps for Problem Solving

1. Identify the goal you are trying to accomplish.

2. Describe the barriers or constraints that are preventing you from achieving your goal—that are creating the problem.

3. Identify different solutions for overcoming the barriers or constraints and hypothesize which solution is likely to be the most effective.

4. Try your solution—either in reality or through a simulation.

5. Explain whether your hypothesis was correct. Determine if you want to test another hypothesis using a different solution.

Steps for Problem Solving for Younger Students

1. What am I trying to do?

2. What things are in my way?

3. What are some things I can do to get around these things?

4. Which solution seems to be the best?

5. Did this solution work? Should I try another solution?

---

the problem-solving process emphasize finding the best solution. Step 3 in the model (Figure 16.2) involves identifying different solutions for overcoming the barriers or constraints and hypothesizing which solution is likely to be *the most effective*. This step requires the problem solver to consider the merits of solutions she has generated. The last step also reinforces the idea of finding the best possible solution. In this step, the problem solver determines whether the hypothesis was correct and if she wants to test another hypothesis using a different solution. A failed solution also sends her back to revisit the first steps in problem solving: perhaps to rethinking a goal, reevaluating constraints, or trying another solution.

Use Familiar Content to Teach Students the Steps for Problem Solving

In their daily lives, students frequently encounter messy problems that require them to define goals, identify constraints, and consider possible solutions. You can use these common situations to introduce and guide students through the steps of problem solving. How many students have missed the bus after their parents left for work? What's the goal—getting to school on time, or taking a day off and making sure their parents don't find out? If the goal is to get to school, what are the possible constraints—no driver's license, no car, no friends with a car, too far to walk? How can the obstacles be overcome—ask a neighbor for a ride, call a cab, ride brother's a bike? Students can hypothesize possible outcomes for each of these solutions. Applying a set of steps to problems like this one helps students understand problem solving as a systematic process.

Give Students Graphic Organizers for Problem Solving

Students can use graphic organizers like the one in Figure 16.3 as a visual tool to help them understand and use the process of problem solving.

Guide Students As Needed

When students are first learning to solve problems, you might clearly identify the desire goal and the constraints or limiting conditions. At first, you might also help students analyze how the constraints or limiting conditions affect the situation and collaborate with students to generate possible solutions. When students first begin problem solving, they might also need help identifying available resources and information.

After students have had some practice with problem solving, you might give them more

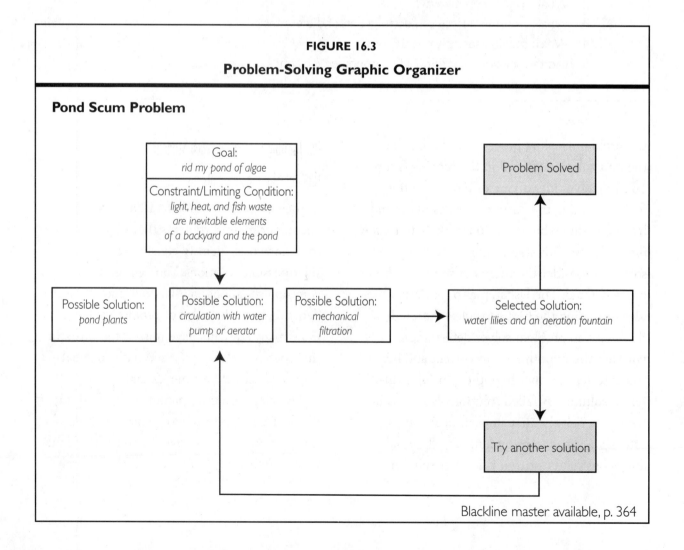

FIGURE 16.3

Problem-Solving Graphic Organizer

Pond Scum Problem

Goal: *rid my pond of algae*

Constraint/Limiting Condition: *light, heat, and fish waste are inevitable elements of a backyard and the pond*

Possible Solution: *pond plants*

Possible Solution: *circulation with water pump or aerator*

Possible Solution: *mechanical filtration*

Selected Solution: *water lilies and an aeration fountain*

Problem Solved

Try another solution

Blackline master available, p. 364

FIGURE 16.4

Results Template—Problem Solving

My hypothesis about the best solution

I think this idea will work because

After I completed the problem-solving process, I found

As a result of doing this task, I learned

---

freedom. You might suggest a problem to students and allow them to carry out all the steps from clarifying the goal to evaluating the solution they tried. You might check in with students after each step, or allow them to come to you for assistance when they need it.

Ask Students to Explain Their Hypotheses and Conclusions

Explaining their thinking helps students to enhance their understanding of the process they are using and their use of the steps involved. You can use several methods to help students explain their hypotheses and conclusions:

- Give students a results template, Figure 16.4, that asks them to explain their work and what they learned.

- Use sentence stems to prompt students' thinking about the problem-solving process:
  I think if I try _____,
  then _____ will
  happen.
- Let students use audiotapes to record their thinking as they go through the steps in the problem-solving process and to describe what they learned.

Tools to Facilitate Problem Solving in the Classroom

Before using our recommendations in your classroom practice, consider a hypothetical situation or problem to check your understanding of the previous discussion by completing the exercise in Figure 16.5 (p. 214). It will give you

FIGURE 16.5

Checking My Understanding—Problem Solving

Imagine you are a high school student, and your teacher gives you the following task.

Charlotte Brontë wants her 19th century female protagonists to live in a way that goes beyond the traditional themes and social customs that seem to control their fictional destinies. But she also wants her new novel, *Jane Eyre*, to sell. Quite a dilemma. But Ms. Brontë has an idea—she'll solicit ideas from her readers.

First, you must determine what the limiting conditions that you, as a female writer of 19th century fiction with a female protagonist, will face. Next, think of different ways of scripting Jane Eyre's life in a way that allows the character to break from tradition yet does not offend readers so much that the book will not sell. From your ideas, select two or three solutions that, given the chance, you would have shared with Ms. Brontë. Hypothesize what might have happened—to Brontë, to book sales, to those who read the book—if she used your suggestions.

What knowledge would you need to be able to complete this task?

What challenges and issues do you think you would have to confront as you worked? How would you overcome these challenges?

If you had been given the opportunity to practice using the steps of the problem-solving process presented in Figure 16.2, p. 211, to what extent would that have helped you generate the hypotheses required for this task?

an opportunity to apply what you have learned. The other assessment and planning tools that follow will help you guide your students in the process of solving problems in the classroom.

Assessing the Impact on Students

Rubrics are one tool you can use to gauge students' progress. Sample rubrics are provided below in Figure 16.6 for evaluating students' progress in using the process of problem solving. These rubrics can be revised, when appropriate, for students to use as part of the self-assessment process to help them reflect on their work.

Planning Classroom Activities and Assessing Myself

Answering a series of questions will help you discover how you might use the strategies for solving problems presented in this module. You can use the Planning for Problem Solving Worksheet, Figure 16.7 (p. 216), to guide your thinking when planning for asking students to use problem solving.

Rubrics help assess student learning. You can assess yourself too—how effectively you use strategies to guide problem solving in your classroom. Use Figure 16.8 (p. 217) to evaluate your use of problem solving.

FIGURE 16.6

Rubrics for Problem Solving

Problem-Solving Rubric

4   The student selects the solution that is the most effective for overcoming the obstacle or constraint and accurately explains why it is the most effective of the possible solutions.

3   The student selects the solution that is the most effective for overcoming the obstacle or constraint but does not explain why it is the most effective of the possible solutions.

2   The student selects a solution that overcomes the obstacle or constraint, but it is not the most effective solution given the options.

1   The student selects a solution that does not overcome the obstacle or constraint.

0   Not enough information to make a judgment.

Problem-Solving Rubric for Younger Students

4   The student picks a solution that is the best one for getting around the things that are in the way. The student tells why it is the best solution.

3   The student picks a solution that is the best for getting around the things that are in the way, but the student does not tell why it is the best solution.

2   The student picks a solution that gets around the things that are in the way, but the solution is not the best one.

1   The student picks a solution that does not get around the things that are in the way.

0   The student does not try to do the task.

FIGURE 16.7

Planning for Problem Solving Worksheet

What knowledge will students be learning?

Do I need to set aside time to teach students the process of problem solving? How will I teach them the process?

Will I ask students to use a graphic organizer?

How much guidance will I provide students?

How will students explain their hypothesis and communicate their conclusions?

How will I monitor how well students are doing with problem solving?

What will I do to help students who are not using problem solving effectively?

FIGURE 16.8
Assessing Myself—Problem Solving

I clearly communicate the knowledge students will use for the problem solving activity.

Not at all   To a great extent

| 0 | 1 | 2 | 3 | 4 |

I make sure students know how to use the process of problem solving.

Not at all   To a great extent

| 0 | 1 | 2 | 3 | 4 |

I make sure students understand the graphic organizers for problem solving.

Not at all   To a great extent

| 0 | 1 | 2 | 3 | 4 |

I give students an appropriate amount of guidance for the activity.

Not at all   To a great extent

| 0 | 1 | 2 | 3 | 4 |

Over time, I collect evidence about my students' proficiency at using problem solving.

Not at all   To a great extent

| 0 | 1 | 2 | 3 | 4 |

Module Reflection

Review your responses to the questions in the Reflecting on My Current Beliefs and Practices—Problem Solving worksheet, Figure 16.1 (p. 210). How has this module affected your thinking about teaching and learning? Use the space provided to record your thoughts.

- Reading this information affirms some of what I already knew about problem solving

- Now, I better understand some things about problem solving

- I think I will change how I use problem solving in my classroom

DECISION MAKING

Generating and testing hypotheses may not seem connected to making a decision. However, making a decision generally entails making a prediction and weighing that prediction against other possible alternatives. For example, when choosing the best or worst representative of a specific category, such as the worst movie of the 1990s, students will likely make a prediction and weigh the merits of that prediction against other possible alternatives. They might consider several movies on the basis of such attributes as the quality of the dialogue, the camera work, and how good or bad the actors are.

Before reading "Recommendations for Classroom Practice," take some time to reflect on your current practices and beliefs about decision making by completing the worksheet in Figure 17.1 (p. 220). This will give you a basis for comparison as you read about the strategies in the module.

Recommendations for Classroom Practice

Decision making is a complex process that students will need to learn about and practice. In this module, we discuss several approaches to use in the classroom:

- giving students a model for the process,
- using familiar content to teach students the steps for decision making,

- giving students graphic organizers for decision making,
- giving students guidance as needed, and
- asking students to explain their hypotheses and conclusions.

Give Students a Model for the Process

Students can examine hypothetical situations using a structured decision-making process that requires them to use their understanding of alternatives and potential criteria to predict what decision will or should be made. Students can follow steps, such as those shown in Figure 17.2 (p. 221), in a process for making decisions.

Students must understand the concept of *criteria* to use this decision-making process. Criteria differ somewhat from characteristics. Characteristics are neutral; criteria are value laden. We use characteristics to compare cars, or plays, or presidential candidates' stances on the issues. We use criteria to choose a car to buy, to decide which play to see, or to decide which candidate to vote for. When comparing cars, we might use characteristics such as price, color, engine size, type of transmission, number of doors, and drive wheels. If we are choosing a car to buy, we restate the characteristics as criteria: under $30,000, silver, eight-cylinder, manual transmission, four doors, and four-wheel drive. Criteria reflect preferences and values.

FIGURE 17.1

Reflecting on My Current Beliefs and Practices—Decision Making

What is the purpose of asking students to make decisions?

What kinds of decision-making activities do I use with my students?

What questions do I have about decision making?

FIGURE 17.2

Model for Decision Making

Steps in the Process of Decision Making

1. Describe the decision you are making and the alternatives you are considering.
2. Identify the criteria that will influence the selection, and indicate the relative importance of the criteria by assigning an importance score from a designated scale (e.g., 1–4).
3. Rate each alternative on a designated scale (e.g., 1–4) to indicate the extent to which each alternative meets each criterion.
4. For each alternative, multiply the importance score and the rating and then add the products to assign a score for the alternative.
5. Examine the scores to determine the alternative with the highest score.
6. Based on your reaction to the selected alternative, determine if you need to change any importance scores or add or drop criteria.

Steps in the Process of Decision Making for Younger Students

1. What am I trying to decide?
2. What are my choices?
3. What are important criteria for making this decision?
4. How important is each criterion?
5. How well does each of my choices match my criteria?
6. Which choice best matches with criteria?
7. How do I feel about the decision? Do I need to change any criteria and try again?

Use Familiar Content to Teach Students the Steps for Decision Making

As with many thinking and reasoning skills, students use decision making all the time. What they don't do all the time is use a rigorous and systematic process for making decisions like the one just described. In order to help them learn this process, you can use common, everyday decision-making situations to introduce the steps.

For example, many high school students will face the decision of choosing a college to attend. Walking students through an example of choosing a college can help them understand the steps in decision making. Students will need to consider possible alternatives, and determine criteria for making the decision. For some students, one criterion might be "close to home," while for others, a criterion might be "far from home." Other criteria might include low cost, a good environmental engineering program, solid academic reputation of the institution, a good football team, or a conservative campus culture. As students complete each step of the decision-making process, they will begin to see that alternatives and criteria vary for different people. Further, the importance of

FIGURE 17.3

Graphic Organizer—Decision Making

Best Citizen

Which character would best fulfill the personal and civic responsibilities of a good citizen?

Criteria	Alternatives					
	Henry Fleming *Red Badge of Courage*		Scout Finch *To Kill a Mockingbird*		Holden Caulfield *Catcher in the Rye*	
individual responsibility	2 × 2	4	2 × 3	6	2 × 1	2
adheres to moral principle	3 × 1	3	3 × 4	12	3 × 4	12
respects rights of others	4 × 2	8	4 × 2	8	4 × 1	4
honest	3 × 1	3	3 × 2	6	3 × 3	9
respects the law	4 × 1	4	4 × 1	4	4 × 2	8
TOTAL		22		36		35

Blackline master available, p. 365

each criterion will vary according to a student's values and preferences. Therefore, an important consideration for students might be explaining the rationale for their choices. Working through real-world examples such as this one helps students become familiar with the key concepts and steps of decision making.

Give Students Graphic Organizers for Decision Making

Students can use graphic organizers like the one in Figure 17.3 as a visual tool to help them understand and use the process of decision making.

Guide Students As Needed

When students are first learning to use the decision-making process, you might clearly identify the alternatives and the criteria for making the decision. At first, you might also walk students through the process of assigning values to each criterion and determining the extent to which each alternative meets each criterion. Remember, the multiplication required in Step 4 of the process (see Figure 17.2) might be tricky for younger students. For younger students, each criterion might be limited to a value of one so students will not have to deal with multiplication at all. They can simply add up the scores for each alternative.

After students have had some practice with the decision-making process, you might give them more freedom in decision-making tasks. You might suggest a decision to students but allow them to identify alternatives and criteria as a class. Or, you might assign the decision and alternatives and allow students to choose their own criteria. Gauge your students' abilities with the process of decision making and give them as much support or freedom as they need to execute the process successfully.

Ask Students to Explain Their Hypotheses and Conclusions

Explaining their thinking helps students to enhance their understanding of the decision-making process and their use of the steps involved. You can use several methods to help students explain their hypotheses and conclusions:

- Give students a results template, Figure 17.4, that asks them to explain their work and what they learned.
- Use sentence stems to prompt students' thinking about the decision-making process: I think if I change criterion from_____ to _____, then_____ will happen.
- Let students use audiotapes to record their thinking as they go through the steps in the decision-making process and to describe what they learned.

FIGURE 17.4

Results Template—Decision Making

My hypothesis about the best alternative:

I think this idea will work because

After I completed the decision-making process, I found

As a result of doing this task, I learned

Tools to Facilitate Decision Making in the Classroom

Before using our recommendations in your classroom practice, consider a hypothetical situation or problem to check your understanding of the previous discussion by completing the exercise in Figure 17.5 (p. 225). It will give you an opportunity to apply what you have learned. The other assessment and planning tools that follow will help you guide your students in the process of making decisions in the classroom.

Assessing the Impact on Students

Rubrics are one tool you can use to gauge students' progress. Sample rubrics are provided in Figure 17.6 (p. 226) for evaluating students' progress in using the process of decision making. These rubrics can be revised, when appropriate, for students to use as part of the self-assessment process to help them reflect on their work.

Planning Classroom Activities and Assessing Myself

Answering a series of questions will help you discover how you might use the strategies for making decisions presented in this module. You can use the Planning for Decision Making Worksheet, Figure 17.7 (p. 227), to guide your thinking when planning for asking students to use decision making.

Rubrics help assess student learning. You can assess yourself too—how effectively you use strategies to guide decision making in your classroom. Use Figure 17.8 (p. 228) to evaluate your use of decision making.

FIGURE 17.5

Checking My Understanding—Decision Making

What is the most important communication mechanism invented? Use the decision-making matrix to get started, and then add your own criteria.

Criteria	Alternatives					
	telephone	e-mail	telegraph	wireless phone	fax	Internet chat
No. of people affected						
Accessibility						
Cost for basic service						

What issues arose as you engaged in this decision-making task?

What insights did you gain about the decision-making process?

What knowledge would students need to do this task?

FIGURE 17.6

Rubrics for Decision Making

Decision-Making Rubric

4 The student uses significant and relevant criteria to select the most appropriate option. The student clearly and concisely explains in detail why the option selected is the most appropriate.

3 The student uses relevant criteria to select the most appropriate option and explains why the option selected is the most appropriate.

2 The student uses criteria that are related to the situation but not the most relevant, or selects an option that is not the most appropriate, given the criteria.

1 The student uses criteria that are unrelated to the situation.

0 Not enough information to make a judgment.

Decision-Making Rubric for Younger Students

4 The student uses important criteria to select the best option. The student clearly explains why the option selected is the best. The student uses details in the explanation.

3 The student uses criteria to select the best option. The student explains why the option selected is the best.

2 The student uses criteria that are related to the situation but not the most important. Or, the student picks an option that is not the best for the criteria.

1 The student uses criteria that are not related to the situation.

0 The student does not try to do the task.

FIGURE 17.7

Planning for Decision Making Worksheet

What knowledge will students be learning?

Do I need to set aside time to teach students the process of decision making? How will I teach them the process?

Will I ask students to use a graphic organizer?

How much guidance will I provide students?

How will students explain their hypothesis and communicate their conclusions?

How will I monitor how well students are doing with decision making?

What will I do to help students who are not using decision making effectively?

FIGURE 17.8

Assessing Myself—Decision Making

I clearly communicate the knowledge students will use for the decision-making activity.

Not at all   To a great extent

| 0 | 1 | 2 | 3 | 4 |

I make sure students know how to use the process of decision making.

Not at all   To a great extent

| 0 | 1 | 2 | 3 | 4 |

I make sure students understand the graphic organizers for decision making.

Not at all   To a great extent

| 0 | 1 | 2 | 3 | 4 |

I give students an appropriate amount of guidance for the activity.

Not at all   To a great extent

| 0 | 1 | 2 | 3 | 4 |

Over time, I collect evidence about my students' proficiency at using decision making.

Not at all   To a great extent

| 0 | 1 | 2 | 3 | 4 |

Module Reflection

Review your responses to the questions in the Reflecting on My Current Beliefs and Practices—Desicion Making worksheet, Figure 17.1 (p. 220). How has this module affected your thinking about teaching and learning? Use the space provided to record your thoughts.

● Reading this information affirms some of what I already knew about decision making

● Now, I better understand some things about decision making

● I think I will change the way I use decision making in my classroom

HISTORICAL INVESTIGATION

Students engage in historical investigation when they construct and investigate a plausible scenario for an event from the past about which there is no general agreement. For example, there are conflicting versions of Roosevelt's role in events that led up to the bombing of Pearl Harbor. To engage in historical investigation, a student would have to understand the circumstances surrounding the bombing of Pearl Harbor, generate a hypothesis about Roosevelt's role in that event, and collect evidence that supports or refutes this hypothesis.

Historical investigation is not something that students do because *they* are confused about an event. Rather, the investigation grows out of confusions or contradictions found in information available about the topic. Students will not find quick answers to historical investigations. They can't just go to a book or a Web site and look up the answer. When students work on a historical investigation, they must use available resources to *construct* a resolution to the confusions.

Before reading "Recommendations for Classroom Practice," take some time to reflect on your current practices and beliefs about historical investigation by completing the worksheet in Figure 18.1 (p. 231). This will give you a basis for comparison as you read about the strategies in the module.

Recommendations for Classroom Practice

Historical investigation is a complex process that students will need to learn about and practice. In this module, we discuss several approaches to use in the classroom:

- giving students a model for the process,
- using familiar content to teach students the steps for historical investigation,
- giving students graphic organizers for historical investigation,
- guiding students as needed, and
- asking students to explain their hypotheses and conclusions.

Give Students a Model for the Process

Questions such as "What really happened?" and "Why did this happen?" motivate historical investigations. However, there are no quick and easy answers to these questions. In fact, the process of constructing a resolution can be quite complicated. Students can use a structured process as shown by the steps in Figure 18.2 (p. 232) to guide them through historical investigations. The process emphasizes constructing a hypothetical scenario and finding evidence to support or refute this scenario.

Collecting evidence is probably the most important part of the historical investigation

FIGURE 18.1

Reflecting on My Current Beliefs and Practices—Historical Investigation

What is the purpose of asking students to use historical investigation?

What kind of historical investigation might apply to the content areas I teach?

What questions do I have about historical investigation?

process. You should directly teach this concept to students. They will need to work with a variety of resources to clearly identify what is already agreed upon about the topic and to describe exactly the confusions and contradictions. Students might work with primary sources, interviews, various news sources, and resources that might be obscure or difficult to find. When students first begin historical investigation, they will likely need assistance locating materials as well as determining which materials to look for.

Students might also need instruction about how to interpret specific materials. It is not uncommon for student to confuse evidence with opinion. Other considerations for students interpreting resources include the reliability of source information, the motives and perspectives of authors, the comprehensiveness of arguments and documentation, and credibility and bias.

Use Familiar Content to Teach Students Steps for Historical Investigation

It may not be obvious, but historical investigation is a common occurrence in today's society. To underscore its importance, you might present students with some well-known examples such as the inquiry into the events of the assassination of John F. Kennedy or the inquiry into what actually happened when the *Titanic* sank.

To give students practice in the historical investigation process, you might identify an event in the local newspaper and ask students to generate hypotheses about what occurred. Students could then collect evidence about their hypotheses.

Give Students Graphic Organizers for Historical Investigation

Students can use graphic organizers such as the one in Figure 18.3 (p. 233) as a visual tool to

---

FIGURE 18.2

Model for Historical Investigation

Steps in the Process of Historical Investigation
1. Clearly describe the historical event to be examined.
2. Identify what is known or agreed upon and what is confusing or contradictory.
3. Based on what you understand about the situation, offer a hypothesis.
4. Seek out and analyze evidence to determine if your hypothetical scenario is plausible.

Steps in the Process of Historical Investigation for Younger Students
1. What historical event do I want to explain?
2. What do people already know about this event?
3. What confuses people about this event?
4. What suggestions do I have for clearing up these confusions?
5. How can I explain my suggestions?

FIGURE 18.3

Graphic Organizer—Historical Investigation

George Washington and the Cherry Tree

Concept or Scenario:
Did George Washington chop down the cherry tree?

Known or Agreed Upon:
The story is meant to teach children a lesson.

Confusions or Contradictions:
Other stories exist, too.

Specifics:
- The story about George Washington chopping down a cherry tree was published in a book by Mason Locke Weems in 1809.

- George Washington was a popular figure and many stories were told about him

Specifics:
- There is a story about his mother's favorite colt dying while George was riding it. George told the truth and did not try to hide the fact that he had been riding the colt.

Resolution:
The cherry tree story was probably made up. But the important part of the story is what matters. It is meant to teach us to tell the truth.

Blackline master available, p. 366

help them understand and use the process of historical investigation.

Guide Students As Needed

Historical investigation is a complex process. To execute it effectively, students must gather information, sometimes from primary sources, synthesize material, ask relevant questions, and determine the credibility of sources. A full-blown historical investigation could take several days or even weeks for students to complete. You can adapt historical investigation tasks to meet the needs of your students and the demands of your schedule. Students might work as a group to generate and test hypotheses for an investigation. You might ask the class to generate hypotheses together, then choose and test a hypothesis individually. As discussed earlier, you might also assist students with resource gathering and other research tasks to make the process more efficient and to help students build the necessary skills for this type of task.

For younger students, you might adjust the complexity of historical investigation. As illustrated in the graphic organizer about George Washington and the cherry tree (Figure 18.3, p. 233), younger students might explore cultural and historical confusions about famous people. For example, did George Washington really chop down a cherry tree? What happened to Amelia Earhart? Investigation tasks such as these can help younger students to develop their skills at conducting research and broaden the way they think about history.

Ask Students to Explain Their Hypotheses and Conclusions

Explaining their thinking helps students to enhance their understanding of the historical investigation process and their use of the steps involved. You can use several methods to help students explain their hypotheses and conclusions:

- Give students a results template, Figure 18.4 (p. 235), that asks them to explain their work and what they learned.
- Use sentence stems to prompt students' thinking about the historical investigation process: I think if I had found evidence about _____, then I would have concluded _____.
- Let students use audiotapes to record their thinking as they go through the steps in the historical investigation process and to describe what they learned.

Tools to Facilitate Historical Investigation in the Classroom

Before using our recommendations in your classroom practice, consider a hypothetical situation or problem to check your understanding of the previous discussion by completing the exercise in Figure 18.5 (p. 236). It will give you an opportunity to apply what you have learned. The other assessment and planning tools that follow will help you guide your students in the process of historical investigation in the classroom.

FIGURE 18.4

Results Template—Historical Investigation

My hypothesis about what actually happened:

I think this occurred because

After I gathered evidence, I found

As a result of conducting this historical investigation, I learned

---

FIGURE 18.5

Checking My Understanding—Historical Investigation

Read the following classroom scenario that sets the stage for a historical investigation and then answer the questions that follow.

When teaching her world history students about the Great Depression, Mrs. Belvin took the opportunity to engage her students in an investigation about what caused the Great Depression. The class discussed events leading up to the Depression, and Mrs. Belvin presented some of the commonly held views about the cause, including

- The decline in investment spending. In simple terms, proponents of this theory believe people invested less and saved more, so investment fell short of savings, causing the level of public income to fall. As a result, consumers spent less, so businesses produced less and, in turn, cut workers' pay or laid off workers. As workers made less or lost jobs, they spent even less, and so on, creating a downward spiral of income.

- The high tariff (Smoot-Hawley Tariff) passed during the Hoover administration. A simple summary of this argument is that the United States passed this tax on goods imported from other countries, but, at the same time, the United States was making loans to other countries and trying to export goods. As a result, other countries imposed high taxes on U.S. exports. These countries could not make enough money to buy American products or pay back their loans.

- Poor monetary policy. Some economists believe that the federal government interfered too much with the country's money supply (monetary policy) to keep the price level from falling. Economists who support this argument think the government did not give the economy time to self-correct.

Although Mrs. Belvin did not expect her students to resolve a disagreement that economic historians have debated for years, she thought the investigation would help her students gain an in-depth understanding of the historic issues and economic concepts related to the Great Depression.

Now, what would you do? Imagine you are a student in Mrs. Belvin's class. Looking at the steps of historical investigation, Mrs. Belvin has provided the historical event that you will investigate—cause of the Great Depression. She has also provided the background for disagreements about the historical event. Offer your hypothesis about what caused the Great Depression:

Now, describe your next steps. Would you need to refine your hypothesis? How would you go about that process? Once you are satisfied with your hypothesis, what steps would you take to test it?

-

-

-

Assessing the Impact on Students

Rubrics are one tool you can use to gauge students' progress. Sample rubrics are provided in Figure 18.6 for evaluating students' progress in using the process of historical investigation. These rubrics can be revised, when appropriate, for students to use as part of the self-assessment process to help them reflect on their work and experience.

Planning Classroom Activities and Assessing Myself

Answering a series of questions will help you discover how you might use the strategies for historical investigation presented in this module. You can use the Planning for Historical Investigation Worksheet, Figure 18.7 (p. 238), to guide your thinking when planning for asking students to use historical investigation.

Rubrics help assess student learning. You can assess yourself too—how effectively you use strategies to guide historical investigation in your classroom. Use Figure 18.8 (p. 239) to evaluate your use of historical investigation.

FIGURE 18.6

Rubrics for Historical Investigation

Rubric for Historical Investigation

4 The student thoroughly and accurately identifies what is known about the subject of the investigation and presents a well-articulated and logical resolution to the confusions or contradictions associated with the situation.

3 The student accurately identifies what is known about the subject of the investigation and presents a logical resolution to the confusions or contradictions associated with the situation.

2 The student presents a partial description of what is known about the subject of the investigation and/or only partially addresses the confusions or contradictions.

1 The student's description of what is known about the subject of the investigation is severely flawed.

0 Not enough information to make a judgment.

Rubric for Historical Investigation for Younger Students

4 The student finds out in detail what the student people already know about the historical event. The student gives a complete and logical solution to the confusions.

3 The student finds out what people already know about the historical event. The student gives a logical solution to the confusions.

2 The student finds out part of what people already know about the historical event. Or, the student does not give a complete solution to the confusions.

1 The student makes a lot of mistakes in the description of what people already know about the historical event.

0 The student does not try to do the task.

FIGURE 18.7

Planning for Historical Investigation Worksheet

What knowledge will students be learning?

Do I need to set aside time to teach students the process of historical investigation? How will I teach them the process?

Will I ask students to use a graphic organizer?

How much guidance will I provide students?

How will students explain their hypothesis and communicate their conclusions?

How will I monitor how well students are doing with historical investigation?

What will I do to help students who are not using historical investigation effectively?

FIGURE 18.8

Assessing Myself—Historical Investigation

I clearly communicate the knowledge students will use for the historical investigation activity.

Not at all   To a great extent

0   1   2   3   4

I make sure students know how to use the process of historical investigation.

Not at all   To a great extent

0   1   2   3   4

I make sure students understand the graphic organizers for historical investigation.

Not at all   To a great extent

0   1   2   3   4

I give students an appropriate amount of guidance for the activity.

Not at all   To a great extent

0   1   2   3   4

Over time, I collect evidence about my students' proficiency at using historical investigation.

Not at all   To a great extent

0   1   2   3   4

Module Reflection

Review your responses to the questions in the Reflecting on My Current Beliefs and Practices—Historical Investigation worksheet, Figure 18.1 (p. 231). How has this module affected your thinking about teaching and learning? Use the space provided to record your thoughts.

● Reading this information affirms some of what I already knew about historical investigation

● Now, I better understand some things about historical investigation

● I think I will change the way I use historical investigation in my classroom

EXPERIMENTAL INQUIRY

Many educators associate the process of experimental inquiry with generating and testing hypotheses in science. But we can practice this strategy across the disciplines to help students use knowledge meaningfully. We can use the same process that drives inquiry in science classes to describe observations, generate explanations, make predictions, and test them in humanities classes, liberal arts, or the fine arts.

Before reading "Recommendations for Classroom Practice," take some time to reflect on your current practices and beliefs about experimental inquiry by completing the worksheet in Figure 19.1 (p. 242). This will give you a basis for comparison as you read about the strategies in the module.

Recommendations for Classroom Practice

Experimental inquiry is a complex process that students will need to learn about and practice. In this module, we discuss several approaches to use in the classroom:

- giving students a model for the process,
- using familiar content to teach students the steps for experimental inquiry,
- giving students graphic organizers for experimental inquiry,
- giving students guidance as needed, and

- asking students to explain their hypotheses and conclusions.

Give Students a Model for the Process

Researchers and scientists spend their lifetimes engaging in experimental inquiry. Making careful observations, developing explanations, and designing and carrying out experiments are complex processes, so students will need guidance and opportunities to practice. Although many students have a general understanding of the experimental inquiry process, you might use a set of steps like those in Figure 19.2 (p. 243) to guide them.

Perhaps the most difficult parts of the process are Steps 2 and 3 (refer to Figure 19.2). Step 2 is highly inductive. That is, students must be able to provide a viable explanation for something they have observed. This process requires students to use what they already know and usually results in identifying or generating some rule or principle. Step 3 is more deductive. In this step, students use the rule or principle to make a prediction. Here again, students must use prior knowledge—an understanding of the concepts and principles—to predict what might happen. In this step, students are applying their knowledge to new situations.

FIGURE 19.1

Reflecting on My Current Beliefs and Practices—Experimental Inquiry

What is the purpose of asking students to use experimental inquiry?

What kinds of experimental inquiry activities might apply to the content areas I teach?

What questions do I have about experimental inquiry?

Use Familiar Content to Teach Students the Steps for Experimental Inquiry

Many students have heard the story of how Benjamin Franklin used a kite and a metal key to confirm that lightning is electricity. Students may not have considered how Franklin came to carry out this experiment. In fact, he followed the steps in experimental inquiry: he made observations, generated a hypothesis based on what he knew about electricity, designed a plan to test his hypothesis, and conducted an experiment. Showing students how experiments they have seen or heard about fit the model for experimental inquiry can help them understand the steps in the process.

Give Students Graphic Organizers for Experimental Inquiry

Students can use graphic organizers like the one in Figure 19.3 (p. 244) as visual tools to help them understand and use the process of experimental inquiry.

FIGURE 19.2

Model for Experimental Inquiry

Steps in the Process of Experimental Inquiry
1. Observe something that interests you, and describe what has occurred.
2. Explain what you have observed. What theories or rules could explain what you have observed?
3. Based on your explanation, make a prediction.
4. Set up an experiment or activity to test your prediction.
5. Explain the results of your experiment in light of your explanation. If necessary, revise your explanation or prediction or conduct another experiment.

Steps in the Process of Experimental Inquiry for Younger Students
1. What do I see or notice?
2. How can I explain it?
3. Based on my explanation, what can I predict?
4. How can I test my prediction?
5. What happened? Is it what I predicted? Do I need to try a different explanation?

(Adapted from *Dimensions of Learning*, Marzano et al., 1997)

FIGURE 19.3

Experimental Inquiry Graphic Organizer

Ben Franklin's Kite Experiment

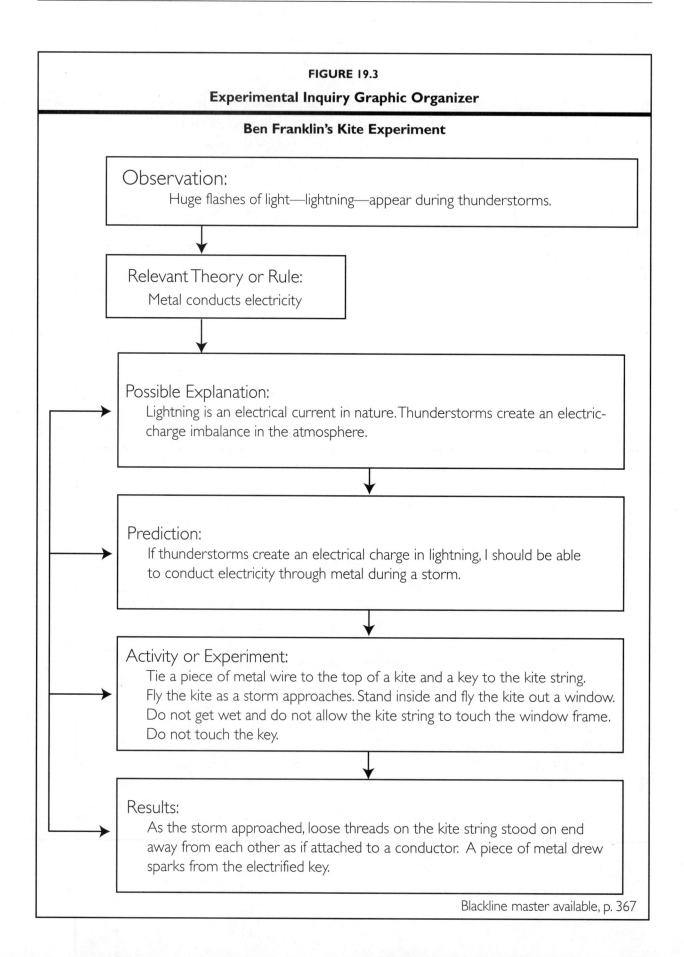

Observation:
> Huge flashes of light—lightning—appear during thunderstorms.

Relevant Theory or Rule:
> Metal conducts electricity

Possible Explanation:
> Lightning is an electrical current in nature. Thunderstorms create an electric-charge imbalance in the atmosphere.

Prediction:
> If thunderstorms create an electrical charge in lightning, I should be able to conduct electricity through metal during a storm.

Activity or Experiment:
> Tie a piece of metal wire to the top of a kite and a key to the kite string. Fly the kite as a storm approaches. Stand inside and fly the kite out a window. Do not get wet and do not allow the kite string to touch the window frame. Do not touch the key.

Results:
> As the storm approached, loose threads on the kite string stood on end away from each other as if attached to a conductor. A piece of metal drew sparks from the electrified key.

Blackline master available, p. 367

Ask Students to Explain Hypotheses and Conclusions

Explaining their thinking helps students to enhance their understanding of the experimental inquiry process and their use of the steps involved. You can use several methods to help students explain their hypotheses and conclusions:

- Give students a results template, Figure 19.4, that asks them to explain their work and what they learned.
- Use sentence stems to prompt students' thinking about the process:
My observations reveal _____ .
I think if I do_____,
then _____ will happen.

- Let students use audiotapes to record their thinking as they go through the steps in the experimental inquiry process and to describe what they learned.

Tools to Facilitate Experimental Inquiry in the Classroom

Before using our recommendations in your classroom practice, consider a hypothetical situation or problem to check your understanding of the previous discussion by completing the exercise in Figure 19.5 (p. 246). It will give you an opportunity to apply what you have learned. The other assessment and planning tools that follow will help you guide your

---

FIGURE 19.4

Results Template—Experimental Inquiry

My hypothesis about what would happen is

I think this will occur because

After I tried this idea, I found

As a result of this task, I learned

FIGURE 19.5

Checking My Understanding—Experimental Inquiry

We typically teach and use experimental inquiry in science class, although we can conduct experimental inquiry in any subject area. Following is an example from a language arts class. Read the example and then try to generate another nontraditional use of the experimental inquiry process.

Mrs. Collier was weary of trying to convince her students of the importance of revising and editing their writing. Many students simply completed single drafts and then turned in their work, frequently using technology to add graphics in an attempt to impress Mrs. Collier and earn points. Finally, she decided to guide students in an experiment. Students worked in groups to create two versions of a persuasive piece of writing—one not well written, but with colorful graphics, and one with no graphics, but well written. Students then hypothesized how people reading them would rate the work in terms of how persuaded they were by it. Each group designed a plan for getting different groups of people to read each piece and then rate it.

---

students in the process of experimental inquiry in the classroom.

Assessing the Impact on Students

Rubrics are one tool you can use to gauge students' progress. Sample rubrics are provided in Figure 19.6 (p. 247) for evaluating students' progress in using the process of experimental inquiry. These rubrics can be revised, when appropriate, for students to use as part of the self-assessment process to help them reflect on their work.

Planning Classroom Activities and Assessing Myself

Answering a series of questions will help you discover how you might use the strategies for experimental inquiry presented in this module. You can use the Planning for Experimental Inquiry Worksheet, Figure 19.7 (p. 248), to guide your thinking when planning for asking students to use experimental inquiry.

Rubrics help assess student learning. You can assess yourself too—how effectively you use strategies to guide your students in experimental inquiry in your classroom. Use Figure 19.8 (p. 249) to evaluate your use of experimental inquiry.

FIGURE 19.6

Rubrics for Experimental Inquiry

Rubric for Experimental Inquiry

4   The student designs and conducts an experiment that insightfully tests a well-articulated hypothesis. The student fully and accurately explains the results in light of the hypothesis. The student makes recommendations about how the experiment should be refined.

3   The student designs and conducts an experiment that adequately tests a hypothesis. The student explains the results in light of the hypothesis.

2   The student designs and conducts an experiment that is related to the situation but does not adequately test the hypothesis.

1   The student does not design and conduct an experiment, or designs one that has no relationship to the hypothesis.

0   Not enough information to make a judgment.

Rubric for Experimental Inquiry for Younger Students

4   The student designs and carries out an experiment that does a good job of testing the hypothesis. The student completely explains the results. The student also makes suggestions about how to improve the experiment.

3   The student designs and conducts an experiment that does a good job of testing the hypothesis. The student correctly explains the results.

2   The student designs and conducts an experiment, but the experiment does not do a good job of testing the hypothesis. Or, the student does not correctly explain the results.

1   The student does not design and conduct an experiment. Or, the student designs an experiment that does not match the hypothesis.

0   The student does not try to do the task.

FIGURE 19.7

Planning for Experimental Inquiry Worksheet

What knowledge will students be learning?

Do I need to set aside time to teach students the process of experimental inquiry? How will I teach them the process?

Will I ask students to use a graphic organizer?

How much guidance will I provide students?

How will students explain their hypothesis and communicate their conclusions?

How will I monitor how well students are doing with experimental inquiry?

What will I do to help students who are not using experimental inquiry effectively?

FIGURE 19.8

Assessing Myself—Experimental Inquiry

I clearly communicate the knowledge students will use for the experimental inquiry activity.

Not at all | | | | | To a great extent

0   1   2   3   4

I make sure students know how to use the process of experimental inquiry.

Not at all   To a great extent

0   1   2   3   4

I make sure students understand the graphic organizers for experimental inquiry.

Not at all   To a great extent

0   1   2   3   4

I give students an appropriate amount of guidance for the activity.

Not at all   To a great extent

0   1   2   3   4

Over time, I collect evidence about my students' proficiency at using experimental inquiry.

Not at all   To a great extent

0   1   2   3   4

Module Reflection

Review your responses to the questions in the Reflecting on My Current Beliefs and Practices—Experimental Inquiry worksheet, Figure 19.1 (p. 242). How has this module affected your thinking about teaching and learning? Use the space provided to record your thoughts.

- Reading this information affirms some of what I already knew about experimental inquiry

- Now, I better understand some things about experimental inquiry

- I think I will change the way I use experimental inquiry in my classroom

INVENTION

When we think of inventions, we tend to think *big*: the light bulb, cotton gin, telephone, automobile, airplane, computer. But, an invention doesn't have to be an elaborate mode of transportation or communication. Many a roll of duct tape has been sacrificed to create an inspired invention that responds to a pressing need. We need invention in situations where we find ourselves asking, "Shouldn't there be a better way to. . . ?" After all, this question was the driving force behind those big inventions.

The idea of *inventing* a product or a process might intimidate some students. They, too, will tend to think *big* when you mention invention: the skateboard, the snowboard, the mobile phone, e-mail, the Internet. Let students know that although some inventions change the world, some inventions make one small thing a little better. Students will feel less intimidated by the invention process if they know you aren't expecting them to invent the wheel and if they know that they can use it in their daily lives.

Before reading "Recommendations for Classroom Practice," take some time to reflect on your current practices and beliefs about invention by completing the worksheet in Figure 20.1 (p. 252). This will give you a basis for comparison as you read about the strategies in the module.

Recommendations for Classroom Practice

Invention is a complex process that students will need to learn about and practice. In this module, we discuss several approaches to use in the classroom:

- giving students a model for the process,
- using familiar content to teach students the steps for invention,
- giving students graphic organizers for invention,
- guiding students as needed, and
- asking students to explain their hypotheses and conclusions.

Give Students a Model for the Process

People invent products or processes to fulfill specific needs. The invention process involves hypothesizing what might work, developing the idea, and testing the invention. For example, students might use their understanding of the principles of the cardiovascular and muscular systems to invent a new form of exercise. During this process, they must hypothesize what might work, develop the idea, and then conduct tests to determine if their idea does, in fact, work. Invention often demands generating and testing multiple hypotheses until one proves effective. You can

FIGURE 20.1

Reflecting on My Current Beliefs and Practices—Invention

What is the purpose of asking students to invent something?

What kinds of invention activities do I use with my students?

What questions do I have about invention?

FIGURE 20.2

Model for Invention

Steps in the Process of Invention

1. Describe a situation you want to improve or a need you want to respond to.
2. Identify specific standards for the invention that would improve the situation or meet the need.
3. Brainstorm ideas and hypothesize the likelihood that each will work.
4. If your hypothesis suggests that a specific idea might work, begin to draft, sketch, and then create the invention.
5. Develop your invention to the point that you can test your hypothesis.
6. If necessary, revise your invention until it reaches the standards you have set.

Steps in the Process of Invention for Younger Students

1. What do I want to make? Or what do I want to make better?
2. What standards do I want to set for my invention?
3. What is the best way to make a rough draft of my invention?
4. How can I make my rough draft better?
5. Does my invention meet the standards I have set?

---

guide students' work by providing them with explicit steps, as shown in Figure 20.2, for the process of invention.

Use Familiar Content to Teach Students Steps for Invention

The idea of inventing a product or a process might seem abstract to some students, but you can find many concrete examples of inventions to share with them as you teach the steps for the process. Where would we be without the washing machine? Or the automobile? Or the light bulb? Students can answer questions about these inventions that will help them understand the process. For example, What need motivated the invention? What standards did the inventors set? How has the invention improved something?

You can lead students through the steps in the invention process using an example of a famous invention such as the telephone. Alexander Graham Bell received the patent for the telephone, but Thomas Edison improved Bell's invention. Bell's telephone worked only over short distances of two to three miles, so Edison set out to improve this situation. The standard for Edison was to improve the phone so that it carried speech clearly with no distance limitations. Edison created hundreds of models, constantly looking for alternatives and ways to improve the product. His first attempt worked over 107 miles—from New York City to Philadelphia. Eventually, he improved the telephone so that distance was no longer a factor.

Give Students Graphic Organizers for Invention

Students can use graphic organizers like the one in Figure 20.3 (p. 255) as visual tools to help them understand and use the process of invention.

Guide Students As Needed

The first time students use invention with content knowledge, they will probably need close guidance. At first you might identify the situation that needs improvement along with the standards for the invention. Eventually, and even ideally, you will want to give students more freedom in using the invention process. Even when students have a great deal of freedom, however, it is still advisable to closely monitor their work and provide feedback to them as they are using the process.

Ask Students to Explain Their Hypotheses and Conclusions

Explaining their thinking helps students to enhance their understanding of the invention process and the steps involved. You can use several methods to help students explain their hypotheses and conclusions:

- Give students a results template that asks them to explain their work and what they learned (see Figure 20.4).
- Use sentence stems to prompt students' thinking about the process:
  A need I want to address is _____
  _____.
  I think if I change _____
  _____,
  then _____ will happen.
- Let students use audiotapes to record their thinking as they go through the steps in the invention process and to describe what they learned.

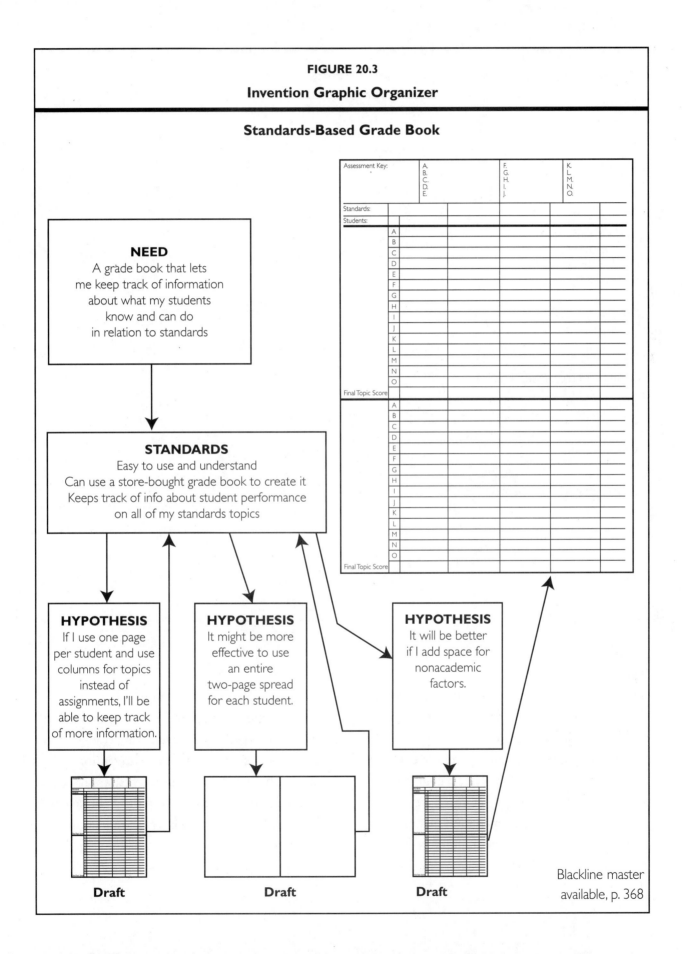

FIGURE 20.3

Invention Graphic Organizer

Standards-Based Grade Book

NEED
A grade book that lets
me keep track of information
about what my students
know and can do
in relation to standards

STANDARDS
Easy to use and understand
Can use a store-bought grade book to create it
Keeps track of info about student performance
on all of my standards topics

HYPOTHESIS
If I use one page
per student and use
columns for topics
instead of
assignments, I'll be
able to keep track
of more information.

HYPOTHESIS
It might be more
effective to use
an entire
two-page spread
for each student.

HYPOTHESIS
It will be better
if I add space for
nonacademic
factors.

Draft

Draft

Draft

Blackline master
available, p. 368

FIGURE 20.4

Results Template—Invention

My hypothesis about the invention that will improve the situation

I think this idea will work because

After I tried this idea, I found

As a result of this invention process, I learned

Tools to Facilitate Invention in the Classroom

Before using our recommendations in your classroom, consider a hypothetical situation or problem to check your understanding of the previous discussion by completing the exercise in Figure 20.5 (pp. 257–258). It will give you an opportunity to apply what you have learned. The other assessment and planning tools that follow will help you guide your students in the process of invention in the classroom.

Assessing the Impact on Students

Rubrics are one tool you can use to gauge students' progress. Sample rubrics are provided in Figure 20.6 (p. 259) for evaluating students' progress in using the process of invention. These rubrics can be revised, when appropriate, for students to use as part of the self-assessment process to help them reflect on their work.

FIGURE 20.5

Checking My Understanding—Invention

The following activity is designed to engage you in the invention process. As you work through the activity, notice what knowledge you need to create an invention that meets a stated need. Pay particular attention to what you have to do with that knowledge as you generate a hypothesis and plan for testing it.

Think about your school. Describe a situation you want to improve or a need to which you want to respond.
Examples

• Scheduling for students to use the computer lab doesn't work well. I want to improve the system.

• My grade book doesn't work very well now that I am keeping records according to how students perform on standards. I need to find a better way to keep records.

•

•

•

Describe specific standards for the invention that would improve the situation or meet the need.
Examples

• Students should be able to use the computer lab after school, during their free periods, or during time allotted for individual work in a class. Time in the computer lab should be maximized for students, and a technical support person should always be available for them.

• My record-keeping methods need to reflect what my students know and should be convenient for scoring assessments aligned with standards.

•

•

•

(continued on p. 258)

FIGURE 20.5 (CONTINUED)

Checking My Understanding—Invention

Brainstorm ideas and hypothesize the likelihood that each will work.

Examples

• We can rotate the teacher schedule for after-school detention assignments with after-school computer lab assignments. We can use knowledgeable students as technical support for the lab. That way, teachers can plan lessons or grade papers while supervising the lab, but they won't necessarily have to provide the computer support.

• I can redesign my grade book so that it's based on standards instead of assignments. Every time an assignment addresses a standard, I'll insert a score for that standard. This method will require more space for each student, but it should work.

•

•

•

If you think a specific idea might work, begin to draft, sketch, and then create the invention. Develop your invention to the point that you can test your hypothesis. If necessary, revise your invention until it reaches the standards you have set. Describe the steps you followed.

•

•

•

Reflect on the steps you went through to create this invention. How do you think you would prepare students for a similar task?

FIGURE 20.6

Rubrics for Invention

Invention Rubric

4   The student develops an invention that improves a situation or meets a specific need. The student sets and exceeds high standards for the invention.

3   The student develops an invention that improves a situation or meets a specific need. The student sets and meets standards for the invention.

2   The student develops an invention, but the invention does not clearly improve a situation or meet a specific need. The student sets but does not meet standards for the invention.

1   The student attempts to develop an invention, but the invention does not improve a situation or meet a specific need. The student does not set and meet standards for the invention.

0   Not enough information to make a judgment.

Invention Rubric for Younger Students

4   The student creates an invention that meets a specific need. The student sets high standards for the invention. The invention goes beyond the standards.

3   The student creates an invention that meets a specific need. The student sets standards for the invention and meets them.

2   The student creates an invention, but it does not clearly meet a need. Or, the student does not meet standards for the invention.

1   The student tries to create an invention, but it does not meet a need. The student does not set and meet standards for the invention.

0   The student did not try to do the task.

Planning Classroom Activities and Assessing Myself

Answering a series of questions will help you discover how you might use the strategies for invention presented in this module. You can use the Planning for Invention Worksheet, Figure 20.7 (p. 261), to guide your thinking when planning for asking students to use the invention process.

Rubrics help assess student learning. You can assess yourself too—how effectively you use strategies to guide invention in your classroom. Use Figure 20.8 (p. 262) to evaluate your use of invention in your classroom and with students.

FIGURE 20.7

Planning for Invention Worksheet

What knowledge will students be learning?

Do I need to set aside time to teach students the process of invention? How will I teach them the process?

Will I ask students to use a graphic organizer?

How much guidance will I provide students?

How will students explain their hypothesis and communicate their conclusions?

How will I monitor how well students are doing with invention?

What will I do to help students who are not using invention effectively?

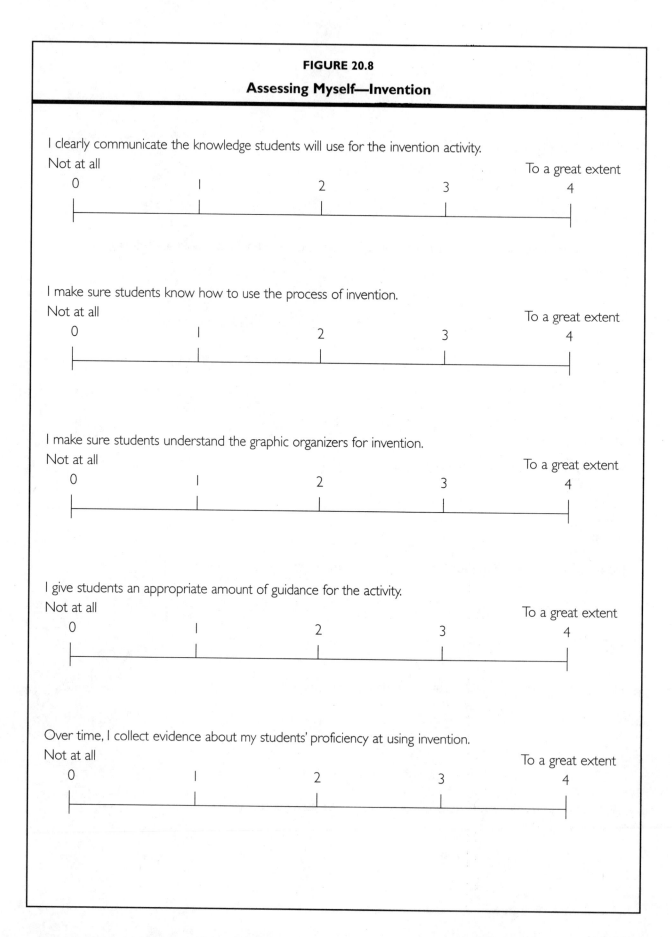

FIGURE 20.8

Assessing Myself—Invention

I clearly communicate the knowledge students will use for the invention activity.

Not at all | | | | To a great extent

0 1 2 3 4

I make sure students know how to use the process of invention.

Not at all | | | | To a great extent

0 1 2 3 4

I make sure students understand the graphic organizers for invention.

Not at all | | | | To a great extent

0 1 2 3 4

I give students an appropriate amount of guidance for the activity.

Not at all | | | | To a great extent

0 1 2 3 4

Over time, I collect evidence about my students' proficiency at using invention.

Not at all | | | | To a great extent

0 1 2 3 4

Module Reflection

Review your responses to the questions in the Reflecting on My Current Beliefs and Practices—Invention worksheet, Figure 20.1 (p. 252). How has this module affected your thinking about teaching and learning? Use the space provided to record your thoughts.

- Reading this information affirms some of what I already knew about invention

- Now, I better understand some things about invention

- I think I will change the way I use invention in my classroom

9

CUES, QUESTIONS, AND ADVANCE ORGANIZERS

Study Group Tip

If you are using this handbook in a study group, your group might want to read and discuss the research summary about cues, questions, and advance organizers in the companion book, *Classroom Instruction That Works*.

Accessing what students already know enhances their learning about new content. This process is commonly referred to as "accessing prior knowledge." Imagine you are reading an article about the best vacation spots in France. When you read the title of the article, you might pause for a moment before reading the article and recall the last vacation you took— what you liked about it and what you did not like about it. Recalling your experience provides a context for reading the article. It allows you to compare and contrast what is stated in the article with what you already know. Although mature learners usually access their prior knowledge automatically, K–12 students must sometimes be reminded and even helped to access what they already know. In this section, we discuss cues and questions as ways of helping students access and use their prior knowledge.

Research shows that cues and questions should focus on what is important, not on what is unusual. When using questions in the classroom, teachers should focus on "higher-level" questions because they produce deeper learning. Also, waiting briefly before accepting responses from students increases the depth of students' answers. We also know questions are effective learning tools even when asked before a learning experience. In this section, we offer strategies and suggestions for using what research tells us works in the classroom. We encourage you to use these and other approaches to using cues, questions, and advance organizers to enhance students' learning.

List of Figures

CUES AND QUESTIONS

Cues are explicit reminders or hints about what students are about to experience. For example, a teacher is giving students a cue when she explains that the article they are about to read on the civilizations of Mesopotamia and the Indus Valley will contain some information they already know about civilizations, but that they should also look for new information. Telling students the topic of the article helps trigger what they already know—what they might have learned in class or outside of school. Reminding them to look for new information in the article establishes expectations for students.

Questions perform about the same function as cues. For example, prior to reading the article on Mesopotamia and the Indus Valley, the teacher might ask students questions that elicit what they already know about the topic: What are the characteristics of urban development in ancient Mesopotamia? What environmental and cultural factors influenced the development of civilization in the Indus Valley? Even the best-designed lesson requires students to fill in a lot of missing information. Questions can greatly aid students in this process. Higher-level questions require students to analyze information and have more effect on learning than questions that ask students to recall or recognize information. A higher-order question asks students to restructure information or apply what they know.

Before reading "Recommendations for Classroom Practice," take some time to reflect on your current practices and beliefs about cues and questions by completing the worksheet in Figure 21.1 (p. 268). This will give you a basis for comparison as you read about the strategies in the module.

Recommendations for Classroom Practice

In this module, we discuss several approaches to use in the classroom:

- focusing important information,
- using explicit cues,
- asking inferential questions, and
- asking analytic questions.

Focus on Important Information

Ideally, cues and questions trigger students' memories. For example, What do I already know about fairy tales? What do I already know about adding numbers? What do I already know about the Civil War in the United States?

Sometimes you might begin a unit or lesson by presenting information or asking questions related to something unusual—even bizarre—about the content. Although this method can effectively gain students' attention, pointing out the bizarre might also distract

FIGURE 21.1

Reflecting on My Current Beliefs and Practices—Cues and Questions

What is the purpose of using cues and questions in the classroom?

When do I use cues with my students?

What kinds of questions do I use with my students?

What questions do I have about using cues and questions in my classroom?

students so that they have a difficult time refocusing on what is important. For example, when beginning a unit on space and the solar system, a teacher might begin by asking students what they know about UFOs and stories of alien sightings. This activity might be fun, but students might then have a difficult time drawing out their scientific knowledge about space. We recommend that during planning, teachers identify what is important in the unit or lesson and then create appropriate questions and cues to use at the beginning of lessons.

Use Explicit Cues

As stated earlier, students are more likely to learn if they connect new information to what they already know—their prior knowledge. There is no reason to be subtle or ambiguous with students as you prepare them for a unit or lesson. Sometimes a direct approach can be most effective: simply tell them what they are about to learn, and then help them identify and discuss what they already know and predict what they think they will learn.

The best-known structured approach to eliciting prior knowledge is called KWL. In this model, the "K" reminds the students to answer the question, "What do I already **know** about this topic?" For example, when students are thinking about Mesopotamia, they might recall that they know that Mesopotamia lies between two rivers and that this location helped it become a great ancient civilization. The "W" cues them to answer, "What do I **want** to know?" Students might want to know what raw materials people had to work with in ancient Mesopotamia, what the great achievements of Mesopotamia were, and what the major differences between Mesopotamia and

the Indus Valley were. After the learning experience, students answer the question, "What did I **learn**?" After reading the article, students might answer the questions they had and record any other important information they have learned. Teachers have reported that when they use explicit cues like those in the KWL strategy, students begin to use the strategy when they are working in small groups or even when they are studying alone.

Ask Inferential Questions

Inferential questions help students fill in gaps from a lesson, an activity, or a reading. You can design specific questions aimed at stimulating students' questions. Figure 21.2 (pp. 270–271) gives examples of inferential questions that you can construct for things, people, actions, events, and states.

Ask Analytic Questions

Some questions require students to analyze and even critique the information presented to them. As with inferential questions, analytic questions often require students to use prior knowledge in addition to the new information that is being presented. Figure 21.3 (p. 272) gives some examples of analytic questions designed around highly analytic thinking and reasoning skills.

Tools to Facilitate Cues and Questions in the Classroom

Before using our recommendations in your classroom practice, consider a hypothetical situation or problem to check your understanding

FIGURE 21.2

Inferential Questions That Require Students to Make Inferences

Things and People

What action does this thing or person usually perform?

What action does the U.S. press secretary usually perform?

What action is usually performed on this thing?

What action is usually performed on a desktop computer?

How is this thing usually used?

How is a spreadsheet usually used?

What is this thing part of?

What is the large intestine part of?

What is the process for making this thing?

What is the process for mining gold?

What particular taste, feel, smell, or sound does this thing have?

What particular smell does sulfuric acid have?

What particular color, number (or quantity), location, or dimensionality does this thing have?

What particular molecular arrangement does H_2O have?

How is this thing usually sold?

How is a consumer service usually sold?

What particular emotional state does this person have?

What is the emotional state of Macbeth after the murder of the king?

Does this thing have a particular value?

What is the value of Mary Cassatt's (1892) The Bath (La Toilette)?

When this thing is used, does it present a particular danger to other things or to people? What is it?

What danger might using a lathe present to things or people?

Actions

What thing or person usually performs this action?

Who usually designs the structure of a large office building?

What effect does this action have on the taste, feel, sound, or look of this thing?

What effect does placing sodium bicarbonate, $NaHCO_3$ (common baking soda), into water have on the chemical composition of the sodium bicarbonate?

How does this action typically change the emotional state of a person?

How does a peaceful, long vacation typically change the emotional state of a person?

How is the value of a thing changed by this action?

How is the value of a novel changed when it is turned into a movie?

How does this action change the size or shape of a thing?

How does a flood change the size or shape of a river bank?

How does this action change the state of a thing?

How does United States monetary policy affect inflation?

FIGURE 21.2 (CONTINUED)

Inferential Questions That Require Students to Make Inferences

Events

What people are usually involved in this event?

What people are usually involved in a barn raising?

During what season or time of year does this event usually take place?

During what season do the gazelles typically migrate from Serengeti National Park west and then north into the Masai Mara?

On what day of the week does this event usually take place?

On what day of the week does an election usually take place?

At what time of day does this event usually take place?

At what time of day do owls usually hunt for food?

Where does this event usually take place?

Where do the Olympic Games usually take place?

At what point in history did this event take place?

At what point in history did the Russian Revolution take place?

What equipment is typically used in this event?

What equipment is typically used when flying a Navy fighter plane?

How long does this event usually take?

How long does a corn harvest in Iowa usually take?

States

What is the basic process involved in reaching this state?

What is the basic process involved in becoming hypothermic?

What changes occur when something reaches this state?

What changes occur when someone becomes hypothermic?

FIGURE 21.3

Analytic Questions

Analytic Skills

Analyzing Errors

Identifying and articulating errors in the logic of information.

What are the errors in reasoning in this information?

How is this information misleading?

How could it be corrected or improved?

Constructing Support

Constructing a system of support or proof for an assertion.

What is an argument that would support the following claim?

What are some of the limitations of this argument or the assumptions underlying it?

Analyzing Perspectives

Identifying and articulating personal perspectives about issues.

Why would someone consider this to be good (or bad, or neutral)?

What is the reasoning behind this perspective?

What is an alternative perspective, and what is the reasoning behind it?

---

of the previous discussion by completing the exercise in Figure 21.4 (p. 273). It will give you an opportunity to apply what you have learned. The other assessment and planning tools that follow will help you guide your students with cues and questions in the classroom.

Assessing the Impact on Students

Rubrics are one tool you can use to gauge students' progress. Of all the cueing and questioning techniques presented in this module, analytic questions most lend themselves to student assessment. Sample rubrics are provided in Figures 21.5 (p. 274), 21.6 (p. 275), and 21.7 (p. 275) for evaluating students' progress in using the three types of analytic questions presented in this module. These rubrics can be revised, when appropriate, for students to use as part of the self-assessment process to help them reflect on their work.

FIGURE 21.4

Checking My Understanding—Cues and Questions

A teacher might present the following learning goals to students. Read each goal and answer the questions.

Learning Goal: During the Civil War unit, the teacher wants students to understand that when people who live in a region put a different value on a resource, conflict results.

What questions or cues might you use to elicit students' prior knowledge about this topic?

What are some questions or cues that relate to some unusual aspect of the Civil War but might distract students from the learning goal?

What analytic questions might you use that would require students to use the information presented plus what they already know?

Learning Goal: During the unit on classical musicians, the teacher wants students to understand that musicians, such as Mozart and Bach, were able to create music that stimulates emotions and mental pictures in listeners.

What questions or cues might you use to elicit students' prior knowledge about this topic?

What are some questions or cues that relate to some unusual aspect of these musicians but might distract students from the learning goal?

What analytic questions might you use that would require students to use the information presented plus what they already know?

FIGURE 21.5

Rubrics for Analyzing Errors

Analyzing Errors Rubric

4   The student identifies major as well as less subtle errors in reasoning in the information and explains clearly and in detail how the information is misleading and can be improved.

3   The student identifies the major errors in reasoning in the information and explains how the information is misleading and can be improved.

2   The student identifies some of the errors in reasoning in the information. The student explains how the information is misleading in a way that is unclear or illogical. Or, the student does not explain how the information can be improved.

1   The student does not identify the errors in reasoning in the information. The student does not explain how the information is misleading or can be improved.

0   Not enough information to make a judgment.

Analyzing Errors Rubric for Younger Students

4   The student finds important mistakes in reasoning in the information. The student also finds smaller mistakes. The student uses details and tells why the information is misleading. The student also tells how the information can be improved.

3   The student finds the important mistakes in reasoning in the information. The student tells why the information is misleading. The student tells how the information can be improved.

2   The student finds some of the mistakes in reasoning in the information. The student's explanation is not clear. Or, the student does not tell how the information can be improved.

1   The student does not find any mistakes in reasoning in the information. The student does not tell how the information can be improved.

0   The student does not try to do the task.

Planning Classroom Activities and Assessing Myself

Answering a series of questions will help you discover how you might use the strategies for cues and questions presented in this module. You can use the Planning for Cues and Questions Worksheet, Figure 21.8 (p. 276), to guide your thinking when planning for cues and questions in your classroom.

Rubrics help assess student learning. You can assess yourself too—how effectively you use strategies for cues and questions in your classroom. Use Figure 21.9 (p. 277) to evaluate your use of cues and questions.

FIGURE 21.6

Rubrics for Constructing Support

Constructing Support Rubric

4 The student presents a well-articulated and detailed argument that has no errors in logic.

3 The student presents a well-articulated argument that has no errors in logic.

2 The student presents an argument that makes a point but is not well articulated or has some significant errors in logic.

1 The student presents an argument that makes no clear point or has so many errors in logic that it is invalid.

0 Not enough information to make a judgment.

Constructing Support Rubric for Younger Students

4 The student makes a clear argument with lots of details. The argument does not have any mistakes in logic.

3 The student makes a clear argument. The argument does not have any mistakes in logic.

2 The student makes an argument that makes a point but is not clear. Or, the student makes an argument that has some big mistakes.

1 The student makes an argument that makes no clear point. Or, the student makes an argument that has so many mistakes that it is incorrect.

0 The student does not try to do the task.

FIGURE 21.7

Rubrics for Analyzing Perspectives

Analyzing Perspectives Rubric

4 The student accurately explains in detail the key reasons or logic, as well as more subtle reasons, underlying several perspectives on the issue.

3 The student accurately explains the key reasons or logic underlying several perspectives on the issue.

2 The student explains the reasons or logic underlying perspectives on the issue in a way that reveals some misconceptions about the perspectives.

1 The student explains the reasons or logic underlying perspectives on the issue in a way that reveals severe misconceptions about the perspectives.

0 Not enough information to make a judgment.

Analyzing Perspectives Rubric for Younger Students

4 The student correctly tells the important reasons behind several points of view on the topic. The student also tells some reasons that are not the big reasons.

3 The student correctly tells the important reasons behind several points of view on the topic.

2 The student explains the reasons behind points of view on the topic in a way that shows some mistakes.

1 The student explains reasons behind points of view on the issue in a way that has so many errors that it does not make sense.

0 The student does not try to do the task.

FIGURE 21.8

Planning for Cues and Questions Worksheet

What knowledge will students be learning?

What cues will I use?

What questions will I use?

- ☐ targeted questions
- ☐ analytic questions
  - analyzing errors
  - constructing support
  - analyzing perspectives
  - other_____
- ☐ other _____

How will I monitor the effect of the cues and questions on students' learning?

What will I do to improve the effect of cues and questions on students' learning?

FIGURE 21.9

Assessing Myself—Cues and Questions

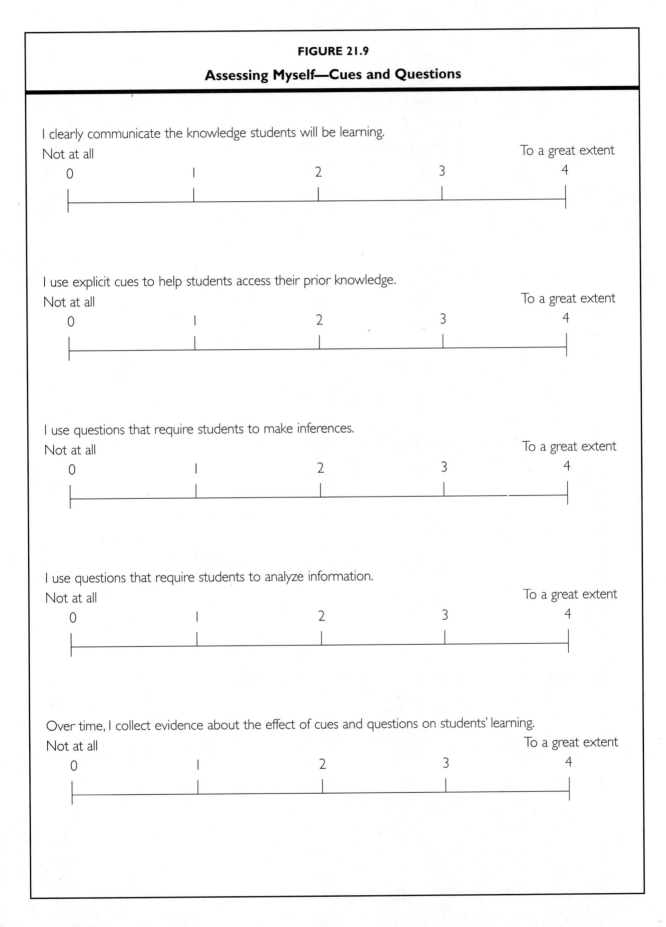

I clearly communicate the knowledge students will be learning.

Not at all   To a great extent

0   1   2   3   4

I use explicit cues to help students access their prior knowledge.

Not at all   To a great extent

0   1   2   3   4

I use questions that require students to make inferences.

Not at all   To a great extent

0   1   2   3   4

I use questions that require students to analyze information.

Not at all   To a great extent

0   1   2   3   4

Over time, I collect evidence about the effect of cues and questions on students' learning.

Not at all   To a great extent

0   1   2   3   4

Module Reflection

Review your responses to the questions in the Reflecting on My Current Beliefs and Practices—Cues and Questions worksheet, Figure 21.1 (p. 268). How has this module affected your thinking about teaching and learning? Use the space provided to record your thoughts.

- Reading this information affirms some of what I already knew about cues and questions

- Now, I better understand some things about cues and questions

- I think I will change how I use cues and questions in my classroom

ADVANCE ORGANIZERS

We often see what we expect to see. To illustrate, consider a 1981 study by Brewer and Tryens. These researchers brought 30 students individually into a room and told them it was the office of a professor who was conducting an experiment. Each student was asked to wait for a short while. After 35 seconds, the students were taken to another room and asked to write down everything they could recall about the office. The researchers hypothesized that students would remember those items they expected to see in a professor's office regardless of whether they were there or not. In other words, they hypothesized that students' prior knowledge would influence what they perceived. That is precisely what happened. Twenty-nine of 30 students remembered that the office had a desk and a chair, but only eight recalled that it had a bulletin board and a skull; and nine students recalled that the office had books, although it did not. The students remembered what they expected to see regardless of whether it was there or not.

This experiment and others done in the classroom show that we can influence what students will learn from an experience by helping them connect what they already know to what they need to know. Further, this experiment suggests that because prior knowledge can change or distort students' perceptions, we need to anticipate what prior knowledge might influence a learning experience and try to maximize the potential *positive* influence on students' learning.

An advance organizer is a tool teachers can use to this end. Advance organizers are organizational frameworks teachers present to students prior to teaching new content to prepare them for what they are about to learn. Advance organizers take the surprise out of what is to come, help students retrieve what they already know about a topic, and focus them on the new information.

Before reading "Recommendations for Classroom Practice," take some time to reflect on your current practices and beliefs about cues and questions by completing the worksheet in Figure 22.1 (p. 280). This will give you a basis for comparison as you read about the strategies in the module.

Recommendations for Classroom Practice

As with cues and questions, advance organizers should focus on essential information, especially when unusual or bizarre aspects of the topic might distract students. Advance organizers can, of course, help students get ready to learn facts and details about a topic, but you can use advance organizers more effectively if you help students get ready to *use* the information. For example, if students are getting ready to read mystery stories, an advance organizer could prepare them to find examples of foreshadowing or

FIGURE 22.1

Reflecting on My Current Beliefs and Practices—Advance Organizers

What kinds of advance organizers do I use with my students?

What kinds of information do I include in advance organizers? Why do I include this information?

What questions do I have about using advance organizers?

characterization. Advance organizers, whether preparing students to learn details or to process information at a higher level, can take many formats. In this module, we discuss several approaches to use in the classroom:

- using expository advance organizers,
- using narrative advance organizers,
- teaching students skimming as a form of advance organizers, and
- teaching students how to use graphic advance organizers.

Use Expository Advance Organizers

Expository advance organizers are straightforward descriptions of the new content that students will be learning. You can provide these descriptions orally or in written form, but, as with all advance organizers, you should emphasize important content, not the strange or fantastic. In some cases an expository advance organizer might include text and pictures for clarification of complex information. For example, suppose a physical education teacher is planning to teach her students to play cricket and wants to show an instructional video of a cricket match. She knows that because many students have never seen a cricket match, they will be fascinated by the peculiarities of the game and how different it is from the sports they know. Although she wants students to enjoy the match, she also wants them to learn more about offensive and defensive strategies, rules, and movement skills in an unfamiliar game. To make sure students will attend to the information related to these topics, she gives students an expository advance organizer, Figure 22.2 (pp. 282–283).

Use Narrative Advance Organizers

Narrative advance organizers are stories. Although stories won't always come to mind when you are preparing students for new information, they are an effective way to help students make personal or real-world connections with the new content. Stories can make something distant or unfamiliar—such as a time in history, a scientific discovery, or a complex math concept—seem personal and familiar. For example, suppose students in a social studies class are studying the concepts of perspective, motive, and bias and how to interpret and use primary source documents. The teacher might share the personal story in Figure 22.3 (p. 284). Stories like this one can stimulate student's thinking and help them make personal connections to new information.

Teach Students to Skim

Skimming information before reading can be a powerful form of advance organizer. Skimming allows students to preview important information they will encounter later by focusing on and noting what stands out in headings, subheadings, and highlighted information. Expository information is particularly suited to skimming because chapters in textbooks, articles in magazines, and other informative texts commonly include headings, bold terms, pictures with captions, inset quotations, and other helpful clues about the information presented.

Many students don't make it a practice to skim a chapter in a textbook or an article in a magazine before they begin to read. They simply start reading and proceed quickly

FIGURE 22.2
Expository Advance Organizer—Cricket

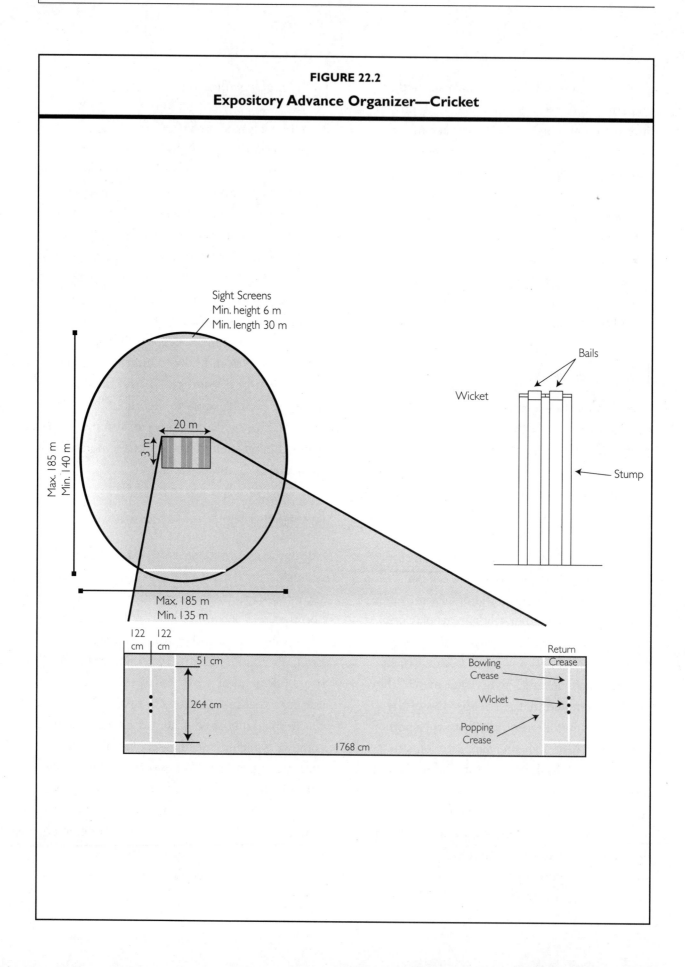

Sight Screens
Min. height 6 m
Min. length 30 m

Bails

Wicket

Stump

Max. 185 m
Min. 140 m

20 m

3 m

Max. 185 m
Min. 135 m

122 cm | 122 cm

51 cm

264 cm

1768 cm

Return Crease

Bowling Crease

Wicket

Popping Crease

FIGURE 22.2 (CONTINUED)
Expository Advance Organizer—Cricket

Cricket Rules

The Basics

Two teams, 11 players each

Teams bat in innings and try to score runs

After each team has batted an equal number of innings (one or two), the team with the most runs wins. (In cricket, **innings** refers to one or more rounds of play.)

Playing the Game

Fielders:

> All eleven players take the field
>
> One fielder is the **bowler,** who stands at one end of the pitch
>
> One fielder is the **wicket-keeper,** who squats behind the wicket at the opposite end of the pitch. The wicket-keeper is the only one who wears gloves for catching the ball.

Batsmen:

> Two take the field
>
> **Striker** stands in front of the wicket, near the popping crease, opposite the bowler.
>
> **Nonstriker** stands near the opposite wicket.

Bowler throws the ball at the far wicket, trying to knock down the bails—usually the ball bounces once before it reaches the striker.

Striker tries to hit the ball out of reach of the fielders. If striker has a good hit, he and his partner run and try to change places to score a run. Fielders try to stop runs and get the batsmen out by throwing the ball at the wickets ("run out").

The video will show the 10 different ways of getting out:

Caught	**Hit wicket**
Bowled	**Handle the ball**
Leg before wicket	**Obstructing the field**
Stumped	**Hit the ball twice**
Run out	**Timed out**

Also, watch the video for the following strategies, and add to the list:

Defensive Strategies	**Offensive Strategies**
Fast bowling	**Block**
Spin bowling	**Cross bat**

FIGURE 22.3

Narrative Advance Organizer—Sample Passage

When I was 4 years old, a tornado blew away half of the house my family lived in. My sister, who was 10, and I were the only ones home at the time. My sister had walked me home from school at my insistence—it was raining, and I wanted to use my new Mickey Mouse umbrella. Soon after we arrived home, the tornado sirens started sounding. My sister ran around gathering flashlights and other supplies, as she had learned to do on a field trip to the weather center the week before. We were in the basement hiding behind the couch when the tornado hit the house.

When I was college, I wrote an essay about the tornado and how the experience had affected me. When I shared the essay with my sister, she told me I had the story all wrong.

After the television went black in the middle of the Mickey Mouse Club show, and my sister made me duck behind the couch, I remember being totally quiet and in awe of the whole scene. I popped up my head to look at the windows blowing out, the carpet undulating like a roller coaster, and plaster falling from the ceiling. My sister, on the other hand, recalls me shrieking at the top of my lungs the entire time while she covered my head to protect me. Memories of that day are vivid for both of us—we just happen to have very different perspectives on what happened. I remember being calm and curious, but my sister believes she was the calm one who took charge of the situation and protected me.

---

through the text, often skipping headings, picture captions, and other textual organizers and clues. However, if they understand that headings, subheadings, and bold terms provide an outline of the content, and if they have had practice using these text features to understand the text, they might be more inclined to skim readings as a preview of the text.

Use Graphic Organizers

Graphic organizers can be used effectively as advance organizers because they visually represent information students are about to learn. When the information you are presenting is unfamiliar to students, and when the relationships among the pieces of information are complex, you might want to present students with graphic organizers that have much, if not all, of the information already filled in. Using this tool, students can develop a familiarity with both the information and the relationships among the pieces of information before the initial presentation begins. To illustrate, before students begin reading stories about the legend of King Arthur, a teacher might give students an organizer, Figure 22.4 (p. 285), that displays the various pieces of the legend that students will study.

FIGURE 22.4

Graphic Representation Advance Organizer—King Arthur

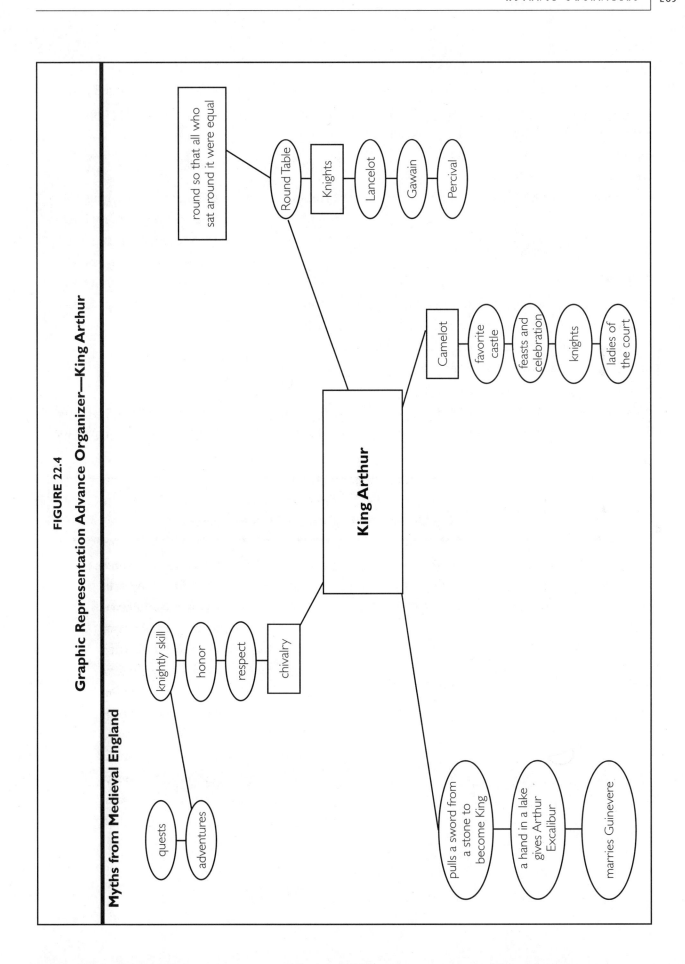

Myths from Medieval England

If you feel students will be able to understand new information on their own, you can provide them with blank organizers. A blank organizer provides conceptual "hooks" on which students can hang ideas that might seem disconnected without the organizer.

Tools to Facilitate Advance Organizers in the Classroom

Before using our recommendations in your classroom practice, consider a hypothetical situation or problem to check your understanding of the previous discussion by completing the exercise in Figure 22.5. It will give you an opportunity to apply what you have learned. The other assessment and planning tools that follow will help you guide your students in using advance organizers in the classroom.

Assessing the Impact on Students

Rubrics are one tool you can use to gauge students' progress. Sample rubrics are provided in Figure 22.6 (p. 287) for evaluating students' progress in using advance organizers. These rubrics can be revised, when appropriate, for students to use as part of the self-assessment process to help them reflect on their work.

Planning Classroom Activities and Assessing Myself

Answering a series of questions will help you discover how you might use the strategies for

---

FIGURE 22.5

Checking My Understanding—Advance Organizers

Imagine that you are preparing students to learn about a particular presidential election. You do not want students to simply become engaged in a discussion or debate during which they express their opinions; therefore, you decide to provide an advance organizer for students to use as you present information.

1. Decide what is important for students to learn. You will need to select a grade level and identify knowledge that is appropriate for that level.

2. Decide what approach you will use for the advance organizer and either briefly describe or sketch it. Explain why you believe the organizer will work.

FIGURE 22.6

Rubrics for Advance Organizers

Advance Organizer Rubric

4 The student understands the major ideas of the topic as well as complex relationships among major elements of the topic and related details.

3 The student understands the major ideas of the topic and related details.

2 The student understands some of the major ideas of the topic.

1 The student has misconceptions about the major ideas of the topic.

0 Not enough information to make a judgment.

Advance Organizer Rubric for Younger Students

4 The student understands the big ideas about the topic. The student also understands connections among different parts of the big ideas and details.

3 The student understands the big ideas about the topic and some details.

2 The student understands some ideas about the topic.

1 The student does not understand the big ideas about the topic.

0 The student does not try to use the advance organizer.

---

advance organizers presented in this module. You can use the Planning for Advance Organizers Worksheet, Figure 22.7 (p. 288), to guide your thinking when planning to use advance organizers in your classroom.

Rubrics help assess student learning. You can assess yourself too—how effectively you use strategies for using advance organizers in your classroom. Use Figure 22.8 (p. 289) to evaluate your use of advance organizers.

FIGURE 22.7

Planning for Advance Organizers Worksheet

What knowledge will students be learning?

What specific important information will I provide students in the advance organizer?

What strategy will I use?

☐ expository advance organizer

☐ narrative advance organizer

☐ skimming

☐ graphic organizer

☐ other_____

How will I monitor how well the advance organizers are helping prepare students for new content?

How will I respond if the advance organizers are not helping some students learn new content?

FIGURE 22.8

Assessing Myself—Advance Organizers

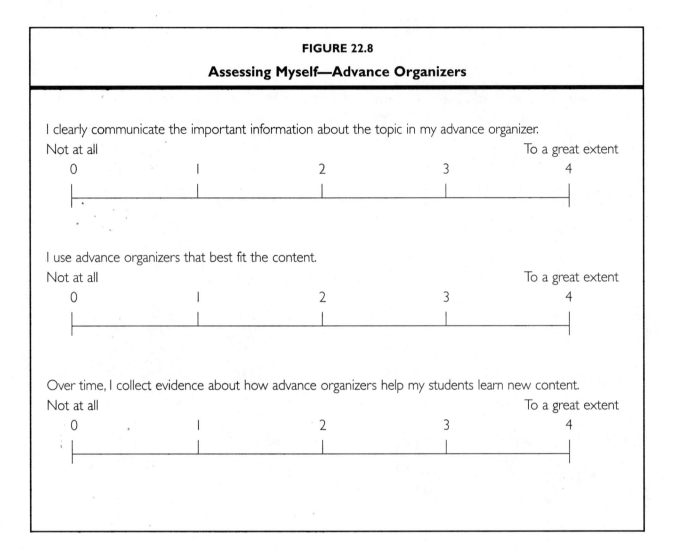

I clearly communicate the important information about the topic in my advance organizer.

Not at all   To a great extent

0   1   2   3   4

I use advance organizers that best fit the content.

Not at all   To a great extent

0   1   2   3   4

Over time, I collect evidence about how advance organizers help my students learn new content.

Not at all   To a great extent

0   1   2   3   4

Module Reflection

Review your responses to the questions in the Reflecting on My Current Beliefs and Practices—Advance Organizers worksheet, Figure 22.1 (p. 280). How has this module affected your thinking about teaching and learning? Use the space provided to record your thoughts.

● Reading this information affirms some of what I already knew about advance organizers

● Now, I better understand some things about advance organizers

● I think I will change how I use advance organizers in my classroom

10

SPECIFIC TYPES OF KNOWLEDGE

The instructional strategies covered in Sections 1–9 work well with all types of knowledge. However, a teacher can use specific instructional strategies for specific types of knowledge. In this section, we consider strategies for four types of knowledge: (1) vocabulary terms and phrases, (2) details, (3) organizing ideas, and (4) skills and processes.

Vocabulary terms are a part of the K–12 classroom. Research shows that direct vocabulary instruction improves students' achievement. When students have instruction in new words, they are more likely to understand the words in context when they encounter them again. In general, students must encounter words in context more than once to learn them. Further, vocabulary instruction is even more powerful when the words are critical to learning new content. Research also indicates that associating an image with a vocabulary term is one of the best ways to learn a new word.

Details are specific pieces of information. In Module 24, we discuss categories of details, including facts, time sequences, cause-and-effect sequences, and episodes. As with vocabulary terms, research indicates students should have systematic, multiple exposures to details. A dramatic enactment of details has the strongest effect on students' learning.

Organizing ideas are the most general type of informational knowledge. In Module 25, we discuss two types of organizing ideas—generalizations and principles. Once students grasp organizing ideas, focus instructional time on having them use organizing ideas in a variety of situations.

Skills and processes both produce some form of result or product. The discovery approach is difficult to use with skills and processes, so when you use a discovery approach, organize examples into categories that represent the different approaches to the skill. Skills are most useful when students learn them to their level of automaticity. Students should practice the parts of a process in their context and be able to control the interaction of the major component skills of a complex process.

List of Figures

VOCABULARY

Direct teaching of vocabulary might be one of the most underused instructional activities in K–12 education. The lack of vocabulary instruction might be a result of misconceptions about what it means to teach vocabulary and its potential effect on student learning. Perhaps the biggest misconception is that teaching vocabulary means teaching formal dictionary definitions. However, as you will learn in this module, you can teach vocabulary without ever mentioning a definition. Another misconception is that teaching vocabulary is "teacher directed"—where the teacher recites definitions and examples and students dutifully record and memorize them—as opposed to "student directed." Teaching vocabulary doesn't have to work that way. In fact, the process can be a highly student-centered, constructivist activity.

Before reading "Recommendations for Classroom Practice," take some time to reflect on your current practices and beliefs about vocabulary by completing the worksheet in Figure 23.1 (p. 294). This will give you a basis for comparison as you read about the strategies in the module.

Recommendations for Classroom Practice

Research indicates that students must encounter words multiple times before they learn them. If students experience words before reading them in context, they have a greater chance of learning the words and understanding them in context. Even a simple technique, such as giving students a list of terms with descriptions and an example used in a sentence, can help them understand and learn new words in context. In this module, we discuss two approaches for teaching vocabulary:

- using a five-step process for teaching vocabulary, and
- asking questions to help students generate information about different types of terms.

Use a Five-Step Process for Teaching Vocabulary

An instructional sequence that gives students multiple exposures to vocabulary terms in multiple ways is probably the most powerful way to teach new terms and phrases. You can follow a five-step process as shown in Figure 23.2 (p. 295) for teaching new terms and phrases. For example, suppose a teacher wants to use this five-step process for the term "food chain." He might use the process in the following manner:

Step 1: Present students with a brief explanation or description of the new term or phrase.

Food Chain: Feeding relationships that involve the transfer of energy and matter from one organism to another

FIGURE 23.1

Reflecting on My Current Beliefs and Practices—Vocabulary

Reflecting on what you have just read, think about your own classroom and answer the following questions.

What vocabulary do I teach in my classroom?

How do I teach vocabulary to my students? What strategies do I use?

What questions do I have about using vocabulary in my classroom?

FIGURE 23.2

Five-Step Process for Teaching Vocabulary

Step 1. Present students with a brief explanation or description of the new term or phrase.

Step 2. Present students with a nonlinguistic representation of the new term or phrase.

Step 3. Ask students to generate their own explanations or descriptions of the term or phrase.

Step 4. Ask students to create their own nonlinguistic representation of the term or phrase.

Step 5. Periodically ask students to review the accuracy of their explanations and representations.

Step 2: Present students with a nonlinguistic representation of the new term or phrase. (See Figure 23.3, p. 296.)

The teacher explains, "In this picture, you can see that the tree gets energy from the sun and makes its own food. The squirrel eats pine cones from the tree. The snake eats the squirrel. And the owl eats the snake. The general pattern of this food chain works like this: Plants use the sun's energy to make their own food. Some animals eat the plants. Some bigger animals eat the animals that eat the plants. Other animals eat these animals."

Step 3: Ask students to generate their own explanations or descriptions of the term or phrase.

One student writes in her vocabulary notebook: "There's a food chain in my backyard. A bird ate a worm. The worm got its food/energy from the nutrients in the soil. Then my cat ate the bird. In a food chain, plants and animals exchange energy in the form of food."

Step 4: Ask students to create their own nonlinguistic representation of the term or phrase.

The student draws the following representation (Figure 23.4, p. 297) in her notebook.

Step 5: Periodically ask students to review the accuracy of their explanations and representations.

Over the next few days, students learn about a variety of different food chains, including parasite chains. At the end of the week, the teacher sets aside time for students to review their vocabulary terms and to make any additions or revisions.

Ask Questions to Help Students Generate Information About Different Types of Terms

Students might use a vocabulary notebook to keep track of and expand on the new terms and phrases they learn. A vocabulary notebook gives students a place to record explanations and nonlinguistic representations for vocabulary terms. These depictions of terms can be

FIGURE 23.3

Food Chain Representation1

FIGURE 23.4
Food Chain Representation 2

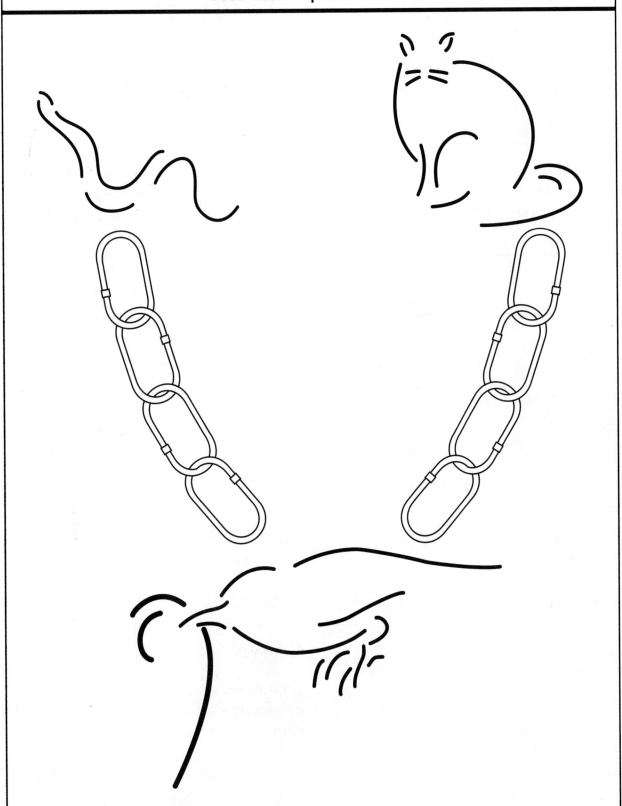

tricky because different types of terms and phrases require different explanations and nonlinguistic representations. You can use questions like those in Figure 23.5 to guide students as they generate information about different types of terms.

Tools to Facilitate Vocabulary Study in the Classroom

Before using our recommendations in your classroom practice, consider a hypothetical situation or problem to check your understanding of the previous discussion by completing the exercise in Figure 23.6 (p. 299). It will give you an opportunity to apply what you have learned. The other assessment and planning tools that follow will help you guide your students study of vocabulary in the classroom.

Assessing the Impact on Students

Rubrics are one tool you can use to gauge students' progress. Sample rubrics are provided in Figure 23.7 (p. 300) for evaluating students'

FIGURE 23.5

Questions About Different Types of Terms

Persons
Mother Teresa
What was her personality?
What important things did she do?
Why did she do these things?
What is her legacy?

Places
Strasbourg, France
Where is it?
What size is it?
What are some of its unique features?
What important events have occurred there?

Things
CAT scan
What is it?
What is its purpose?
What is it used for?
Who uses it?

Events
Presidential Election
When did it occur?
How frequently does it occur?
Who was involved?
What was the outcome?

Abstractions
Postmodernism
What are its essential ideas?
What characterizes it?
What are some examples of it?

FIGURE 23.6

Checking My Understanding—Vocabulary

Imagine you are a student and your teacher gives you the following five words to record in your vocabulary notebook. For each term, write an explanation and create a nonlinguistic representation, then answer the questions that follow.

Vocabulary term	Description	Nonlinguistic representation
Franklin D. Roosevelt		
Alaska		
Compass		
Olympics		
Gravity		

Do you think creating a nonlinguistic representation would be helpful for remembering a vocabulary term? Why or why not?

FIGURE 23.7

Rubrics for Vocabulary

Vocabulary Rubric

4   The student has a complete and detailed understanding of the term. The student generates explanations and descriptions of the term and uses the term in context.

3   The student has a complete understanding of the term and generates explanations and descriptions of the term.

2   The student has an incomplete understanding of the topic or some misconceptions about the meaning of the term. However, the student has a basic understanding of the term.

1   The student has so many misconceptions about the term that the student cannot be said to understand the term.

0   Not enough information to make a judgment.

Vocabulary Rubric for Younger Students

4   The student has a complete and detailed understanding of the term. The student creates explanations and descriptions of the term. The student can use the term in sentences.

3   The student has a complete understanding of the term. The student creates explanations and descriptions of the term.

2   The student does not completely understand the term. The student's explanation shows some mistakes about the meaning of the term.

1   The student does not understand the term. The student makes many mistakes when explaining the meaning of the term.

0   The student does not try to describe the term.

---

progress in learning vocabulary terms. These rubrics can be revised, when appropriate, for students to use as part of the self-assessment process to help them reflect on their work.

Planning Classroom Activities and Assessing Myself

Answering a series of questions will help you discover how you might use the strategies for vocabulary presented in this module. You can use the Planning for Vocabulary Worksheet, Figure 23.8 (pp. 301–302), to guide your thinking when planning for vocabulary in your classroom.

Rubrics help assess student learning. You can assess yourself too—how effectively you use strategies for vocabulary study in your classroom. Use in Figure 23.9 (p. 303) to evaluate your effectiveness with vocabulary study.

FIGURE 23.8

Planning for Vocabulary Worksheet

Unit _____

What vocabulary terms will I teach? Include a brief explanation or description of each.

-

-

-

-

-

-

-

-

(continued on p. 302)

FIGURE 23.8 (CONTINUED)

Planning for Vocabulary Worksheet

What activities will I ask students to do to learn the terms?

☐ Generate their own explanations or descriptions

☐ Create nonlinguistic representations

☐ Ask questions to help students generate information

☐ Other _____

What opportunities will I provide to ensure that students periodically review their vocabulary terms?

How will I monitor how well students are doing with the terms?

What will I do to help students who are struggling with the terms and phrases?

What images will I use to help students learn these vocabulary terms?

FIGURE 23.9

Assessing Myself—Teaching Vocabulary

I identify a few key terms and phrases that students should know prior to each unit of instruction.

Not at all   To a great extent

0   1   2   3   4

I present students with clear descriptions of terms and phrases.

Not at all   To a great extent

0   1   2   3   4

I present students with nonlinguistic representations for the terms and phrases they are learning.

Not at all   To a great extent

0   1   2   3   4

I provide opportunities for students to generate their own descriptions of key terms and phrases.

Not at all   To a great extent

0   1   2   3   4

I provide students with opportunities to generate their own nonlinguistic representations for terms and phrases they are learning.

Not at all   To a great extent

0   1   2   3   4

I provide students with opportunities to review the terms and phrases they are learning.

Not at all   To a great extent

0   1   2   3   4

Over time, I collect evidence about my students' proficiency with the terms and phrases.

Not at all   To a great extent

0   1   2   3   4

Module Reflection

Review your responses to the questions in the Reflecting on My Current Beliefs and Practices—Vocabulary worksheet, Figure 23.1 (p. 294). How has this module affected your thinking about teaching and learning? Use the space provided to record your thoughts.

● Reading this information affirms some of what I already knew about vocabulary terms

● Now, I better understand some things about vocabulary terms

● I think I will change how I use vocabulary in my classroom

MODULE 24

DETAILS

Details are very specific pieces of information. This category of knowledge includes facts, time sequences, cause-and-effect sequences, and episodes.

Facts convey information about the characteristics of a specific:

- person

  Barbara McClintock won the Nobel Prize for Physiology or Medicine in 1983 and became the first woman to be the sole winner of this award.

- place

  Thailand is a country situated in the west of the Indochinese Peninsula of Southeast Asia that extends about 930 miles (1,500 km) from north to south and about 500 miles (800 km) from east to west.

- living or nonliving thing

  My brother's dog, Reuben, weighs more than 150 pounds.

  The Golden Gate Bridge stretches 4,200 feet, and the suspended towers are 746 feet high.

- event

  On May 29, 1953, Edmund Hillary of New Zealand and Tenzing Norgay, a Nepalese Sherpa, ascended the Southeast Ridge of Mount Everest, past South Peak, to the summit.

Time sequences include important events that occurred between two points in time. For example, the events that occurred between Iraq's invasion of Kuwait on Aug. 2, 1990, and the United States's air attacks on Baghdad, Iraq, on Jan. 16, 1991, can be organized as a time sequence. First one thing happened, then another, then another.

Cause-and-effect sequences involve events that generate a product or an effect. A causal sequence can be as simple as a single cause for a single effect. For example, the fact that the team won the game because a certain player threw the ball to another player, who threw the ball to another player to complete the double play, can be organized as a causal sequence. More commonly, however, effects have complex networks of causes; one event affects another, which combines with a third event to affect a fourth, which then affects another. For example, the events leading up to the Russian Civil War (1918–1920) can be organized as a casual sequence.

Episodes are specific events that include

- a setting (i.e., a particular time and place),
- specific participants,
- a particular duration,
- a specific sequence of events, and
- a particular cause-and-effect.

For example, the events of the Whiskey Rebellion in 1794 can be organized as an episode. The rebellion occurred at a particular time and place; it had specific participants; it lasted for a specific duration of time; it involved a specific sequence of events; it was caused by specific events; and it had a specific effect on the country.

Before reading "Recommendations for Classroom Practice," take some time to reflect on your current practices and beliefs about details by completing the worksheet in Figure 24.1 (p. 307). This will give you a basis for comparison as you read about the strategies in the module.

Recommendations for Classroom Practice

During a unit of instruction, students encounter a wide variety of details such as facts and time sequences. In this module, we discuss two approaches to use in your classroom to teach details:

- exposing students to key details multiple times, and
- using dramatic representations of key details.

Expose Students to Key Details Multiple Times

Students are exposed to so many details during a unit of instruction that they cannot process all of this information at a deep enough level to remember and use it later. Therefore, it's a good idea to identify key details that students are expected to know in depth and then to plan your unit so that students are exposed to these details multiple times (at least three), with these exposures no more than two days apart.

To illustrate, assume that a teacher is planning to teach students about the Whiskey Rebellion. She identifies a set of key details surrounding this event and plans several activities to expose students to this set of details. First, since many students are probably unfamiliar with this event in history, she gives them a time sequence graphic organizer (Figure 24.2, p. 308) that sets out the order of important details.

The teacher's plans for the next few days include several activities that reinforce the important details. In class, students watch a video that depicts the events of the rebellion. For homework, the teacher asks students to read a first-person account of the uprising and generate a summary. Over the next few days as students discuss the significance of the Whiskey Rebellion in U.S. history, the teacher connects the details to the broader context of the episode. In this way, students engage in different activities that help them learn about the rebellion from a variety of perspectives.

Use Dramatic Representations of Key Details

Details can be taught in many ways. But, research indicates that a dramatic representation has the biggest effect on student's learning. Students of all ages can benefit from enactments of details. For example, students might act out the process of oxygen and carbon dioxide exchange in the blood, how a food chain works in an ecosystem, or the flow of electricity in a circuit. In a class studying communication systems, a teacher might ask students to represent a cellular phone transmission. To enact the process, students might act out roles as cellular towers, central switching stations, fiber-optic cables, a mobile caller, and the transmission.

FIGURE 24.1

Reflecting on My Current Beliefs and Practices—Details

Reflecting on what you have just read, think about your own classroom and answer the following questions.

What details do I teach in my classroom?

How do I teach details to my students? What strategies do I use?

What questions do I have about using details in my classroom?

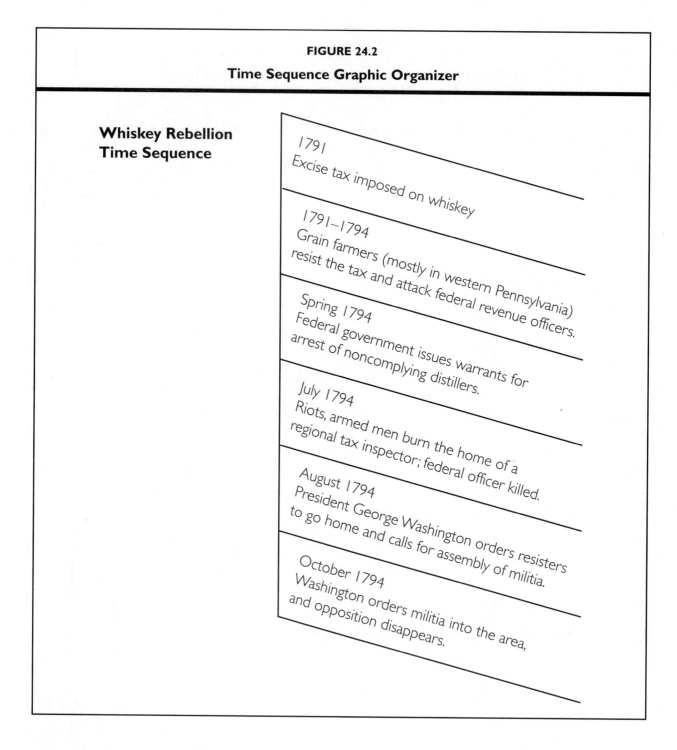

FIGURE 24.2

Time Sequence Graphic Organizer

Whiskey Rebellion Time Sequence

1791
Excise tax imposed on whiskey

1791–1794
Grain farmers (mostly in western Pennsylvania) resist the tax and attack federal revenue officers.

Spring 1794
Federal government issues warrants for arrest of noncomplying distillers.

July 1794
Riots, armed men burn the home of a regional tax inspector; federal officer killed.

August 1794
President George Washington orders resisters to go home and calls for assembly of militia.

October 1794
Washington orders militia into the area, and opposition disappears.

Tools to Facilitate Study of Details in the Classroom

Before using our recommendations in your classroom practice, consider a hypothetical situation or problem to check your understanding of the previous discussion by completing the exercise in Figure 24.3 (p. 309). It will give you an opportunity to apply what you have learned. The other assessment and planning tools that follow will help you guide your students' study of details in the classroom.

FIGURE 24.3

Checking My Understanding—Details

Imagine you are a teacher who is planning to teach the following details to students. For each detail, describe a story you might present to students to help them understand the detail or a type of enactment students might engage in to make the detail come alive for them.

Detail: *The Electoral College has electors from each state who cast votes for the president and vice president of the United States after the general election.*
Story or Enactment:

Detail: *When water freezes, it becomes solid. The molecules in a liquid are loosely packed and move about easily. The molecules in a solid are packed tightly, and movement is limited to vibrations.*
Story or Enactment:

Assessing the Impact on Students

Rubrics are one tool you can use to gauge students' progress. Sample rubrics are provided in Figure 24.4 for evaluating students' progress in learning details. These rubrics can be revised, when appropriate, for students to use as part of the self-assessment process to help them reflect on their work.

Planning Classroom Activities and Assessing Myself

Answering a series of questions will help you use the strategies for details. Use Figure 24.5 (pp. 311–312) to guide you in planning for details in your classroom.

Rubrics help assess student learning and you can assess how effectively you teach these strategies in your classroom by using Figure 24.6 (p. 313).

FIGURE 24.4

Rubrics for Key Details

Key Details Rubric

4   The student has a complete and detailed understanding of the facts, time sequences, cause-and-effect sequences, and episodes important to the topic.

3   The student has a complete understanding of the facts, time sequences, cause-and-effect sequences, and episodes important to the topic.

2   The student has an incomplete understanding or misconception about the key facts, time sequences, cause-and-effect sequences, and episodes important to the topic.

1   The student has an incomplete understanding and so many severe misconceptions about the facts, time sequences, cause-and-effect sequences, and episodes important to the topic that he cannot be said to understand them.

0   Not enough information to make a judgment.

Key Details Rubric for Younger Students

4   The student understands completely the important facts, time sequences, cause-and-effect sequences, and episodes. The student knows details about the important facts, time sequences, cause-and-effect sequences, and episodes.

3   The student understands the important facts, time sequences, cause-and-effect sequences, and episodes.

2   The student does not completely understand the important facts, time sequences, cause-and-effect sequences, and episodes. Or, the student's thinking shows some mistakes about the important facts, time sequences, cause-and-effect sequences, and episodes.

1   The student does not understand the important facts, time sequences, cause-and-effect sequences, and episodes. The student's thinking shows big mistakes about the important facts, time sequences, cause-and-effect sequences, and episodes.

0   The student does not try to do the task.

FIGURE 24.5

Planning for Details Worksheet

Unit _____

What details will I teach during this unit?

☐ Facts

-
-
-

☐ Time Sequences

-
-

☐ Cause-and-Effect Sequences

-
-

☐ Episodes

-
-

(continued on p. 312)

FIGURE 24.5 (CONTINUED)

Planning for Details Worksheet

How will I provide multiple exposures to the details?

How will I use enactments to enhance my students' understanding of the details?

How will I monitor how well students are learning the details?

What will I do to help students who are struggling with the details?

FIGURE 24.6

Assessing Myself—Details

I identify the key details students should learn prior to a unit of instruction.

Not at all   To a great extent

0   1   2   3   4

|————————————|————————————|————————————|————————————|

I present important details in the format of interesting stories or anecdotes.

Not at all   To a great extent

0   1   2   3   4

|————————————|————————————|————————————|————————————|

I have students act out important details.

Not at all   To a great extent

0   1   2   3   4

|————————————|————————————|————————————|————————————|

I expose students to key details multiple times.

Not at all   To a great extent

0   1   2   3   4

|————————————|————————————|————————————|————————————|

Over time, I collect evidence about my students' understanding of key details.

Not at all   To a great extent

0   1   2   3   4

|————————————|————————————|————————————|————————————|

Module Reflection

Review your responses to the questions in the Reflecting on My Current Beliefs and Practices worksheet, Figure 24.1 (p. 307). How has this module affected your thinking about teaching and learning? Use the space provided to record your thoughts.

- Reading this information affirms some of what I already knew about details

- Now, I better understand some things about details

- I think I will change how I use details in my classroom

ORGANIZING IDEAS

Organizing ideas, such as generalizations and principles, are the most general type of informational knowledge. We have not included *concepts* as organizing ideas because, technically defined, they are synonymous with generalizations (see Gagne, 1977). Generalizations are statements for which we can provide examples because they apply to many different situations. For example, the statement, "Mathematical functions describe how changes in one quantity or variable result in changes in another" is a generalization for which we can provide examples:

$$y = 2x + 3$$
$$a = \sqrt{36} - b^2$$
$$z = \sin y$$

Principles are specific types of generalizations that articulate rules or relationships that apply to a number of specific situations. For instance, "Water seeks its own level" is a scientific principle.

Although vocabulary terms and details are important, generalizations help students develop a broad knowledge base because they transfer more readily to different situations. Consider the generalization, "Art reflects and influences culture." We can apply this generalization across countries, situations, and time periods, whereas a fact about Paul Klee's "Twittering Machine" (1922), a specific piece of artwork, does not directly transfer to other situations. This is not to say that details are unimportant. On the contrary, to truly understand generalizations, students must be able to support them with exemplifying facts. For instance, to understand the generalization about the influences of art, students need a rich set of illustrative facts, which may include facts about Klee's "Twittering Machine."

It is easy to confuse some generalizations with some facts. Facts identify characteristics of specific persons, places, living and nonliving things, and events, whereas generalizations identify characteristics about *classes or categories* of persons, places, living and nonliving things, and events. For example, the statement, "My Old English Bull Mastiff, Reuben, is a good watchdog" is a fact. However, the statement, "Mastiffs are good watchdogs" is a generalization. Generalizations also articulate characteristics about abstractions. Specifically, information about abstractions is always stated in the form of generalizations. Generalizations describe the characteristics of classes of

- persons

  Australian aborigines have traditionally lived as hunter-gatherers, but contact with Europeans has radically changed their lifestyle and cultural traditions.
- places

  Alpine tundra exists above timberline on gentle slopes with large meadow areas or on windswept slopes covered with cushion plants. Animal species are limited in alpine tundra environments.

- living and nonliving things
  Diesel engines burn more efficiently and produce fewer pollutants than gasoline-burning engines.
- events
  Rodeos, where riders compete in events such as steer wrestling, calf roping, and bull riding, are popular in the United States and Canada.
- abstractions
  Postmodernism questions the possibility of objectivity and "fixed" meaning.

In general, there are two types of principles found in school-related content: *cause-and-effect principles and correlational principles.* Cause-and-effect principles articulate causal relationships. We can describe pollution as a cause-and-effect principle: Many human activities create pollutants that contaminate the environment. Understanding a cause-and-effect principle involves understanding the specific elements in the cause-and-effect system and the relationships those elements have to one another. To understand the cause-and-effect principle regarding human activities and the contamination of the environment, students must understand the sequence of events that occur, the elements involved, and the type and strength of relationships between and among those elements. In short, understanding a cause-and-effect principle involves understanding a great deal of information.

Correlational principles describe relationships that are not necessarily causal in nature, but in which a change in one factor is associated with a change in another factor. For example, *using a cellular phone while driving an automobile increases the chances of having an accident* is a correlational principle. Again, to understand this principle, a student would have to know specific details about this relationship and understand the general pattern: the number of drivers who have accidents increases as the number of drivers who are using cell phones increases.

These two types of principles are sometimes confused with cause-and-effect sequences. A cause-and-effect sequence applies to a specific situation, whereas a principle applies to many situations. The causes of a specific hurricane in a specific year taken together represent a cause-and-effect sequence. They apply to that specific hurricane only. However, the cause-and-effect principle linking human activities to pollution can be applied to many different types of activities and many types of pollution. Environmental scientists use this principle to make judgments about a variety of situations. The key distinction between principles and cause-and-effect sequences is that principles can be exemplified in a number of situations, whereas sequences apply to a single situation only.

Before reading "Recommendations for Classroom Practice," take some time to reflect on your current practices and beliefs about organizing ideas by completing the worksheet in Figure 25.1 (p. 317). This will give you a basis for comparison as you read about the strategies in the module.

Recommendations for Classroom Practice

In this module, we discuss an approach you can use to teach organizing ideas. The approach is

FIGURE 25.1

Reflecting on My Current Beliefs and Practices—Organizing Ideas

Reflecting on what you have just read, think about your own classroom and answer the following questions.

What organizing ideas do I teach in my classroom?

How do I teach organizing ideas to my students? What strategies do I use?

What questions do I have about using organizing ideas in my classroom?

to help students clear up misconceptions about generalizations and principles.

Clearing Up Misconceptions About Generalizations and Principles

Organizing ideas are "big ideas." Generalizations and principles describe complex relationships or scenarios that apply to different situations, and students need a great deal of information to understand them. It's not surprising that students commonly have misconceptions about them when they first hear them. For example, one generalization about the economy says that during a recession, unemployment rates rise and production declines. If students hear that unemployment rates rose during the month of July, they might think, "Oh no—recession!" But unemployment rates are only part of the complex web of elements that create a recession.

When students have apparent misconceptions about organizing ideas, you might present examples that help them understand the flaws in their thinking. For example, a teacher might anticipate potential misconceptions students might have about the state of the economy during a recession or pick up on students' misconceptions during classroom activities. Students might think that a rise in the unemployment rate means that the economy is headed for a recession. However, this is not always the case. The teacher might give students examples of times in recent history when unemployment rates rose but a recession did not occur. She might also present examples of times when a rise in unemployment rates combined with other factors to signal a full-blown economic downturn. Students need to understand that a variety of factors come in to play with generalizations and principles.

If students seem to understand a generalization or principle accurately, but not in depth, you might describe how it applies in a novel situation. For example, students might discuss the following questions: What conditions would have to occur today for the economy to fall into a recession (or pull out of one)? What happens when unemployment rates fall in a country that does not have a market economy? You also might ask students to come up with new examples or situations in which the principle applies.

Tools to Facilitate Organizing Ideas in the Classroom

Before using our recommendations in your classroom practice, consider a hypothetical situation or problem to check your understanding of the previous discussion by completing the exercise in Figure 25.2 (p. 319). It will give you an opportunity to apply what you have learned. The other assessment and planning tools that follow will help you guide your students in organizing ideas in the classroom.

Assessing the Impact on Students

Rubrics are one tool you can use to gauge students' progress. Sample rubrics are provided in Figure 25.3 (p. 320) for evaluating students' progress in learning generalizations and principles. These rubrics can be revised, when appropriate, for students to use as part of the self-assessment process to help them reflect on their work.

FIGURE 25.2

Checking My Understanding—Organizing Ideas

Identify one generalization and one principle that you might want students to understand related to a specific content area. For each generalization or principle, identify common misconceptions students might have.

Generalization

Common Misconceptions

-

-

-

Principle

Common Misconceptions

-

-

-

FIGURE 25.3

Rubrics for Organizing Ideas

Generalizations and Principles Rubric

4   The student has a complete and detailed understanding of the generalization or principle and generates new or unique examples or applications.

3   The student has a complete and detailed understanding of the generalization or principle and reconstructs or generates key examples or applications.

2   The student has an incomplete understanding of the generalization or principle and is missing some information or has misconceptions about the key examples or applications.

1   The student has an incomplete understanding and so many severe misconceptions about the generalization or principle that he cannot be said to understand it.

0   Not enough information to make a judgment.

Generalizations and Principles Rubrics for Younger Students

4   The student understands completely the generalization or principle. The student comes up with new examples.

3   The student understands the generalization or principle. The student can retell some important examples.

2   The student does not completely understand the generalization or principle. The student is missing some information. Or, the student's thinking shows some mistakes about the generalization or principle or the examples.

1   The student does not understand the generalization or principle. The student's thinking shows big mistakes about the generalization or principle or the examples. Or, the student cannot tell any examples.

0   The student does not try to do the task.

Planning Classroom Activities and Assessing Myself

Answering a series of questions will help you discover how you might use the strategies for organizing ideas in this module. You can use the Planning for Organizing Ideas Worksheet, Figure 25.4 (p. 321), to guide your planning for organizing ideas in your classroom.

Rubrics help assess student learning. You can assess yourself too—how effectively you use strategies for organizing ideas in your classroom. Use Figure 25.5 (p. 322) to evaluate your effectiveness with using organizing ideas in the classroom.

FIGURE 25.4

Planning for Organizing Ideas Worksheet

Unit _____

What organizing ideas will I teach during this unit?

    ☐ Generalization

    ☐ Principle

What misconceptions might students have about the generalization or principle?

What examples will I present to help students clear up misconceptions?

What new or different situations will I present to students to enhance their understanding of the generalization or principle?

How will I monitor how well students understand the generalization or principle?

What will I do to help students who are struggling with the generalization or principle?

FIGURE 25.5

Assessing Myself—Organizing Ideas

I identify key generalizations and principles students should know prior to a unit of instruction.

Not at all   To a great extent

   0   1   2   3   4

I clearly communicate the generalization or principle to students.

Not at all   To a great extent

   0   1   2   3   4

I provide accurate and clear examples to help students clear up misconceptions.

Not at all   To a great extent

   0   1   2   3   4

I provide new or different situations to enhance students' understanding.

Not at all   To a great extent

   0   1   2   3   4

Over time, I collect evidence about my students' understanding of the generalizations or principles.

Not at all   To a great extent

   0   1   2   3   4

Module Reflection

Review your responses to the questions in the Reflecting on My Current Beliefs and Practices—Organizing Ideas worksheet, Figure 25.1 (p. 317). How has this module affected your thinking about teaching and learning? Use the space provided to record your thoughts.

- Reading this information affirms some of what I already knew about organizing ideas

- Now, I better understand some things about organizing ideas

- I think I will change how I use organizing ideas in my classroom

SKILLS AND PROCESSES

As educators, we speak of teaching skills or processes—the writing process, problem-solving skills, the scientific method, basketball skills—but we rarely reflect on what we mean by a skill or process. Processes are similar to skills in some ways and different in other ways. Processes and skills both produce some form of result or product. For example, the *skill* of reading a bar graph leads to a new understanding of the relationship between two variables. The *process* of writing produces a new composition. The difference lies in how we accomplish each. Processes have a much higher tolerance than skills for variation in the steps involved. For example, there are not many ways to go about reading a bar graph, but there are many different ways to engage in the process of writing. We might say that processes are more robust than skills are in terms of how they can be performed.

In technical terms, we can define skills as *tactics* and *algorithms* (Snowman & McCown, 1984). *Tactics* are general rules governing an overall flow of execution, rather than a set of steps that must be performed in a specific order. For example, a tactic for reading data displayed in a chart might address (1) determining what is reported in the rows of the chart, (2) determining what is reported in the columns of the chart, and (3) determining the relationship between the elements in the rows

and columns. When we read a chart, we follow a general pattern to carry out these rules, but we do not have to follow them in a rigid or set order. *Algorithms* are mental skills that have specific outcomes and specific steps. Performing long division is an illustration of an algorithm. Although the steps in a tactic do not have to be performed in a set order, the steps in an algorithm do. Obviously, changing the order in which you perform the steps of long division will dramatically change the answer that is computed.

Before reading "Recommendations for Classroom Practice," take some time to reflect on your current practices and beliefs about skills and processes by completing the worksheet in Figure 26.1 (p. 325). This will give you a basis for comparison as you read about the strategies in the module.

Recommendations for Classroom Practice

In this module, we describe four approaches you might use to help students learn skills and processes:

- facilitating the discovery approach to skills and processes,
- building models,
- shaping skills and processes, and
- internalizing skills and processes.

FIGURE 26.1

Reflecting on My Current Beliefs and Practices—Skills and Processes

---

Reflecting on what you have just read, think about your own classroom and answer the following questions.

What skills or processes do I teach in my classroom?

How do I teach skills or processes to my students? What strategies do I use?

What questions do I have about using skills and processes in my classroom?

Facilitate the Discovery Approach to Skills and Processes

A common misconception in education is that allowing students to discover how to perform a skill or process is always better than directly teaching the skill or process. This idea probably gained favor in reaction to the long-held misconception that drill and practice in specific steps is always the best way to teach skills. The truth about how to teach skills and processes lies somewhere between the "discovery" and "drill-and-practice" techniques. Students learn some skills better through discovery, but they learn other skills better through direct instruction. For example, consider the skills of addition, subtraction, multiplication, and division. Asking students to discover the steps involved in these computation processes makes little sense. Students would probably understand these skills well if they discovered the steps to addition, but this process would take an excessive amount of time. It makes more sense to have students discover strategies for solving specific types of addition problems.

There is no magic list of skills and processes that are best suited for a discovery approach. A useful rule of thumb is that the more variation there is in the steps that students can use to execute a skill or a process effectively (e.g., in the order of the steps, the number of steps, and even the steps themselves), the more amenable the skill or process is to discovery learning. For example, if a student must follow five steps in a specific order to properly use a piece of equipment in a science lab, then you probably shouldn't ask the student to try to discover these five steps and the order of execution. Instead, you might demonstrate those steps and then provide opportunities for students to alter them to suit their individual needs and styles. On the other hand, a tactic students can execute in a number of ways is probably a good candidate for discovery learning.

Build Models

Developing a rough model of the steps involved is the first phase of learning a skill or process. For example, when you first learned to hit a golf ball, someone probably showed you what to do before you actually tried a shot on your own. Your instructor may have demonstrated the proper grip, the proper stance, and how to shift your weight. Likewise, when you first learned long division, someone probably showed you the steps in the process. In short, when we learn a new procedure, we need someplace to start—we need a model. Without an initial model, learning a skill or process can be chaotic and time consuming because it's essentially trial-and-error.

One good modeling process is the "think aloud," a method that involves verbalizing your thoughts as you demonstrate the skill or process. Although it might seem tedious, the "think aloud" process should touch on the important parts of the skill or process. For example, a teacher using think-aloud modeling to help students develop a model of two-column addition might write a problem on the board and then say, "Let's see, the first thing I have to do is add up the numbers in the ones column: 2 plus 3 equals 5, and 7 more equals 12. That's 12 ones, which equals 1 ten and 2 ones. I write down the 2 ones and take the 1 ten over to the tens column. I think I'll put a 1 at the top of the tens column so I don't forget it."

You can use think-aloud modeling for almost any skill or process. For example, in a woodworking class, a teacher can think aloud as she demonstrates how to use a lathe properly, emphasizing not only the steps involved but also the general safety rules to follow. In a French class, a teacher might think aloud as he conjugates a verb or breaks a sentence into its grammatical parts.

Some students may prefer a written set of steps. You can develop steps for skills and processes that give students general guidance. As students practice, they will refine the steps to suit their own way of doing things. To illustrate, Figure 26.2 is a set of steps you might present to students as a model for the skill of reading a bar graph.

With a little thought, you can create a set of general steps for almost any skill or tactic. In a language arts class, a teacher might give students a set of steps for writing a limerick. She might demonstrate each step as she reads them out loud. In an art class, the teacher might post a set of steps for properly caring for animal-hair brushes.

Shape Skills and Processes

Constructing an initial model for a new skill or process is just the first step in learning this type of knowledge. Once you begin to use the skill or process, you'll alter your initial model. You'll figure out what works and what doesn't work, and, in response, you will modify your approach, adding some things and dropping others. This process is called shaping. For example, after you constructed an initial model for performing long division, you began to discover some shortcuts and tricks that made the process work better for you. Similarly, after you first learned how to create text on your word processor, you began to identify ways to use the word processor more efficiently.

One of the most important aspects of the shaping process is identifying and fine-tuning the subcomponents of a complex process. For example, teachers commonly provide a description of the various components involved in writing, sometimes referred to as the process writing approach: (1) prewriting, (2) writing, and (3) revising.

FIGURE 26.2

Steps for Reading a Chart

1. Read the title of the chart. Get a sense of the information that will be in it.
2. Look at the headings for the rows. Identify what is being reported in the rows.
3. Look at the heading for the columns. Identify what is being reported in the columns.
4. Look at each of the data cells in the chart. Identify the value of the data.
5. Make a statement that summarizes the important information in the chart.

However, within each of these major components of the writing process are more specific subcomponents. For example, within the prewriting component of the writing process, students may identify the following subcomponents in their preparations:

- Prewriting
  - Brainstorm ideas
  - Group related ideas, using webs, graphic organizers, or story maps
  - Plan a sequence of ideas and creates an outline
  - Construct critical standards for the written piece
  - Build background knowledge

As the research recommends, students should not practice the subcomponents of a complex process in isolation. It's much more useful to practice them in the context of the entire process. To facilitate this type of practice, you can structure tasks to emphasize a specific subcomponent. The following activities can help students focus on specific subcomponents of a process:

- Help students clearly identify the specific subcomponent (e.g., skill or strategy) they are going to practice and set criteria for evaluating their own progress.
- Give students a variety of assignments over time that require them to use the targeted skill or strategy within the context of the process.
- Encourage students to self-assess, but also give them feedback on the targeted skill or strategy. To help students focus, avoid giving feedback on other aspects of the process.

The importance of shaping a new skill or process cannot be exaggerated. Inattention to this aspect of learning skills and processes is a primary reason for students' failure to effectively use them.

Help Students Internalize Skills and Processes

The last aspect of learning a new skill or process is internalizing it. For some skills and processes, internalizing means learning them to the point where you can use them without much conscious thought. This level of proficiency is called *automaticity* because you use the skill or process automatically. In fact, you must learn many skills and processes to the level of automaticity if they are to be truly useful. Imagine how difficult (and dangerous) driving a car would be if using the brake were not an automatic response.

You can't achieve automaticity in all skills and processes, but you can develop fluency in them. For example, the process of editing is never automatic, but good editors are quite fluent in the language of editing. Although they have to think about what they are doing, they have internalized the necessary skills to such a degree that they can use them with relative ease. In the classroom, then, you should devote a good deal of time and effort to helping students internalize important skills and processes. Setting up a schedule that provides adequate time for students to practice is one effective method for helping students to internalize skills.

Tools to Facilitate Organizing Ideas in the Classroom

Before using our recommendations in your classroom practice, consider a hypothetical situation or problem to check your understanding of the previous discussion by completing the exercise in Figure 26.3. It will give you an opportunity to apply what you have learned. The other assessment and planning tools that follow will help you guide your students in skills and processes in the classroom.

Assessing the Impact on Students

Rubrics are one tool you can use to gauge students' progress. Sample rubrics are provided in Figure 26.4 (p. 330) for evaluating students' progress in using skills and processes. These rubrics can be revised, when appropriate, for students to use as part of the self-assessment process to help them reflect on their work.

Planning Classroom Activities and Assessing Myself

Answering a series of questions will help you discover how you might use the strategies for skills and processes in this module. You can use the Planning for Skills and Processes Worksheet, Figure 26.5 (p. 331), to guide your thinking when planning for skills and processes in your classroom.

Rubrics help assess student learning. You can assess yourself too—how effectively you use strategies for skills and processes in your classroom. Use Figure 26.6 (p. 332) to evaluate your effectiveness with skills and processes.

FIGURE 26.3

Checking My Understanding—Skills and Processes

Think of a skill or process that you can perform with fluency, almost automatically—like driving a car, riding a horse, adding numbers in your head, typing, or reading a book. Think about how you went through the three phases of modeling, shaping, and internalizing as you developed this skill, and then answer the following questions.

How did you build an initial model for this skill or process?

What did you do to shape and adapt the skill?

How did you internalize this skill?

FIGURE 26.4

Rubrics for Skills and Processes

Generic Rubric for Procedural Knowledge

4   The student performs the skill or process accurately and with fluency. The student also understands the key features of the skill.

3   The student performs the skill or process accurately but not automatically.

2   The student makes some significant errors when performing the skill or process but can still do the basic steps.

1   The student makes so many errors when performing the skill or process that the student cannot actually do the skill.

0   Not enough information to make a judgment.

Generic Rubric for Procedural Knowledge for Younger Students

4   The student does the skill correctly and easily. The student also understands the important parts of the skill.

3   The student does the skill correctly but not easily.

2   The student makes some big mistakes when she does the skill, but the student can still do the basic steps in the skill.

1   The student makes so many big mistakes that she cannot do the skill.

0   The student does not try to do the skill.

FIGURE 26.5

Planning for Skills and Processes Worksheet

Unit _____

What skill or process will I teach during this unit?

What will I do to help students build models for the skill or process?

What will I do to help students shape the skill or process?

What will I do to help students internalize the skill or process?

How will I monitor how well students are using the skill or process?

What will I do to help students who are struggling with the skill or process?

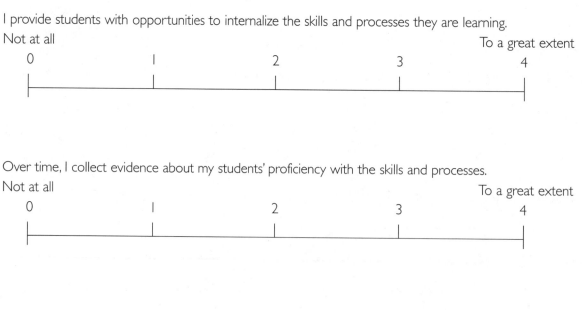

FIGURE 26.6

Assessing Myself—Skills and Processes

I identify specific skills and processes students are to master prior to a unit of instruction.

Not at all   To a great extent

0   1   2   3   4

I present students with models for the skills and processes they are learning.

Not at all   To a great extent

0   1   2   3   4

I provide students with opportunities to shape the skills and processes they are learning.

Not at all   To a great extent

0   1   2   3   4

I provide students with opportunities to internalize the skills and processes they are learning.

Not at all   To a great extent

0   1   2   3   4

Over time, I collect evidence about my students' proficiency with the skills and processes.

Not at all   To a great extent

0   1   2   3   4

Module Reflection

Review your responses to the questions in the Reflecting on My Current Beliefs and Practices—Skills and Processes worksheet, Figure 26.1 (p. 325). How has this module affected your thinking about teaching and learning? Use the space provided to record your thoughts.

- Reading this information affirms some of what I already knew about skills and processes

- Now, I better understand some things about skills and processes

- I think I will change how I use skills and processes in my classroom

11 Putting It All Together

Educators can use the techniques described in Sections 1 through 10 of this handbook in a variety of situations and circumstances. As suggested in the introduction, we encourage you to select whatever techniques you find useful and disregard the rest. However, in this section we make a case that the strategies in this handbook can be organized into an instructional framework that provides structure to what occurs during a unit of instruction.

Many teachers probably remember and still use Madeline Hunter's (1984) framework for "lesson design." Specifically, Hunter recommended that a lesson include the components listed in Figure 11.1.

Hunter's suggestions for lesson design make good sense, and the recommendations in this handbook support her suggestions. However, in this section, we take a different approach. Instead of addressing the characteristics of an effective lesson, we focus on the characteristics of an effective unit. One of the main reasons for our focus on a unit is that lessons, taken day-by-day, might look very different depending on the situation. For example, when a teacher introduces new content, a lesson might include all the elements of Hunter's lesson design. However, when students are applying content knowledge, a lesson could entail having students work independently or in small groups during an entire day with no direct instruction.

In this section, we present a framework for organizing a unit of instruction. A unit is usually organized around a theme, for example "weather" or "great leaders," and commonly takes some weeks to complete. The instructional strategies described in the previous sections can be organized in a way that provides explicit guidance in organizing a unit. Please note that this section is different from the previous sections because it synthesizes much of the previous discussions into a unified whole.

List of Figures

FIGURE 27.1

Elements of Lesson Design

Elements of Lesson Design

Anticipatory set. A mental set that causes students to focus on what will be learned. It may also give practice in helping students achieve the learning and yield diagnostic data for the teacher. *Example:* "Look at the paragraph on the board. What do you think might be the most important part to remember?"

Objective and purpose. Not only do students *learn* more effectively when they know what they're supposed to be learning and why that learning is important to them, but teachers *teach* more effectively when they have that same information. *Example:* "Frequently people have difficulty in remembering things that are important to them. Sometimes you feel you have studied hard and yet you don't remember some of the important parts. Today, we're going to learn ways to identify what's important, and then we'll practice ways we can use to remember important things."

Input. Students must acquire new information about the knowledge, process, or skill they are to achieve. To design the input phase of the lesson so that a successful outcome becomes predictable, the teacher must have analyzed the final objective to identify knowledge and skills that need to be acquired.

Modeling. "Seeing" what is meant is an important adjunct to learning. To avoid stifling creativity, showing several examples of the process or products that students are expected to acquire or produce is helpful.

Checking for understanding. Before students are expected to do something, the teacher should determine that they understand what they are supposed to do and that they have the minimum skills required.

Guided practice. Students practice their new knowledge or skill *under direct teacher supervision.* New learning is like wet cement; it is easily damaged. An error at the beginning of learning can easily "set," so that correcting it later is harder than correcting it immediately.

Independent practice. Independent practice is assigned only after the teacher is reasonably sure that students will not make serious errors. After an initial lesson, students frequently are not ready to practice independently, and the teacher has committed a pedagogical error if unsupervised practice is expected.

Source: Adapted from Hunter, M. (1984) "Knowing, Teaching, and Supervising." In P. Hosford (Ed.) *Using What We Know About Teaching* (pp. 169–192). Alexandria, VA: Association for Supervision and Curriculum Development.

An Instructional Framework for Units

Although a unit of instruction does not have to look a certain way, the sequence presented in Figure 27.2 (pp. 339–340) gives a rough outline of the instructional techniques that might be implemented at the beginning of a unit, during a unit, and at the end of a unit.

As Figure 27.2 shows, we recommend that you think of an instructional unit as involving three general categories of activities: (1) what happens at the beginning of a unit, (2) what happens during a unit, and (3) what happens at the end of a unit. Use the Planning Worksheet for a Unit of Instruction, Figure 27.3 (pp. 341–342), to help guide your thinking when planning units

Instructional Strategies to Use at the Beginning of a Unit

A unit of instruction should begin with at least two distinct activities:

- Identifying clear learning goals (see Section 7)
- Allowing students to identify and record their own learning goals (see Section 7)

To illustrate, an 8th grade language arts teacher might present students with the following five instructional goals during a unit on Mary Shelley's *Frankenstein:*

Learning Goal 1:   Understands elements of character development

Learning Goal 2:   Understands the use of gothic literary devices

Learning Goal 3:   Understands the effects of author's style on a reader

Learning Goal 4:   Writes persuasive compositions

Learning Goal 5:   Uses a variety of sentence structures

As recommended in Section 7 of this handbook, these goals are relatively specific but flexible enough to allow students to identify more specific personal learning goals. For example, when identifying learning goals that relate to the five provided by the teacher, a student might state the following personalized goals:

I want to know what the monster in *Frankenstein* represents.

I want to address two counterarguments when I write my persuasive essay.

You might use the following questions as guidance when planning for the beginning of an instructional unit:

1. What learning goals will I present to students?
2. How will I display these goals so that they are clearly evident throughout the unit?
3. How will I provide guidance for students as they generate their own learning goals?
4. How will students display these goals so that they are clearly evident throughout the unit?

Instructional Strategies to Use During a Unit

Once clear learning goals have been established, instructional strategies have great value

FIGURE 27.2

Planning Guide

When Strategies Might be Used	Instructional Strategies
At the Beginning of a Unit	*Setting Learning Goals* 1. Identify clear learning goals. 2. Allow students to identify and record their own learning goals.
During a Unit	*Introducing New Knowledge* 1. Guide students in identifying and articulating what they already know about the topic. 2. Provide students with ways of thinking about the topic in advance. 3. Ask students to compare the new knowledge with what is known. 4. Ask students to keep notes on the knowledge addressed in the unit. 5. Help students represent the knowledge in nonlinguistic ways, periodically sharing these representations with others. 6. Ask students to work sometimes individually, but other times in cooperative groups. *Practicing, Reviewing, and Applying Knowledge* 1. Assign homework that requires students to practice, review, and apply what they have learned; however, be sure to give students explicit feedback as to the accuracy of all of their homework. 2. Engage students in long-term projects that involve generating and testing hypotheses. 3. Have students revise the linguistic and nonlinguistic representations of knowledge in their notebooks as they refine their understanding of the knowledge. Monitoring Learning Goals 1. Give students feedback and help them self-assess their progress toward achieving their goals. 2. Ask students to keep track of their achievement of the learning goals and of the effort they are expending to achieve the goals. 3. Periodically celebrate legitimate progress toward learning goals.

(continued on p. 340)

FIGURE 27.2 (CONTINUED)

Planning Guide

At the End of a Unit	*Helping Students Determine How Well They Have Achieved Their Goals* 1. Provide students with clear assessments of their progress on each learning goal. 2. Have students assess themselves on each learning goal and compare these assessments with the teacher's assessment. 3. Ask students to articulate what they have learned about the content and about themselves as learners.

FIGURE 27.3

Planning Worksheet for a Unit of Instruction

Planning for the Beginning of an Instructional Unit

• What learning goals will I present to students?

• How will I display these goals so that they are clearly evident throughout the unit?

• How will I provide guidance for students as they generate their own learning goals?

• How will students display these goals so that they are evident throughout the unit?

During a Unit
Planning for Introducing Knowledge

• Which activities will I use to help students identify what they already know about new knowledge?

• What activities will I use to help provide students with advanced organizers for new knowledge?

• What activities will I use to help students make inferences about new knowledge?

• What will I do to help students take notes about the new knowledge?

• What will I do to help students represent the new knowledge in nonlinguistic ways?

• How will I use cooperative learning?

• What will I do to help students identify similarities and differences relative to the new knowledge?

(continued on p. 342)

FIGURE 27.3 (CONTINUED)

Planning Worksheet for a Unit of Instruction

During a Unit
Planning for Students to Review, Apply, and Practice Knowledge
• How will I use homework to help students practice the knowledge that has been presented to them?

• How will I use homework to help students apply the knowledge they are learning?

• What activities will I use to help students generate and test hypotheses about the knowledge they are learning?

• What will I do to help students review and revise the nonlinguistic representations they have made for the knowledge they are learning?

During a Unit
Planning for Monitoring Student Progress Toward Learning Goals
• How will I provide students with systematic feedback on their progress toward learning goals?

• How will I involve students in the feedback process relative to learning goals?

• How will I celebrate and recognize student progress throughout the unit?

Planning for the End of a Unit
• How will I provide a summary evaluation to students for each of the learning goals?

• How will I solicit students' self-evaluations for each learning goal?

• How will I reconcile differences between my evaluation of a student's progress and the self-evaluation?

throughout a unit of instruction. As Figure 27.2 (pp. 339–340) shows, we organize these strategies into three broad categories: (1) introducing new knowledge; (2) practicing, reviewing, and applying knowledge; and (3) monitoring learning goals.

Introducing New Knowledge. Within a unit of instruction, it is useful to distinguish between knowledge new to students and knowledge they have already been exposed to that you will ask them to practice, review, or apply. Of course, knowledge that is new at the very beginning of a unit might be the very knowledge that students review, practice, or apply two weeks into the unit. For example, consider the concept of map projections, which might be introduced in a unit on maps and globes. Assuming that this knowledge was new to students, the following instructional activities would be appropriate:

- Guide students in identifying and articulating what they already know about the topics. (See Section 9.)
- Provide students with ways of thinking about the topic in advance. (See Section 9.)
- Ask students to compare the new knowledge with what is known. (See Section 9.)
- Ask students to keep notes on the knowledge addressed in the unit. (See Section 2.)
- Help students represent the knowledge in nonlinguistic ways, periodically sharing these representations with others. (See Sections 2 and 5.)
- Ask students to work sometimes individually, but other times in cooperative groups. (See Section 6.)

To illustrate, before students watch a video of how various maps are created, the teacher might ask them to briefly share with another student anything they know or think they know about the topic. The teacher might also give students a partially completed graphic organizer as a form of advance organizer. While students watch the video on how maps are created, the teacher might occasionally stop the video and ask inferential questions about various maps. The teacher might also ask students to keep a notebook like that shown in Figure 27.3 (p. 344).

During this process, students record notes generate nonlinguistic representations for their notes. At the end of the demonstration, the teacher might ask students to identify similarities and differences among various map projections, such as the Mercator projection, the Berghaus Star projection, and the Lambert Equal-Area Conic projection. Finally, students might perform some of these activities while working in cooperative groups.

In short, introducing new knowledge can be facilitated by the use of the specific instructional strategies listed above. You might use the following questions to help you plan for introducing new knowledge:

- What activities will I use to help students identify what they already know about new knowledge?
- What activities will I use to help provide students with advanced organizers for new knowledge?
- What activities will I use to help students make inferences about new knowledge?
- What will I do to help students take notes about the new knowledge?

FIGURE 27.4

Combination Notes—Map Projections

MAP PROJECTIONS
only on a globe do you get
true size and shapes

on a map, some
distortion is inevitable

minimize distortion by
using different projections
for different needs

Projections

Cylindrical
treat Earth as cylinder
parallels are horizontal lines
meridians are vertical lines
Mercator projection

Conic
projection of globe on a cone
drawn with point above N or S pole

Planar
part of Earth as flattened disk
as viewed from point at center
of Earth

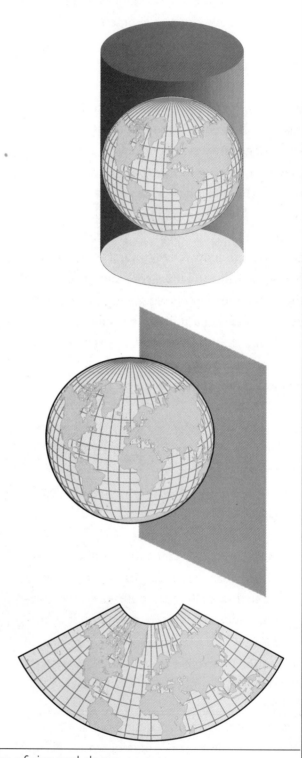

Summary: Map projections cause some distortion of size and shape.
Three types of projections are cylindrical, conic, and planar.

- What will I do to help students represent the new knowledge in nonlinguistic ways?
- How will I use cooperative learning?
- What will I do to help students identify similarities and differences relative to the new knowledge?

Reviewing, Applying, and Practicing Knowledge. After knowledge has been introduced, students must review, apply, and practice if they are to learn the new knowledge effectively. A number of instructional strategies relate to this aspect of learning.

- Assign homework that requires students to review, apply, or practice what they have learned. However, be sure to give students explicit feedback about the accuracy of all their homework. (See Section 4.)
- Engage students in projects that involve generating and testing hypotheses. (See Section 8.)
- Ask students to revise the linguistic and nonlinguistic representations of knowledge in their notebooks as they refine their understanding of the knowledge. (See Sections 2 and 5.)

For example, after introducing the concept of estimating linear measurements in a mathematics class, a teacher might assign homework that requires students to practice this concept by estimating the dimensions of different objects. Or the teacher might assign homework that requires an application of the skill by asking students to solve problems in real-world contexts, such as estimating the amount of carpet needed in a specific situation.

In a social studies class, after introducing students to the concept of conflict and cooperation among individuals, groups, and institutions, a teacher might engage students in an activity that requires them to generate and test hypotheses about this topic. For example, students might engage in a systems analysis of the ways in which conflict and cooperation work within their school or classroom, or they might use the problem-solving process to work through specific conflict scenarios.

Finally, if the teacher has asked students to record nonlinguistic representations of the topic in their notebooks, she might provide time for them to revise those representations—adding new information they might have learned and correcting misconceptions they might have initially had.

The following questions will help you plan how students will review, apply, and practice knowledge:

- How will I use homework to help students practice the knowledge that has been presented to them?
- How will I use homework to help students apply the knowledge they are learning?
- What activities will I use to help students generate and test hypotheses about the knowledge they are learning?
- What will I do to help students review and revise the nonlinguistic representations they have made for the knowledge they are learning?

Monitoring Learning Goals. Monitoring students' progress toward learning goals should occur throughout a unit of instruction. Asking students to monitor their progress toward the goals they and the teacher have constructed increases the likelihood that students will accomplish these goals, and communicates that the established goals are the focal point of the unit. Several instructional strategies facilitate the systematic monitoring of goals:

- Provide students with feedback and help them self-assess their progress toward achieving their learning goals. (See Section 7.)
- Ask students to keep track of their achievement of the learning goals and of the effort they are expending to achieve the goals. (See Section 7.)
- Periodically celebrate legitimate progress toward learning goals. (See Section 3.)

As students work with the knowledge that is the focus of the learning goal, the teacher provides continual feedback on students' progress toward those goals. This process is best done individually. That is, feedback should be provided individually to each student on the learning goals they each set. Using the many rubrics provided in the previous sections of this handbook, the teacher might update his assessment of students' progress every second or third day. Both teacher and students might keep a table or chart of the feedback. The process is made even more powerful in terms of students' learning if students are involved in it. For example, using the same rubrics that the teacher uses, students might systematically evaluate their own progress on the learning goals and compare their self-evaluations with those made by the teacher. Self-assessment worksheets, provided in previous sections of

this handbook, can facilitate this process. Finally, periodically throughout the unit, the teacher might have students describe their progress. Teachers might note and recognize students' progress in a variety of ways, for example by giving specific explanations about what the student has done correctly and incorrectly, asking students to review and comment on one another's homework, and recognizing students for reaching specific learning goals.

The following questions can help you plan for monitoring students' progress toward learning goals during a unit of instruction:

- How will I provide students with systematic feedback on their progress toward learning goals?
- How will I involve students in the feedback process relative to learning goals?
- How will I celebrate and recognize students' progress throughout the unit?

Instructional Strategies to Use at the End of a Unit

A unit of instruction should begin with a focus on learning goals—and it should end with that focus as well. The following activities can provide this focus:

- Give students clear assessments of their progress on each learning goal. (See Sections 3 and 7.)
- Have students assess themselves on each learning goal and compare these assessments with those of the teacher (See Section 7.)
- Have students articulate what they have learned about the content and about themselves as learners. (See Section 7.)

To illustrate, the 8th grade language arts teacher mentioned at the beginning of this section might give each student a summary evaluation of the student's performance on each of the five learning goals. The teacher might ask students to provide their own summaries of their performance on their learning goals. If a student's evaluations differ from the teacher's, the student and teacher might have a conference to determine which of the two summary evaluations is the more accurate. Finally, students might write a description of what they learned relative to the content of the unit and what they learned about themselves as learners.

The following questions might help you plan how to end a unit:

- How will I provide a summary evaluation to students for each of the learning goals?
- How will I solicit students' self-evaluations for each learning goal?
- How will I reconcile differences between my evaluation of students and their self-evaluations?
- How will I engage students in providing a summary of their learning goals at the end of the unit?

Conclusion

This handbook has presented suggestions for classroom practice in nine general categories of instructional strategies. What is more important is that the handbook has required you to (1) examine your use of instructional strategies within these nine categories, (2) test the effectiveness of your current practices, and (3) consider (and possibly try out) new practices. Ultimately, this process of self-examination, testing the effectiveness of what we do, and considering new ways of doing things is the key to success in the classroom. Instructional strategies do not produce effective teaching. Rather, effective teaching is the byproduct of a thoughtful individual, skilled in the art and science of teaching, making decisions about the best practices for her students at all times. Handbooks like this one are tools only. With this acknowledged, we encourage you to continue your exploration into the effectiveness of the instructional strategies presented in this handbook and to consider other strategies. Finally, we encourage you to involve others in your exploration. Nothing is more powerful than a group of dedicated educators sharing their insights about classroom practice. We hope that the *Handbook for Instructional Strategies That Work* has provided and will continue to provide a framework within which individual and joint inquiry about effective teaching can occur.

Appendix

Blackline masters for some of the techniques and strategies appear on the following pages. Whether you work alone or in a study group, adapt the formats to enhance your study and investigation of instructional strategies.

List of Blackline Masters

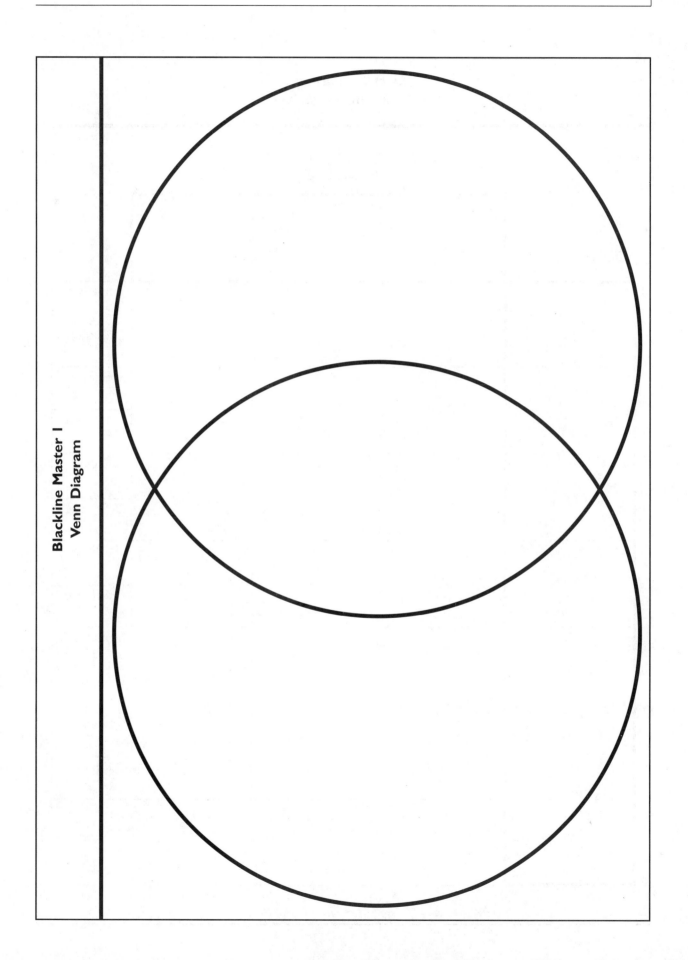

Blackline Master I
Venn Diagram

Blackline Master 2
Comparing Organizer

Items to be compared

Characteristics	A.	B.	C.	
1.				Similarities
				Differences
2.				Similarities
				Differences
3.				Similarities
				Differences
4.				Similarities
				Differences
5.				Similarities
				Differences
6.				Similarities
				Differences
Conclusions				

Blackline Master 3
Classification Organizer

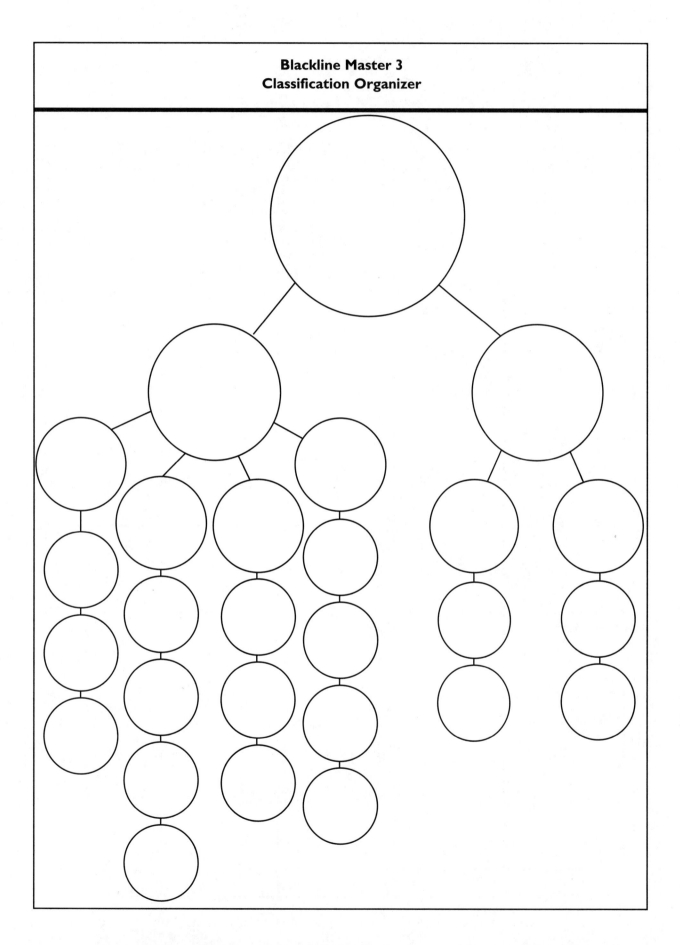

Blackline Master 4
Classifying Organizer

Categories

Items

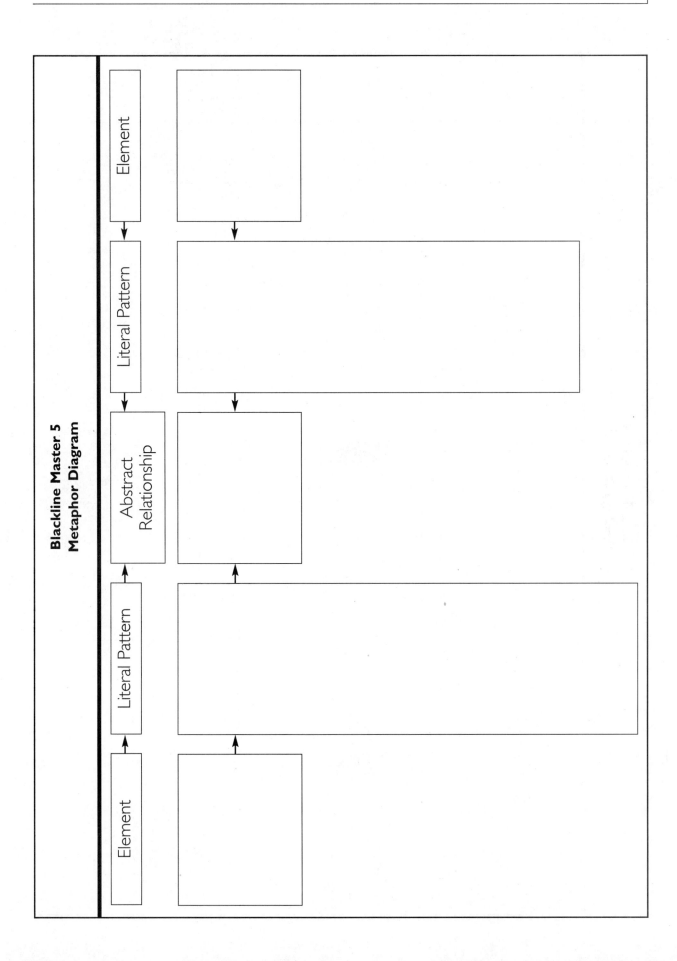

Blackline Master 5
Metaphor Diagram

Element

Literal Pattern

Abstract Relationship

Literal Pattern

Element

Blackline Master 6
Analogy Organizer

A

B

is to

As

C

D

is to

Blackline Master 7
Descriptive Pattern Organizer

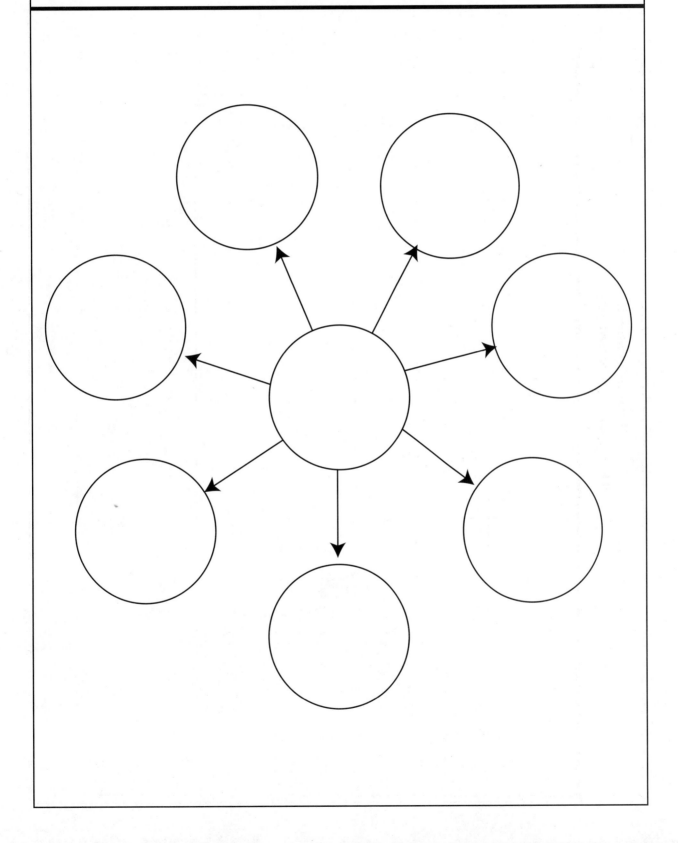

Blackline Master 8
Time Sequence Pattern Organizer

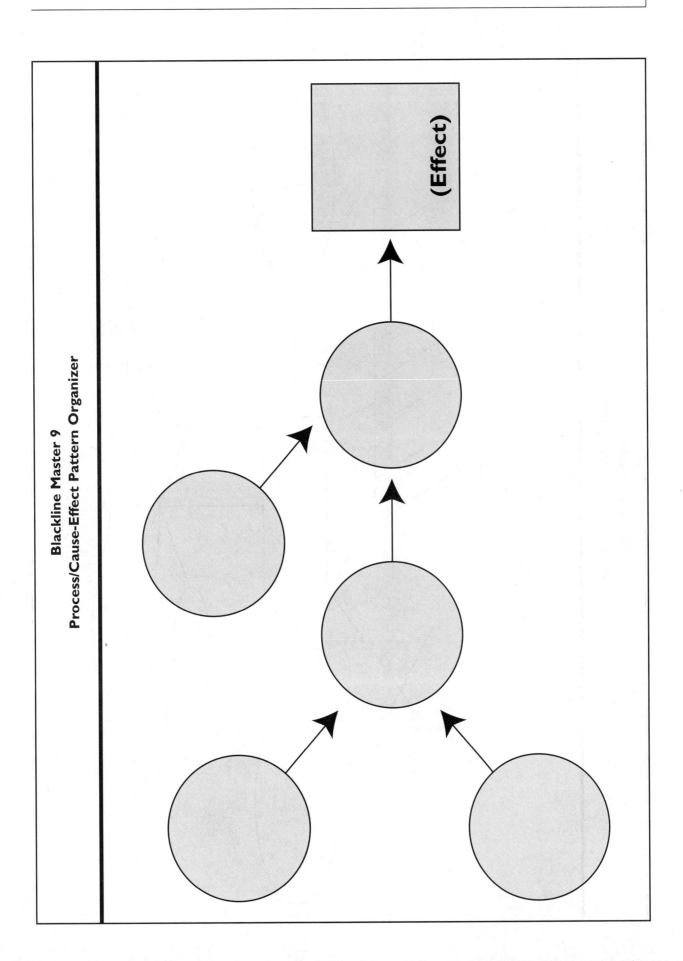

Blackline Master 9
Process/Cause-Effect Pattern Organizer

(Effect)

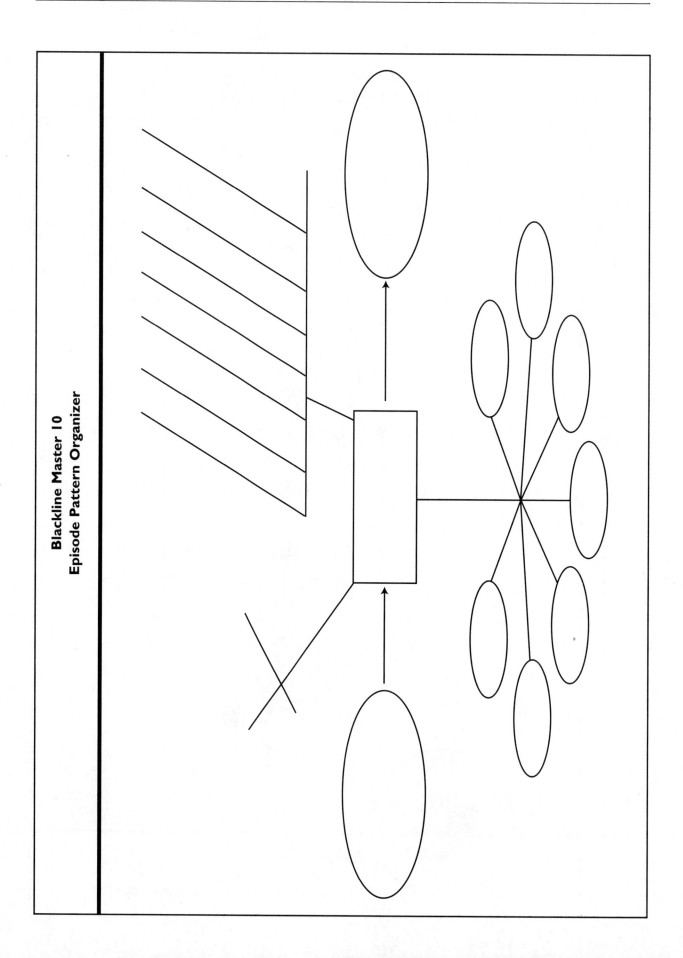

Blackline Master 10
Episode Pattern Organizer

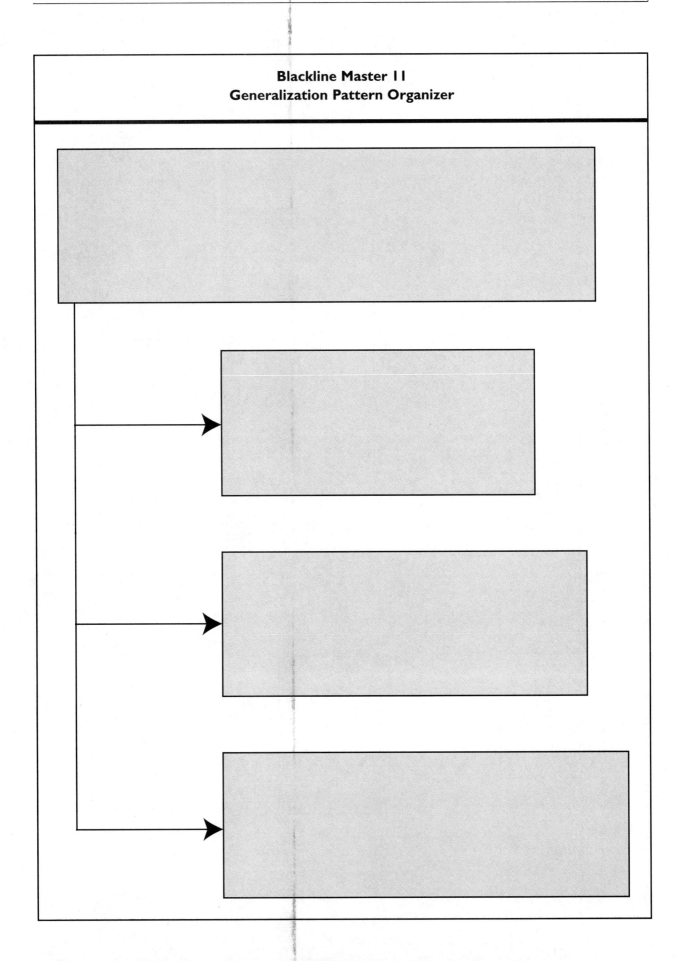

Blackline Master 11
Generalization Pattern Organizer

Blackline Master 12
Concept Pattern Organizer

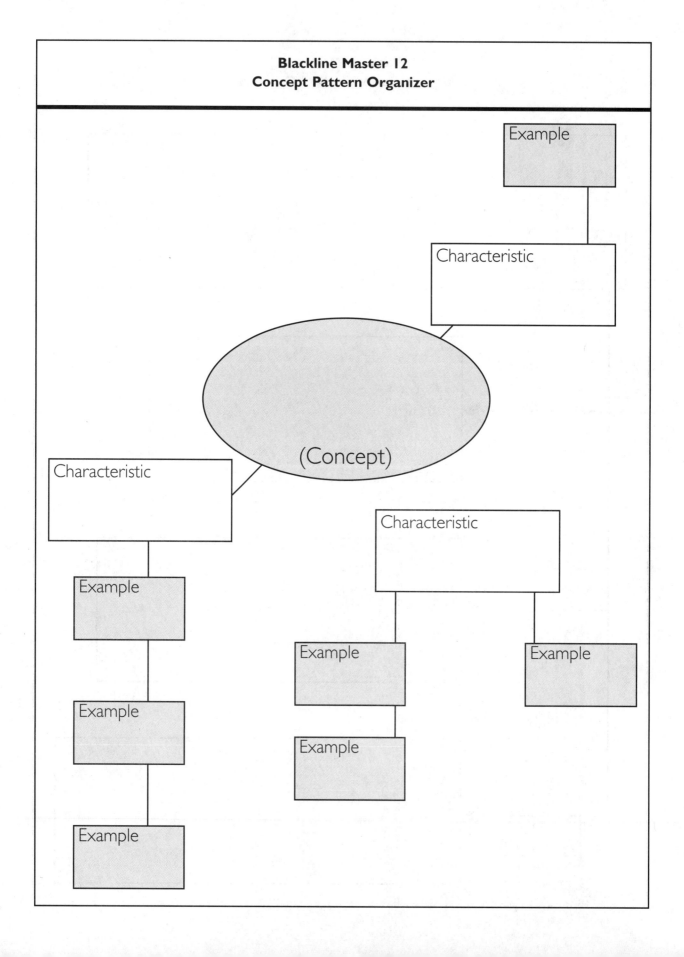

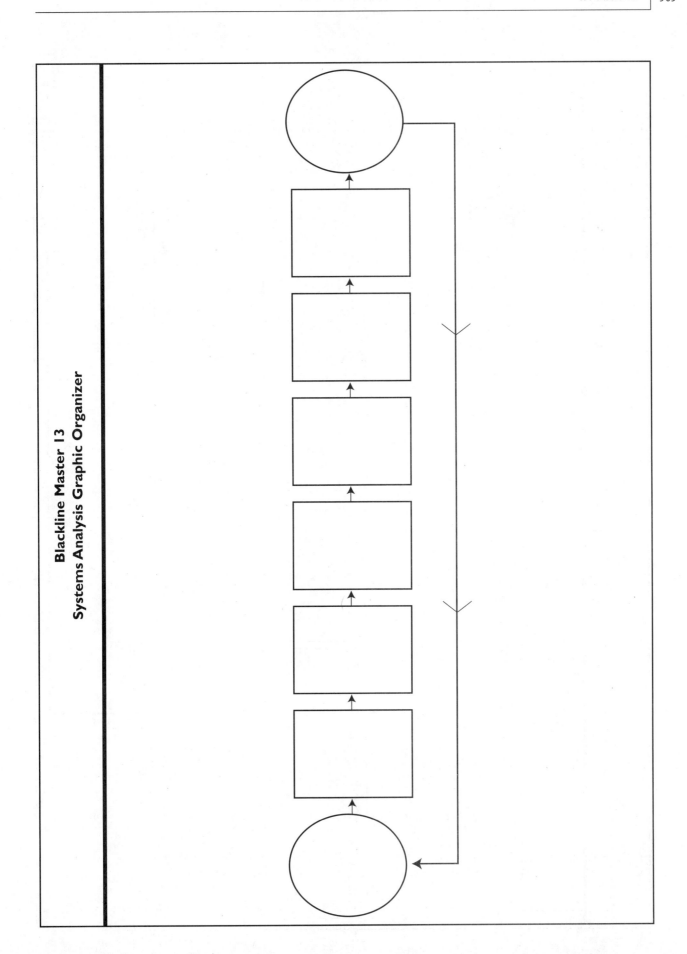

Blackline Master 13
Systems Analysis Graphic Organizer

Blackline Master 14
Problem-Solving Graphic Organizer

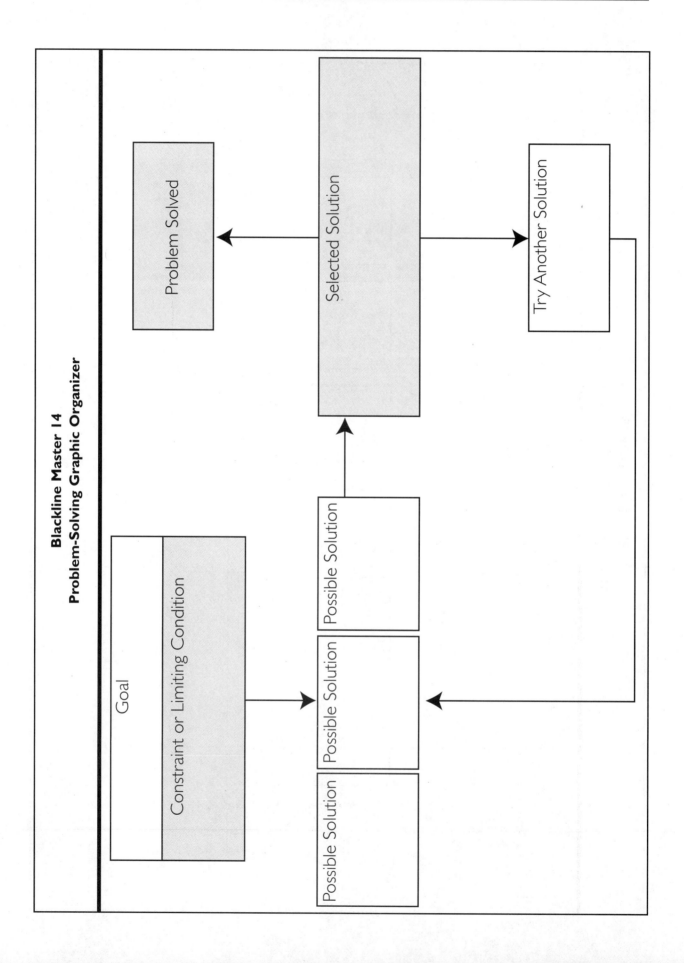

Blackline Master 15
Decision Making Graphic Organizer

Task: _____

Alternatives

Criteria

	Rating	Importance score		Rating	Importance score		Rating	Importance score
___	— ☓ —	Importance score	___	— ☓ —	Importance score	___	— ☓ —	Importance score
___	— ☓ —		___	— ☓ —		___	— ☓ —	
___	— ☓ —		___	— ☓ —		___	— ☓ —	
___	— ☓ —		___	— ☓ —		___	— ☓ —	
___	— ☓ —		___	— ☓ —		___	— ☓ —	

TOTAL

Blackline Master 16

Historical Investigation Graphic Organizer

Concept or Scenario:

General information, known or agreed upon

General confusions or contradictions

Specifics:

Specifics:

Resolution:

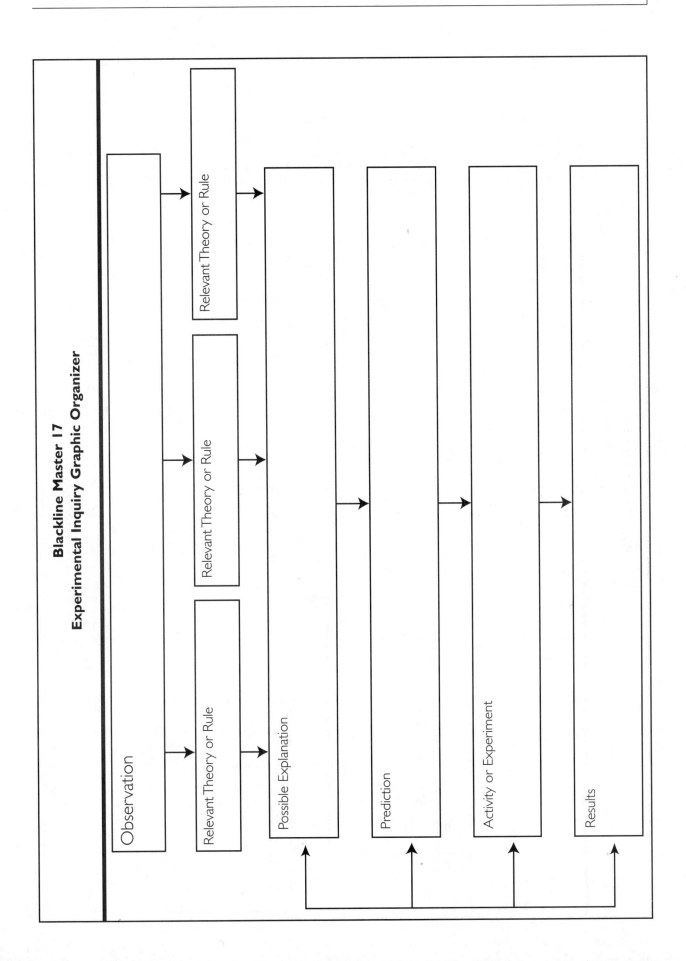

Blackline Master 17
Experimental Inquiry Graphic Organizer

Observation

Relevant Theory or Rule

Relevant Theory or Rule

Relevant Theory or Rule

Possible Explanation

Prediction

Activity or Experiment

Results

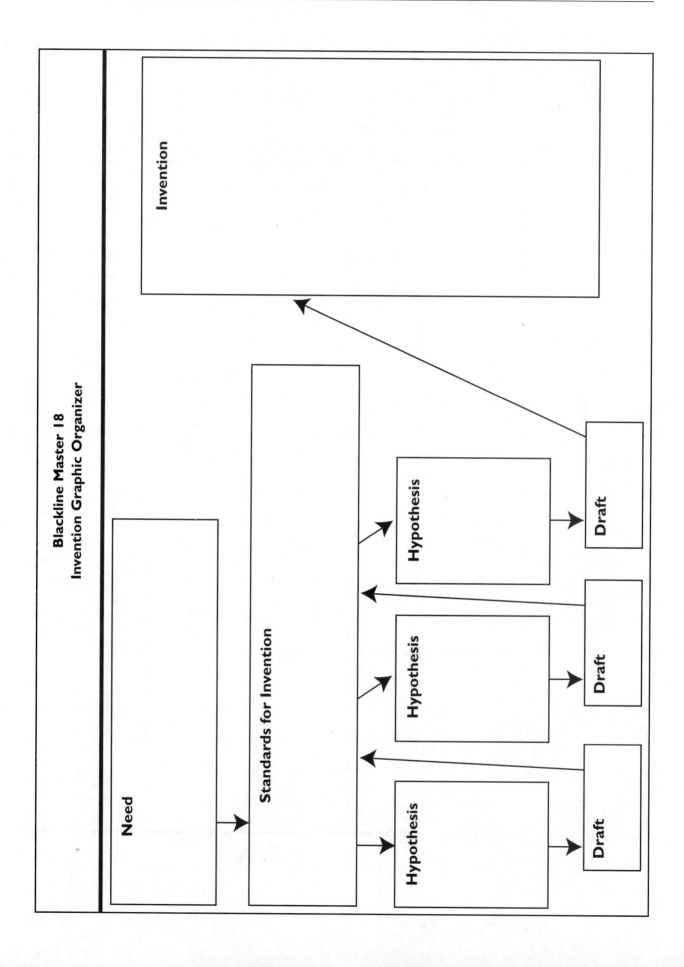

Blackline Master 18
Invention Graphic Organizer

Need

Standards for Invention

Hypothesis

Hypothesis

Hypothesis

Draft

Draft

Draft

Invention

References and Resources

Bogner, D., McCormick, B. J., & Fox, L. R. (2001). Models in science: Student text. *The sun and solar wind.* Retrieved May 4, 20001, from http://www.gensismission.org/educate/sci-module/topics.html

Brophy, J. (1981). Teacher praise: A functional analysis. *Review of Educational Research, 51,* 5–32.

Brown, A. L., Campione, J. C., & Day, J. (1981). Learning to learn: On training students to learn from texts. *Educational Researcher, 10,* 14–24.

Flanders, N. (1970). *Analyzing teacher behavior.* Reading, MA: Addison-Wesley.

Fraser, B. J., Walberg, H. J., Welch, W. W., & Hattie, J. A. (1987). Synthesis of educational productivity research. *Journal of Educational Research, 11*(2), 145–252.

Gagne, R. M. (1977). *The conditions of learning* (3rd ed.). New York: Holt, Rinehart & Winston.

Gerlic, I., & Jausovec, N. (1999). Multimedia: Differences in cognitive processes observed with EEG. *Educational Technology Research and Development, 47*(3), 5–14.

Hattie, J. (1992). Measuring the effects of schooling. *Australian Journal of Education, 36*(1), 5–13.

Hayes, J. R. (1981). *The complete problem solver.* Philadelphia, PA: The Franklin Institute.

Hunter, M. (1984). Knowing, teaching, and supervising. In P. L. Hosford (Ed.), *Using what we know about teaching* (pp. 169–192). Alexandria, VA: Association for Supervision and Curriculum Development.

Johnson, D., Maruyama, G., Johnson, R., Nelson, D., & Skon, L. (1981). Effects of cooperative, competitive, and individualistic goal structures on achievement: A meta-analysis. *Psychological Bulletin, 89*(1), 47–62.

Johnson, D. W., & Johnson, R. T. (1999). *Learning together and alone: Cooperative, competitive, and individualistic learning.* Boston: Allyn & Bacon.

Kintsch, W. (1974). *The representation of meaning in memory.* Hillsdale, NJ: Erlbaum.

Marzano, R. J., Pickering, D. J., & Pollock, J. (2001). *Classroom instruction that works: Research-based strategies for increasing student achievement.* Alexandria, VA: Association for Supervision and Curriculum Development.

Merrett, F., & Thorpe, S. (1996). How important is the praise element in the pause, prompt, and praise tutoring procedures for older, low-progress readers? *Educational Psychology, 16*(2), 193–206.

Naylor, G. (1992). *Bailey's Café.* New York: Vintage Books.

Paivio, A. (1969). Mental imagery in associative learning and memory. *Psychological Review, 76,* 241–263.

Paivio, A. (1971). *Imagery and verbal processing.* New York: Holt, Rinehart & Winston.

Paivio, A. (1990). *Mental representations: A dual coding approach.* New York: Oxford University Press.

Palincsar, A. S., & Brown, A. L. (1984). Reciprocal teaching of comprehension fostering and comprehension monitoring activities. *Cognition and Instruction, 1*(2), 117–175.

Palincsar, A. S., & Brown, A. L. (1985). Reciprocal teaching: Activities to promote reading with your mind. In T. L. Harris & E. J. Cooper (Eds.), *Reading, thinking and concept development: Strategies for the classroom*. New York: The College Board.

Rawls, G., Henry, M., & Krueger, A. (2001). Heat and thermodynamics: Student text. Heat: An agent of change. Retrieved May 4, 2001, from http://www.genesismission.org/educate/scimodule/topics.html

Richardson, A. (1983). Imagery: Definitions and types. In A. A. Sheikh (Ed.), *Imagery: Current theory, research, and application* (pp. 3–42). New York: John Wiley & Sons.

Snowman, J., & McCown, R. (1984, April). *Cognitive processes in learning: A model for investigating strategies and tactics.* Paper presented at the annual meeting of the American Educational Research Association, New Orleans, LA.

Sternberg, R. J. (1977). *Intelligence, information processing and analogical reasoning: The componential analysis of human abilities.* Hillsdale, NJ: Erlbaum.

van Dijk, T. A. (1980). *Macrostructures.* Hillsdale, NJ: Erlbaum.

Van Overwalle, F., & De Metsenaere, M. (1990). The effects of attribution-based intervention and study strategy training on academic achievement in college freshmen. *British Journal of Educational Psychology, 60,* 299–311.

Walberg, H. J. (1999). Productive teaching. In H. C. Waxman & H. J. Walberg (Eds.), *New directions for teaching practice and research,* 75–104. Berkeley, CA: McCutchen.

INDEX

Note: A page number followed by the letter f indicates reference to a figure.

About the Authors

Robert J. Marzano is a private consultant in Aurora, Colorado. He is responsible for translating research and theory into classroom practice. His most recent book, *Classroom Instruction That Works: Research-Based Strategies for Increasing Student Achievement*, published by the Association for Supervision and Curriculum Development (ASCD, 2001), provides the groundwork and theory for this practical handbook. In addition, Marzano headed a team of authors who developed *Dimensions of Learning*, (ASCD) and is the senior author of *Tactics for Thinking* (ASCD) and *Literacy Plus: An Integrated Approach to Teaching Reading, Writing, Vocabulary, and Reasoning* (Zaner-Bloser). Other notable publications address standards as described in the two books *Essential Knowledge: The Debate Over What American Students Should Know* (Marzano, Kendall, & Gaddy/McREL, 1999) and *A Comprehensive Guide to Designing Standards-Based Districts, Schools, and Classrooms* (Marzano & Kendall, ASCD/McREL, 1996). Marzano has also recently completed books entitled *Transforming Classroom Grading* (ASCD, 2000) and *Designing a New Taxonomy of Educational Objectives* (Corwin Press, 2000). He has developed programs and practices used in K–12 classrooms that translate current research and theory in cognition into instructional methods.

Marzano received his B.A. in English from Iona College in New York; an M.Ed. in Reading/Language Arts from Seattle University, Seattle, Washington; and a Ph.D. in Curriculum and Instruction from the University of Washington, Seattle. Marzano was a Senior Fellow with McREL from 1981 until 2001; before that he was a tenured associate professor at the University of Colorado at Denver, and a high school English teacher and department chair.

An internationally known trainer and speaker, Marzano has authored 18 books and more than 150 articles and chapters in books on such topics as reading and writing instruction, thinking skills, school effectiveness, restructuring, assessment, cognition, and standards implementation.

He may be contacted at 7926 S. Roslyn Way, Englewood, CO 80112. Phone: 303-796-7683. E-mail: robertjmarzano@aol.com.

Jennifer S. Norford is a consultant for Mid-continent Research for Education and Learning (McREL). Her 10 years of education experience include classroom teaching, curriculum development, and consultation to K–12 teachers, curriculum coordinators, data and assessment specialists, and technology directors. Norford's work in research and development focuses on instruction and assessment in a standards-based classroom.

Norford has extensive experience developing standards-based materials, analyzing and evaluating materials for alignment with educational standards, developing online models for curriculum, and creating staff development programs and classroom materials. Her research includes meta-analyses with Robert Marzano and extensive data analyses for schools, districts, and intermediate agencies. She has contributed research and writing to numerous publications and products, including ASCD's *Dimensions of Learning Teacher's Manual* (2nd ed.), McREL's *Research into Practice Series*, and *A Comprehensive Guide to Designing Standards-Based Districts, Schools, and Classrooms* (Marzano & Kendall, ASCD/McREL, 1996).

In addition to her research and product development work, Norford manages the Early Literacy Project at McREL. She also provides technical assistance and training for the Early Literacy Advisor, a computerized system that assists classroom teachers in assessing and promoting early literacy development in children ages 4–6.

Norford received a B.A. in English, a B.S. in civil engineering, and an M.A. in English from Virginia Polytechnic Institute and State University. She can be contacted at McREL, 2550 South Parker Road, Suite 500, Aurora, CO 80014. Phone: 303-632-5546. E-mail: jnorford@mcrel.org.

Diane E. Paynter is a principal consultant, Director of Early Literacy, and Director of Consortia at Mid-continent Research for Evaluation and Learning (McREL) in Aurora, Colorado. As an international trainer and researcher, she has worked extensively at the state, district, building, and classroom levels in the areas of standards, curriculum and instruction, assessment, grading and record keeping, and literacy development.

As Director of McREL's Early Literacy Project, she leads a group of researchers in focusing on and training in early literacy development in young children. Additionally, she trains in the areas of integrating the language arts, literature-based reading, process writing, vocabulary instruction, and writing literature-based units aligned with state and district standards.

As Director of Consortia, Paynter works with various consortium across the nation, providing direction, training, materials, and technical support as they move toward aligning curriculum, instruction, and assessment practices to standards.

Paynter is coauthor of many publications, including *Tactics for Thinking* (ASCD), *Dimensions of Learning Teacher's Manual and Trainer's Manual* (ASCD), *Literacy Plus* (Zaner Bloser), *New Approaches to Literacy* (American Psychological Association), *Scaffolding Early Literacy in the Kindergarten and Pre-School Classrooms* (McREL), and *A Framework For Early Literacy Instruction: Aligning Standards To Developmental Accomplishments and Student Behaviors* (McREL). She has also authored many instructional units and articles in well-known publications.

Paynter may be contacted at McREL, 2550 South Parker Road, Suite 500, Aurora, CO 80014. Phone: 303-632-5543. E-mail: dpaynter@mcrel.org.

Debra J. Pickering is a private consultant and Director of Educational Content for TopTutors.com. During more than 25 years in education, she has gained practical experience as a classroom teacher and district staff development coordinator and has done extensive consulting with administrators and teachers, K–12. Her work in research and development centers on the study of learning and the development of curriculum, instruction and assessment that addresses clearly identified learning goals. With a combination of theoretical grounding and practical experience, Pickering works with educators throughout the world who are attempting to translate theory into practice.

Pickering has coauthored a several articles and programs, including Dimensions of Learning Teacher's Manual (2nd ed.) and other materials for ASCD's Dimensions of Learning series, a comprehensive model of learning that provides a framework for developing students into independent learners and complex thinkers.

She received a B.S. degree in English/Drama Education from the University of Missouri, an M.A. in School Administration from the University of Denver, and a Ph.D. in Curriculum and Instruction with an emphasis on Cognitive Psychology from the University of Denver.

Pickering can be contacted at 10098 East Powers Ave., Englewood, CO 80111. Phone: 303-694-9899. E-mail: djplearn@hotmail.com.

Barbara B. Gaddy is managing editor for Mid-continent Research for Education and Learning (McREL) where she oversees the production of publications and other products developed under the regional educational laboratory contract through the U.S. Department of Education.

Gaddy is coauthor of *School Wars: Resolving Our Conflicts Over Religion and Values* (Gaddy, Hall, & Marzano, 1996, Jossey-Bass), ASCD's *Raising Achievement Through Standards* (Gaddy, Marzano, & Checkley, 1998), *Essential Knowledge: The Debate Over What American Students Should Know* (Marzano & Kendall, with Gaddy, 1999, McREL Institute), and *What Works in Classroom*

Instruction (Marzano, Gaddy, & Dean, 2000, McREL). She also contributed to McREL's Research into Practice Series.

Gaddy has been senior editor and project manager for several publications, including *A Comprehensive Guide to Designing Standards-Based Districts, Schools, and Classrooms* (Marzano & Kendall, ASCD/McREL, 1996), ASCD's *Dimensions of Learning Teacher's Manual* (2nd ed., Marzano & Pickering, et al., 1997), and ASCD's *Dimensions of Learning Trainer's Manual* (2nd ed., Marzano & Pickering, et al., 1997). She was also project manager of a yearlong McREL contract to assist the Florida Department of Education in developing curriculum frameworks in seven content areas.

In addition to her work at McREL, Gaddy has written extensively for other education organizations and institutions of higher education. She received a B.S. in marketing management from Miami University (Oxford, Ohio) and an M.A. in mass communications and journalism from the University of Denver. Gaddy can be contacted at McREL, 2550 South Parker Road, Suite 500, Aurora, CO 80014. Phone: 303-632-5517. E-mail: bgaddy@mcrel.org.

Related ASCD Resources: Instructional Strategies That Work

ASCD stock numbers are noted in parentheses.

Audiotapes

Instructional Approaches of Superior Teachers (#299202) by Lloyd Campbell

Planning Units Around Essential Understanding & Questions (#298294) by Lynn Erickson

Putting Best Practices to Work on Behalf of Improving Student Learning (#298132) by Kathleen Fitzpatrick

Teaching for the 21st Century (#297247) by Linda Darling-Hammond

Using Dimensions of Learning as a Tool to Increase Student Success (#200120) by James Riedl and Lucinda Riedl

Online Professional Development

Go to ASCD's Home Page (http://www.ascd.org) and click on Training Opportunities:

ASCD Online Tutorials on Standards, Differentiating Instruction, and the Brain and Learning

ASCD Professional Development Online Courses in Differentiating Instruction, Leadership, and the Brain and Learning

Print Products

Becoming a Better Teacher: Eight Innovations That Work (#100043) by Giselle Martin-Kniep

Classroom Instruction That Works: Research-Based Strategies for Increasing Student Achievement (#101010) by Robert J. Marzano, Debra J. Pickering, and Jane E. Pollock

The Differentiated Classroom: Responding to the Needs of All Learners (#199040) by Carol Ann Tomlinson

Dimensions of Learning Teachers' Manual, 2nd Edition (#197133) by Robert J. Marzano, Debra Pickering, and others

Educating Everybody's Children: Diverse Teaching Strategies for Diverse Learners (#195024) edited by Robert Cole

Enhancing Professional Practice: A Framework for Teaching (#196074) by Charlotte Danielson

A Field Guide to Using Visual Tools (#100023) by David Hyerle

A Different Kind of Classroom: Teaching with Dimensions of Learning (#61192107) by Robert J. Marzano

Research You Can Use to Improve Results (#399238) by Kathleen Cotton

Tools for Learning: A Guide for Teaching Study Skills (#61190086) by M. D. Gall, Joyce P. Gall, Dennis R. Jacobsen, and Terry L. Bullock

Understanding by Design (#198199) by Grant Wiggins and Jay McTighe

The Understanding by Design Handbook (#199030) by Jay McTighe and Grant Wiggins

Visual Tools for Constructing Knowledge (#196072) by David Hyerle

Videotapes

Helping Students Acquire and Integrate Knowledge Series (5 videos) (#496065) by Robert Marzano

How to Improve Your Questioning Techniques (#499047), Tape 5 of the "How To" Series

How to Use Graphic Organizers to Promote Student Thinking (#499048), Tape 6 of the "How To" Series

Concept Definition Map (#499262), Tape 5 of The Lesson Collection Video Series: Reading Strategies

Library of Teaching Strategies Part I & II (#614178)

For additional resources, visit us on the World Wide Web (http://www.ascd.org), send an e-mail message to member@ascd.org, call the ASCD Service Center (1-800-933-ASCD or 703-578-9600, then press 2), send a fax to 703-575-5400, or write to Information Services, ASCD, 1703 N. Beauregard St., Alexandria, VA 22311-1714 USA.